To D. Doug Reynolds

D1569129

China's Quest for Political Legitimacy

Challenges Facing Chinese Political Development

Series Editor: Sujian Guo, Ph.D.
San Francisco State University

In an attempt to reflect the rapidly changing political environment of the People's Republic of China, editor Sujian Guo has assembled a book series to present specialized areas of research in current Chinese political studies. Incorporating theoretical, empirical, and policy research on contemporary Chinese politics both domestically and internationally, this series contemplates the Chinese past, present, and future by utilizing interdisciplinary perspectives to approach issues related to Chinese politics, economy, culture, social development, reform, the military, legal system, and foreign relations. Aimed at bringing a greater understanding of the current Chinese political climate to Western audiences, this series is focused on the emerging voices of Chinese scholars and their perspectives on the ever-changing Chinese diaspora.

Recent titles in the series are:

The Dragon's Hidden Wings: How China Rises with Its Soft Power, by Sheng Ding

"Harmonious World" and China's New Foreign Policy, by Sujian Guo and Jean-Marc F. Blanchard

China in Search of a Harmonious Society, edited by Sujian Guo and Baogang Guo

Greater China in an Era of Globalization, edited by Sujian Guo and Baogang Guo

Toward Better Governance in China, edited by Baogang Guo and Dennis Hickey

Dynamics of Local Governance in China during the Reform Era, edited by Tse-Kang Leng and Yun-han Chu

Dancing with the Dragon: China's Emergence in the Developing World, edited by Dennis Hickey and Baogang Guo

Online Chinese Nationalism and China's Bilateral Relations, edited by Simon Shen and Shaun Breslin

Multidimensional Diplomacy of Contemporary China, edited by Simon Shen and Jean-Marc F. Blanchard

Thirty Years of China-U.S. Relations: Analytical Approaches and Contemporary Issues, edited by Sujian Guo and Baogang Guo

Environmental Protection Policy and Experience in the U.S. and China's Western Regions, edited by Sujian Guo, Joel J. Kassiola, and Zhang Jijiao

China's Quest for Political Legitimacy: The New Equity-Enhancing Politics, by Baogang Guo

China's Quest for Political Legitimacy

The New Equity-Enhancing Politics

Baogang Guo

LEXINGTON BOOKS
A division of
ROWMAN & LITTLEFIELD PUBLISHERS, INC.
Lanham • Boulder • New York • Toronto • Plymouth, UK

Published by Lexington Books
A division of Rowman & Littlefield Publishers, Inc.
A wholly owned subsidiary of The Rowman & Littlefield Publishing Group, Inc.
4501 Forbes Boulevard, Suite 200, Lanham, Maryland 20706
http://www.lexingtonbooks.com

Estover Road, Plymouth PL6 7PY, United Kingdom

Copyright © 2010 by Lexington Books

All rights reserved. No part of this book may be reproduced in any form or by any
electronic or mechanical means, including information storage and retrieval systems,
without written permission from the publisher, except by a reviewer who may quote
passages in a review.

British Library Cataloguing in Publication Information Available

Library of Congress Cataloging-in-Publication Data

Guo, Baogang, 1960–
 China's quest for political legitimacy : the new equity-enhancing politics / Baogang
Guo.
   p. cm. — (Challenges facing Chinese political development)
 Includes bibliographical references and index.
 ISBN 978-0-7391-2258-7 (cloth : alk. paper)
 1. Legitimacy of governments—China. 2. China—Politics and government—2002– 3.
Elite (Social sciences)—China. I. Title.
 JQ1510.G856 2010
 320.951—dc22
                    2010022260

℗™ The paper used in this publication meets the minimum requirements of American
National Standard for Information Sciences—Permanence of Paper for Printed Library
Materials, ANSI/NISO Z39.48-1992.

Printed in the United States of America

To Wen Jiang and Melissa Guo

Contents

List of Figures

List of Tables

List of Chinese Phrases

ai min	爱民	show affection to the people
baogong tou	包工头	labor contractors
baogong zhi	包工制	contract-labor system
baoshengong zhi	包身工制	slave-labor contract system
bao-jia	保甲	an ancient neighborhood watch system
bianfa	变法	reform
buyu min zhengli	不与民争利	do not fight profits with people
bu zhenglun	不争论	no debate
Can Zheng Hui	参政会	National Participation Conference
da tong	大同	the great harmony
dai	代	generation
dilei Zhen	地雷阵	minefield
ernai	二奶	mistress
fengtian chengyun	奉天承运	in the name of heaven
Houhai	后海	name of a residential subdivision in Shenzhen
hou minsheng	厚民生	improving people's livelihood
Jingtai Fenghua	鼎太风华	name of a residential subdivision in Shenzhen
Feng Zehu	丰泽湖	name of a residential subdivision in Shenzhen
geming	革命	revolution
Gongshanlian	工商联	All China Federation of Industry and Commerce
Han Fei Zi	韩非子	a book written by Han Fei
ji min	济民	help the people when they are in need
jiangu gongping	兼顾公平	equity second
jun pin fu	均贫富	distribute wealth equally
jun zi	君子	gentleman
Kuomintang	国民党	The Nationalist Party
li min	利民	benefitting people
like siwei	理科思维	scientific reasoning

Liu Fu	六府	six types of wealth, including water, fire, metal, wood, earth, and grain
minben	民本	putting people first
Minjian	民建	China National Democratic Construction Association
Minmeng	民盟	China Democratic League
mohu gongzi	模糊工资	obscure wage
Qiu Jun	邱浚	a scholar from Ming Dynasty
renmin	人民	people
ren zhi	仁治	rule by virtue
renrou sousuo	人肉搜索	"human flesh search"
sanshi	三事	ancient governing philosophy, including "cultivating virtue, using people's talent, and taking care people's livelihood"
"zheng zai Yangmin"	政在养民	the way of governance lives in nurturing people
Shenmu	神木	a county in Shaanxi province
shachu yitiao xuelu	杀出一条血路	open a blood-filled passageway
Taohuayuan	桃花源	name of a residential subdivision in Shenzhen
tian ming	天命	mandate of heaven
tianxia weigong	天下为公	what is under heaven is for all
wang min	网民	"netizens"
wei min zuo zhu	为民做主	government for the people
wenke siwei	文科思维	humanist reasoning
wumao dang	五毛党	"fifty-cent party" official online commentators
xian chang banli hui	现场办理会	face-to-face decision meeting
yamen	衙门	government institutions
yangmin	养民	nurturing people
yansaihu	言塞湖	"artificial lake of blocked speeches"
yi ren wei ben	以人为本	put people first
yi min wei ben	以民为本	put people first
yi wu wei ben	以物为本	put material things first
yi shen wei ben	以神为本	put divinity first
yi yuan hua	一元化	unified leadership
yangzhenggong	养成工制	probation-labor system
Yueliangwan	月亮湾	name of an expressway in Shenzhen
xuetu zhi	学徒制	apprentice-labor system

xiang-li	乡里	an ancient neighborhood watch system
xiaoyi youxian	效益优先	efficiency first
xinfang	信访	letter-writing and visits
Xinfangju	信访局	Complaints Receiving Bureau
Xun Zi	荀子	an ancient political thinker
zheng dao	政道	"way of politics"
zhengqi fenkai	政企分开	separation of government from enterprises
zhi dao	治道	"way of governance"
Zhigongdang	致公党	China Zhi Gong Party
zhiqing	知青	educated youth
zhongmin	重民	pay more attention to the people
Zhong Nanhai	中南海	the location of the central government's headquarters
Zhongyong	中庸	the way of means

Acknowledgments

For many years, I have observed that liberal political theories, especially the liberal theories of political legitimacy, are ill-equipped to render a satisfactory explanation of political development in China. Being a scholar trained in both Chinese history in mainland China and political science in the United States, I have the language skill, cultural understanding, and scholarly preparation to undertake such a daunting task of bridging the gap between Chinese political traditions and Western political philosophy. My mission in writing this book is to decipher the unique Chinese cognitive model of political legitimation that has provided moral and empirical support to various political regimes throughout Chinese history, including the contemporary communist state.

This book is an accumulation of my research on the issue of political legitimacy for more than a decade. Many of the earlier ideas were presented to various academic conferences. Many similar ideas have appeared in papers or book chapters published during this period. However, this book project allows me to take a more systematic look at this topic. My researches conducted for this book have resulted in many revisions and changes to the ideas and models I developed before. Focusing on the political changes since the turn of this century allows me to narrow my scope of research to the ongoing changes taking place in China. However, no matter how hard I have tried, political development in China always surprises me. But overall, I believe the analytical framework I developed in this book offers a useful tool to the analyses of current as well as future political changes in China. But like other macro level political theories, it can always be challenged and revised by empirical evidence and field researches.

Needless to say, such an endeavor would be impossible without the assistance and help from many colleagues and friends of mine. I am grateful to many people and institutions that have helped me over the years of my scholarly endeavor. First, my thanks go to my college, Dalton State College. As a teaching institution, the college has only limited resources available to its faculty members to conduct research. I am fortunate to have a team of very supportive administrators, such as Dr. John Hutcheson, Dr. Mary Nielson, Dr. Norm Presse and Dr. Judy Cornett, who have given me much encouragement and the needed financial resources to attend academic conferences and conduct field research. I want to thank Dalton State College Foundation for supporting some of my research activities as well. Many of my colleagues, such as Sujian Guo, He Li, Andrew Jack Waskey, Jean-Marc Blanchard, Dennis Hickey, Pat Carmoney, Hongying Wang, Tang Jun, Guanghui Zhou, Yalin Tang, Yuchao Zhu, John James Kennedy, Zhenxu Wang, Gabe T. Wang, Urban Cleaves, Jeffrey P. Blick, and Penny Prime, have commented on some of my chapters or provided research references to my research projects. I want to thank the *Journal of Chinese*

Political Science, American Review of China Studies, and *China Currents* for giving me permissions to use some of the published works contained in my previous publications carried by these journals. I want to thank Lee Hysan Foundation for offering me the Lee Hysan Visiting Scholar Grant to support my research conducted at the University Service Center for China Studies (USC) at Chinese University of Hong Kong (CUHK) in summer 2009. Professor Xiao Jin, the assistant director of the USC, graciously shared with me her unpublished research report on the environmental protection projects undertaken by the ALEX SEE Ecological Association.

Special thanks also go to Dr. George Jones who spent many hours commenting and proofreading most of my chapters. My gratitude also goes to Dr. Norm Presse who also served as a second reader to proofread some chapters of this book, and Kathy Payne who provided secretarial assistance in the production of this book. I am deeply in debt to my family, my wife Wen Jiang and my daughter Melissa Guo, who have tolerated me for my long absence from my family duties during time of my research trips and for being patient with me for my devotion to the project.

Chapter 1
Introduction:
A Theory of Political Legitimacy

China seems to be in a state of constant change in our recent memory. Since the beginning of this new millennium, the reform in China has taken yet another turn. The prolonged emphasis on growth and efficiency are questioned, and the "economy-first" developmental mentality is being challenged. The new consensus among the top leaders in Beijing seems to be that the existing model of development has run its full course and is reaching the end of its glory. They have recently adopted a new approach toward development called "scientific development," which emphasizes balances between men and nature (sustainability), rich and poor (equality), economy and social development (harmonious society).

This new model of development has been applauded by many in the international community. Journalist Joshua Cooper Ramo has coined a new term, "Beijing Consensus," to highlight the difference between the Chinese model and the conventional approach towards development. Ramo defines this new consensus as an equity-driven, peaceful and high quality growth, and places this new model of development as an alternative to the so-called "Washington Consensus" that is essentially efficiency-driven market fundamentalism.[1] According to Ramo, "the emergence of a Beijing consensus for development marks an important change for China, a shift from a reform process that was young and susceptible to externalities to one that is now self-fulfilling, cranking like a chain reaction and more determined by its internal dynamics than by the external pushes. . . ."[2] John Naisbitt, a well-known American scholar of future studies, even predicts that a new "vertical democracy," which combines the bottom-up mass participation with the top-down central command, is emerging in China, and is likely to become an alternative to the Western style of "horizontal democracy."[3]

My primary interest in writing this book is to seek theoretical and empirical understanding of the dynamics of China's recent political development and its implication for the enduring question of political legitimacy. As political scientists trained in the United States, many of us are accustomed to applying Western theories of legitimacy and related analytical frameworks to the study of China. We often find that these theories and frameworks offer little help in explaining the complexity of events that took place in China and, in particular, the prolonged political stability in the country in recent decades. Part of the problem is that many Western observers consider the communist regime in Beijing to be illegitimate and thus predict falsely its collapse repeatedly. It has puzzled many why a regime whose legitimacy is not derived from voters' choices in free and competitive elections can still enjoy overwhelming public support as revealed by many recent empirical studies.[4]

The argument developed in this book is that the issue of political legitimacy must be understood within the context of Chinese cognitive patterns. Liberal political theories are more or less Euro-centric and need to expand their theoretical and empirical reach to account for political tradition in non-western societies. In the case of China, the importance of traditional beliefs, norms and values can never be overstated. The importance of ethics in political discourse, the obligation of the state to secure the welfare of the people, the need for a strong state in maintaining a unitary system of government, and the cultivation of political and social harmony through consensus building, concurrent accord, and individual sacrifice continue to shape the modern day belief system in Chinese government and politics. To a certain extent, these cultural traditional are incompatible with the adversarial, anti-state, and competition-based liberal democracy.[5]

Dynamics of Chinese Politics

The starting points of our theory-building effort should begin with an inquiry of cognitive patterns of political legitimacy found in various cultures. A cognitive pattern is a unique way of processing information, applying knowledge and changing preferences. There has been relatively little attention paid by political scientists about the importance of mind, reasoning, perceptions, metaphor, framing, masking, memory and learning in shaping people's affection about their political leaders and institutions. Legitimacy is a subjective feeling about the rightfulness of exercising political control. Obtaining affectionate feeling towards a regime involves intensive cognitive processing by human brains. The level of affection an individual develops determines the level of political support the individual will manifest. However, neuroscience, psychology, and linguistics cannot provide all the answers. Political science as a behavior science has a larger role to play in deciphering the myth about political legitimation. To accomplish this task, we will borrow two economic concepts: efficiency and equity.

Efficiency, Equity, and the Trade-Off

Efficiency and equity are two well-developed economic concepts in the study of microeconomics. To borrow these concepts and apply them in a macro-level political inquiry can be somewhat challenging. We need to redefine them first as distinctively political concepts with political meaning. Efficiency in economic terms refers typically to the level of non-wasteful allocation, utilization and distribution of resources, while equity refers to a fair distribution of the opportunities and outcome of the fruits of the growth.

As a political concept, efficiency can be understood as effectiveness of governance, which in turn can be measured by institutional capacity, regulatory quality, rule of law, and corruption control and prevention. The concept of efficiency deals with optimum allocation of political and economic resources. Government planning, strengthening the legal system, and improvement of governing capacities can cut down waste and bureaucratic red tape, and rationalize the distribution of resources. Although political elite and professional can play a leading role in the politics of efficiency-enhancement since scientific and managerial skills can assist greatly in the task, the market is still considered the most effective mechanism in facilitating individual decision making. In a market economy, individual and group interests are becoming more and more diversified. The scientific and managerial elite are poorly equipped to have a handle on the complexity of social problems. Human emotions and myriad moralities can render their mechanical views of nature and scientific rationalism useless.

The concept of equity is generally associated with good governance. It implies a fair share of political influence of various political actors whose interests are at stake. Market economy, whether it is socialist or capitalist, produces a diversified economic ownership. The owners of the market assets, big or small, will naturally want to become stakeholders of the political decision making process that may hurt, protect, enhance, and promote their economic and social interests. Many political actors tend to perceive politics as a zero-sum game in the marketplace, in which you get what you fight for. Stakeholders will demand political openness and opportunities to defend and promote their legitimate self-interests. As Samuel Huntington pointed out, most political crises in developing countries are crises of political participation.[6] To prevent these crises, governments of all kinds have openly endorsed some form of democracy as a way to broaden the scope of participation. However, too much or too little participation can both trigger political instability. While liberal democracy supports electoral democracy in which voters have the choice to elect their political leaders, the supporters of deliberative democracy focus their attention on facilitating good governance and promote various schemes of citizens' direct involvement in political decision-making processes. Voice and accountability, transparency, level of public deliberation, and sound public policy consequently become the best indicators to measure the level of citizen participation and the degree of political equity in a given political system.

Achieving efficiency and equity are important goals of politics. However, political trade-off can occur in the process of attaining these two goals. Economists such as Arthur M. Okun have long observed the phenomenon of the equity-efficiency trade-off.[7] According to him, efforts to improve efficiency can compromise equity, and excessive welfare distribution will lower growth rate, and reduce economic efficiency.[8] However, to many, an efficient government always takes precedence over good governance. According to Alexander Hamilton, the dilemma of building a democratic government is that there must be an effective government first before the government can be shared with the majority.

> If men were angels, no government would be necessary. If angels were to govern men, neither external nor internal controls on government would be necessary. In framing a government which is to be administered by men over men,

the great difficulty lies in this: you must first enable the government to control
the governed; and in the next place oblige it to control itself.[9]

This is especially true for a nation facing the challenge of state building. As
Samuel P. Huntington declared in the opening paragraph of his widely read
book, *Political Order in Changing Societies*, "the most important political distinction among countries concerns not their form of government but their degree
of government." According to Huntington, "the function of government is to
govern" and "a weak government, a government which lacks authority, fails to
perform its function and is immoral in the same sense in which a corrupt judge,
a cowardly soldier, or an ignorant teacher is immoral."[10] The main point raised
in his book is that if social mobilization outpaces the development of political
institutions, social chaos may occur.

Extreme egalitarianism orchestrated by communist states in the 1950s and
1960s led to incentive trap, free riding, high operating costs and official corruption. However, extreme inequality that existed in many developing countries
also led to social unrest, erosion of social cohesion, and instability. Furthermore,
society does not share the same vision of what is fair and what is not. What is
considered by some to be an efficient allocation or distribution may be deemed
by others as unfair or unjust ones. These conflicting views of equity may distort
market conditions and produce income polarization and consequently jeopardize
a regime's political stability.[11]

This book treats these two concepts as interrelated, yet conflicting values, in
our political analysis. Three general assumptions will be tested in the rest of this
book. First, political leaders tend to focus on one of the two political goals at a
given time based on their perception of what are the dominant issues or problems. The concerns over the possible trade-off will prevent leaders from pursuing both with the same amount of effort and rigor.

Secondly, there seems to be a cyclical pattern of political development in
the Chinese society evolving around the attainment of these two fundamental
values. The trade-off between the two values leads to an upward spiral and results in a periodical shift in the society's value-orientation and developmental
patterns. The maximization of one value always produces its own negation and
repudiation. In Western democracy, politics tends evolve around a liberal-
conservative dichotomy. However, the same political dynamism also manifested
itself consistently in Chinese political development in recent Chinese history.
The conflicts between socialist vs. revisionist, the left vs. the right, the reformer
vs. the conservative, and the neoliberal vs. the new left are good examples of
these two value orientations.

Thirdly, the driving force for the paradigm shift in decision-makers' value-
orientation system is politicians' needs to acquire new bases of political legitimacy. Political leaders, who worry continuously about the security of their political power, do have an interest in seeking either tacit approval or explicit support
for their political decisions from the people. They know too well that "mandate
of heaven" exists only in the heart and mind of the people and can vanish just as
the flowing water rocks a small boat.

Two Types of Politics

Because of the two inherently contradicting value orientations, there are two types of politics developed around the two types of value orientations: one is the politics of efficiency; the other, the politics of equity. While the politics of efficiency is designed to fight against inefficiency, waste, and the arbitrary interference of social and economic life by political forces, the politics of equity is a struggle against social costs and negative externalities of market forces. Each type of politics consists of a unique governing philosophy, a group of unusual political elite, and a set of new public policies.

The governing philosophy consists of a set of political ideas or a scheme of interpretations[12], and usually involves the use of some metaphors by political leaders to frame political exchanges and policy deliberation. It can also be used to mask the differences in interests between the rulers and the governed. Confucianism and legalism served as core value system in traditional Chinese governing philosophies. In modern politics, Maoism served as the governing philosophy in the first thirty years of the history of the People's Republic of China (PRC). Deng Xiaoping Theory and pragmatism were the dominant governing philosophy for the three decades of reform since the end of 1978. This book will examine the new governing philosophy of the post-Deng era.

The governing elite in this book refers to a set of political leaders who make up the top political leaders in the Chinese Community Party (CCP) and its state apparatus. They are the main advocates and carriers of a regime's governing philosophy. However, there are many subgroups of political elite in China. Each subgroup is a product of its own historical time and conditions. As one subgroup replaces the previous subgroup, new governing philosophy is developed. The twentieth century is an age of revolution for China. Many groups of revolutionary elite emerged during this era. Their struggles and quarrels shaped the direction of Chinese modernization process. During the era of the Republic of China, it was the efficiency-oriented *Kuomintang* (KMT, the Nationalist Party) fought with the equity-conscious CCP. During the era of economic development since the founding of the PRC, the CCP revolutionary elite continued to wield their influences, but the new efficiency-driven technical and managerial elite gradually replaced the revolutionary ones. Since the end of the Cultural Revolution, the political elite with engineering backgrounds slowly replaced the radical revolutionaries. Their relentless pursuit of the modernization and development has resulted in impressive economic and social progress in every aspect of Chinese society. However, after three decades of technocracy, the scientific elite have run out of steam. Faced with the mounting social problems such as income disparities, social unrests, ethnic tensions, and environment degradation, a new post-technocrat elite group has begun their ascendance to the power core within CCP. In Chapters 2 and 3 of this book, we will explore the governing philosophy of this new breed of Chinese leaders and the characteristics of the post-engineer elite group.

If the issues of who governs stands as the heart of all politics, then public policies are the output of the decision making process that is guided by the governing philosophy and formulated by the ruling elite. A group of revolutionary elite armed with authoritarian governing philosophy tends to place emphasis on control, command, and mass campaign. A group of engineer-based scientific elite may use an entirely different set of decision rules. They are more likely to emphasize efficient allocation, mechanical balance, and market regulation. The rise of humanist elite will bring about a new set of decision-making rules. Their mission is to bring people back in the equilibrium and stop the alienation of the people from the economic development. Will the decision making process be more open and more democratic? Part three of this book will analyze several public policy issues to reveal the new orientation of the new ruling elite.

This book is about the new politics of equity. It will be organized around these three main themes: the governing philosophy, the post-engineer elite group, and the new set of public policies. The understanding of this new politics will not only give us a clear sense of direction as to where Chinese politics is headed but also help us understand the driving motivation of these changes; i.e., the need for political legitimacy. Now, let us turn our attention to our dependent variable in this study: political legitimacy.

A Chinese Cognitive Model of Political Legitimacy

Legitimacy is a prerequisite for power and a moral foundation of authority. Historically, two types of legitimacy theory have been developed.[13] The consensus theory of legitimacy believes that the acceptance of political order is voluntary. A defining set of norms, values, beliefs, and public interests provide the basis of objective justice. Consent is the key ingredient of legitimacy. The consensus theory was first developed by Aristotle[14] and then followed by Thomas Hobbes, John Locke, and Jean-Jacque Rousseau,[15] and in modern time, by Talcott Parsons and Seymour M. Lipset.[16]

The conflict theory of legitimacy believes that the acceptance of a political order is instrumental governed by rational self-interests. Ideology, myth, and ritual are necessary means to justify the rulers' right to govern. According to some, shared norms and values are not a necessary condition for political support since political leaders can manipulate legitimacy by making the unacceptable acceptable, by masking the real interests of the rulers, and by framing the political debates through using metaphors or propaganda.[17] David Easton divided political support into diffuse support (learned loyalty based on prevailing norms) and specific support (support based on their own rational assessment of specific policy that has a direct effect on their lives). In his words, the learned loyalty cannot last if there is an "output failure."[18] Niccolò Machiavelli and Karl Marx are surprisingly similar in their account of the conflict views of legitimacy.[19] Other scholars such as Max Weber and Jügen Habermas adopted a mixed interpretation of legitimacy which combines elements of both consensus and conflict theories.[20]

Through a careful review of classic Chinese literature on political legitimacy, we find that Chinese traditional political theorists tend to hold a two-dimensional view of political legitimacy. The consensual aspect is reflected in the notion of "Mandate of Heaven" and benevolent politics. We will call this dimension the original justification which emphasizes the tacit moral support of rulers' right to govern. The instrumental dimension is reflected in the idea of *yang min* (nurturing people), *li min* (benefiting people) and *hou min* (enriching the people). Let us call this dimension the utilitarian justification which focuses heavily on the exchange between tacit public support and the well-being and happiness of the people.[21] Let us examine each dimension with some details.

Original Justification

In traditional Chinese political theory, the original justification can be articulated by using four Chinese concepts: Mandate of Heaven (*tian ming*),[22] rule by virtue *(ren zhi)*,[23] put people first *(min ben)*,[24] and global oneness (*tianxia weigong*).[25]

Mandate of Heaven: The notion that a ruler's right to govern derives from a supernatural force is as old as human civilization. Starting from the Western Zhou Dynasty, ancient Chinese emperors always legitimized their political power by "*tian*" or Heaven (*fengtian chengyun*). The Mandate of Heaven is based on the following assumptions: heaven grants a ruler's right to rule; there is only one Heaven; the emperor is the son of the Heaven, therefore, his rule is divine rule. The similar ideas can also be found in other civilizations. French orator Jacques-Benigne Bossuet reinforced medieval notions of kingship in his theory of the "Divine Right of Kings." He argued that certain kings ruled because God chose them and that these kings were accountable to no one except God.[26] Max Weber called this type of numinous legitimacy the "traditional domination,"[27] which is no longer an important ingredient of modern political legitimacy.

Rule by Virtue: While recognizing the importance of mandate of heaven, Confucianism emphasizes the importance of "virtue" or benevolence in the exercise of political power. Confucius believed that the ruler's virtue and the contentment of the people, rather than power, should be the true measurement of a ruler's political success.[28] In the Confucian paradise of the Great Harmony (*da tong*),[29] there was a system of moral hierarchy in which an emperor is supposed to be the most virtuous man on earth. Since virtue can be nurtured through education, all government officials should be recruited from "gentlemen" (*jun zi*) or learned scholars. Mencius pushed this virtue-based political idealism even further.[30] He believed that government was primarily an exercise of ethics. The rule of a truly moral king, according to him, was characterized by his benevolence towards his people.

Popular Consent: Although legitimate rulers demand people's voluntary submission to their authorities, the Chinese understanding of the relationship between the ruler and the people suggests that rulers must constantly seek popular approval, not by way of expressed public opinions, but through winning the hearts and minds of the people. This understanding is reflected in Mencius's *min ben* ideas. *Min ben* can be translated as "regarding the people as the roots of the state" or simply "put the people first." This concept resembles the concept of popular consent without its legalist tone. It focuses, instead, primarily on the need to look after the interests of the people and govern for the people.[31] Consider the following quotation from Mencius:

> Here is the way to win the empire: win the people and you win the empire.
> Here is the way to win the people: win their hearts and you win the people.
> Here is the way to win their hearts: give them and share with them what they like, and do not do to them what they do not like. The people turn to a humane ruler as water flows downward and beasts take to wilderness. [32]

Min ben has two meanings: First, people's interests are of utmost importance. Second, rulers must follow the will of the people; show respect for people's needs; let people be the principal decision makers of their own life. After all, according to Mencius, people's interests are above the rulers' interests. Most significantly, *min ben* gives the traditional concept of "Mandate of Heaven" a new meaning, namely, the acceptance of a ruler by the people shall be a true test of the will of Heaven. Mencius even suggested that people had a right to overthrow a ruler who forfeited his mandate.[33]

Global Oneness: This is the unique aspect of the Chinese traditional idea of good society. *Tianxia weigong* can be literally translated into global oneness or community ownership of the public sphere. It embraces the idea of equality, social justice and great harmony (*da tong*). It considers the people to be the collective ownership of the state, and public interests are above the rulers' own self interest. Confucius's ideal society is filled with happiness, harmony, justice and equality,

> When the great way prevails, the world is equally shared by all. The talent and virtue are elected. Mutual confidence was emphasized and brotherhood was cultivated. Therefore, people regard all parents as their own, and treat all children as their own. The elders can live in happiness, the adults are employed by their talent, the youths can grow and educate. Widows and widowers, orphans, childless, ills and invalids are all well taken care of.[34]

The idea of equality is deeply embedded in Chinese political thoughts. China was known to be one of the most populated countries on earth for the past two millenniums. Scarcity of material resources such as arable land and food caused periodic problems of famine. Concentration of landownership became a chronicle social problem. Peasants always dreamed of land ownership and equal economic distribution. Justice was always understood as a fair distribution of economic wealth to all. Mencius understands this fairly well. He points out that people are not afraid of scarcity of wealth but instead the unequal distribution of it. To ensure equal land distribution, he strongly recommended the well-field system—a communal land system supposedly used during the Zhou Dynasty (1046-256 BC)—as a way of ensuring equal distribution of lands. Xu Xing, one of the Agriculturists in the period of Warring States (403-221 BC), went even further by advocating social equality. He imagined a society with no distinction between those who worked with their minds and those who worked with their hands as well as between the rulers and the ruled.[35]

The idea of *jun pin fu* is reflected in the writings of many political thinkers. Generally speaking it has two meanings. First, excessive inequality in wealth distribution can cause instability. If the rich are left unregulated, they may become arrogant and uncontrollable. Similarly, if the poor is not provided for, rebellions may be produced. Second, government should take an active role in the necessary redistribution of wealth. There are two ways to deal with the problem of inequality. One is the radical redistribution through the use of force. Many peasant leaders in history believed in that approach. The other is the regulatory approach which tolerates the inequality but which requires that wealth be redistributed through taxation and regulation. In short, the idea of *jun pin fu* reflects the populist tradition in the Chinese political culture.

Utilitarian Justification

Moral bases of power provide the justification for who should govern. However, how to maintain people's belief that the rulers have a right to govern is more difficult than propagating a moral justification. The modern rationalist school of thought believes that people will be happy and supportive of the government only if their needs are satisfied. Therefore by satisfying people's utilitarian needs it will help enhance a government's legitimacy. According to Jeremy Bentham, a British philosopher of the late eighteenth century, the principle of utility dictates an individual's approval or disapproval of a government's legitimacy. The legitimacy of a government, in this view, lies in its ability to maximize an individual's happiness and minimize his/her pain.[36] Utilitarianism as a moral principle associated virtue with well-being of the people, and believes that a morally right course of action in any situation is the one that produces the greatest balance of benefits over harms for everyone affected. It tests the legitimacy of the government not by its intention, but by the consequences of its decisions.[37]

The Chinese Confucianist and the Legalist all agree that ordinary people are motivated primarily by their own profits and self-interests. To strengthen the "Mandate of Heaven," the Confucianist believes that rulers must make decisions on behalf of the people (*weimin zuozhu*), and that those decisions must not do harm to the well-being of the people. As summarized by one of the officials in the Ming Dynasty, "peace lies in the prosperous of the community and stability lies in the happiness of the people."[38] Ancient Chinese political writers even came up with three specific policy recommendations (*sans hi*), which include benefiting people (*li min*), nurturing people (*yang min*), and improving people's livelihood (*hou minsheng*).[39]

Benefiting the People: The concept of "*li min*" can be found in many Chinese classics. According to the book *Han Fei Zi*, "Profit is his [the ruler–added] means of winning over people."[40] *Li min* means asking rulers to give primary consideration to the welfare of the people. It is closely related to the concept of people's livelihood (*min sheng*). A good ruler should not be preoccupied with benefiting himself and indulging in his personal luxury and comfort. Instead, he should be concerned with the welfare of his subjects first. Government should not take profits away from the people (*"buyu min zhengli"*). Among the good deeds mentioned in the classics are those that state that rulers should not tax people heavily, should make sure people have enough food, shelter, and clothing, and should control floods and relieve poverty, etc.

According to *Shangshu*, an ancient book on Chinese history, the key to good governance lies in providing means for people to make a living (*"zhengzai Yangmin"*). The key to nurture people is by making people prosperous. According to Xun Zi, "without a thriving public, there will be no way to foster people's good feeling."[41] One of the ways to nurture people is to accumulate their wealth and resources (*liu fu*).[42] Another way is to make it a government responsibility to provide people with employment opportunity and to regulate the big business and big monopolies, and to accumulate wealth among people. Ming Dynasty scholar Qiu Jun proposed ten policy recommendations to Ming rulers about how to implement the idea of nurturing people. He wanted rulers to improve production, help people own property and plan their wealth, take people's business seriously, enhance their capacity, be concerned about the poor, help people with their suffering, wipe out evil forces that harm people, and let people do what they do the best.[43] This belief in the government's role as a provider of benefits has enabled rulers in China to play a more active role in managing the economy.[44] Ultimately, to enrich people is the highest goal of government action.[45] The state will be at peace if all families and individuals are prosperous.[46]

However, the concept of utility is not only limited to economic interests—money, wealth, and profits. Reputation, respect, and power are also higher levels of utility.[47] According to Maslow's theory of hierarchical human needs, people pursue different needs at different stages of their lives. When their basic level of needs, such as physiology (food, water, sex, and sleep) and security (body, employment, resources, family, health, and property), are met, they will want to fulfill their higher level of needs, such as love/belong (friendship, family, intimacy), esteem (confidence, recognition, achievement, and respect), and self-actualization (morality, creativity, leadership, and power). To put simply, a well-fed person can still be frustrated if his or her higher cravings are not satisfied.[48] Even though a person is better off than he was before, he can still feel unsatisfied if his neighbor is doing better than he is. This relative deprivation, as it is often referred to, can still contribute to the weakening of utilitarian justification of a regime.[49] Therefore, utilitarian basis of political legitimacy is much more complex than the original justification.

Overall, utilitarian justification emphasizes the importance of the happiness of the people, their livelihood, their well-being, and their political influence. Modern political utility theory also emphasizes the importance of achievement and effectiveness of the government as a way of legitimatizing the government. In his study of social conditions for democracy, Seymour Martin Lipset considers the effectiveness and legitimacy of the political system to be of crucial importance.[50] Samuel P. Huntington also emphasizes the importance of achievement in maintaining legitimacy.[51] For the rulers, the strategy of enhancing people's utility is aimed at gaining their political support. The interests of the government may not be the same as the interests of the people.

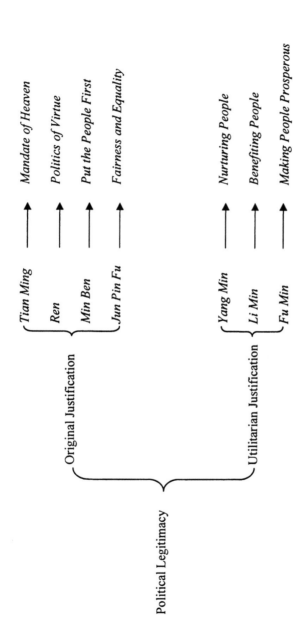

Figure 1.1 Chinese Cognitive Model of Political Legitimacy

Source: The earlier version of this model was contained in my paper on "Political Legitimacy in China's Transition," *Journal of Chinese Political Studies* 8:1-2, (Fall 2003):1-16. This model has been modified since then.

Based on the preceding discussion, we can summarize the Chinese cognitive model of political legitimacy as follows: a ruler, who has the mandate of Heaven, exercising benevolence, showing respect to his subjects, and maintaining a fair distribution of wealth can be rewarded with the affection of the people, even if it is merely a tacit one. A ruler must also understand that he must not do harm to the people, and promote policies that will benefit and enrich the people, and allow the people to do what they do the best. This unique cognitive model mixed both the consensual and conflict theories we discussed earlier (see Figure 1.1).

As a traditional pattern of cognition, there are undoubtedly many limits in its analytical strength in interpreting modern-day political behaviors. The moral basis of original justification is built upon an authoritarian ideology, namely the Mandate of Heaven and Confucianism, and the governing philosophy is government for the people. The moral basis of the utilitarian justification is tacit consent instead of explicit consent that is called for in the modern rational-legal legitimacy. Chinese traditional political theorists focus too much on the low level of utility of the people; they pay little attention to the people's higher-level needs for participation and expression. Despite its limits, contemporary Chinese rulers continue to draw wisdom form this traditional cognitive model, which makes it still relevant to our study of the transitional and developmental politics in China.

This cognitive model of political legitimacy combined with the two types of politics we discussed earlier provides an analytical and theoretical framework for this book. We will examine how the ruling party has used various official ideologies to strengthen its original justification and the economic and its social achievements to enhance its utilitarian appeal. As a simplified political theory, its key hypotheses can be further tested though empirical studies. Before analyzing the new politics of equity, we need to put the emerging politics into some perspective. Let us examine the politics that precedes it first. An in-depth analysis of the latest evolution from an efficiency-driven growth model to an equity-driven one will serve as a testing ground for this new theory.

Chapter Outlines

This book is about the creation of a new politics of equity and the quest for new bases of political legitimacy. After more than two decades of elite-guided, efficiency-driven economic reform, Chinese politics seems to enter into a new phrase: the struggle for equity. The market-driven development has demoralized Chinese society and Chinese politics. Rampant corruption has eroded official ethics. The widening gaps between the rich and the poor have resulted in an escalating number of social unrests. The continued tight grip of power by the authoritarian technocrats has frustrated the emerging middle class who want to have more voices in the decision making process. To restore public confidence and to strengthen its political legitimacy, leaders in Beijing are busy in contemplating new reform schemes designed to address their innate deficiency in equity in their society. An era of equity-driven politics has arrived.

The revival of the politics of equity is part of the political cycle that has characterized Chinese politics in modern history. The immense effort to maximize efficiency has compromised equity and fairness. The politics of equity differs significantly from the politics of efficiency. Equity is a function of political power. An unbalanced distribution of political power will lead to political as well as economic inequality. If the institutions that produce the inequality in power and wealth are not reformed, the goal of equity will be unattainable. If so, then the goal of strengthening the regime's legitimacy is equally unattainable. Political reform and a gradual opening up of the political participation may offer a promising solution to the problem of equity.

The rest of the book will be divided into three parts. Part one will examine the new governing philosophy and the new humanist elite. Chapter 2 focuses on the reorientation of China's developmental strategy, especially on the deliberate effort made by the third and fourth generation of political leaders to strengthen the original justification of the communist rule through inventing a new consensus theory, namely the "scientific development perspective." A comparative analysis of the value orientation of the third and the fourth generation leaders reveals some major shifts in the guiding governing philosophy of the fourth generation leaders. Scientism, humanism, and populism stand as cores of the new value orientation. The new value orientation tries to break away from the utility-based justification, and return to the traditional human-centered justification.

Chapter 3 analyzes three generations of elite politics in China and their system of legitimation. The first generation refers to the revolutionary old guards who fought for China's independence and equality. Their value orientation was based on Marxist ideology, the proletarian dictatorship peasant revolution, and socialism. They shared one thing in common, namely, their humanist background—most of them were intellectuals, teachers, and lawyers. The second generation was led by a first generation leader, Deng Xiaoping. They were mostly engineers. Their political legitimacy was based on meritocracy, technocracy, and pragmatism. The third generation of Chinese political elite is a mixture of managerial elite and humanistic elite. They will be the main players in the new politics of equity.

Part two of this book will examine the development of deliberative democracy in China. Chapter 4 focuses on the deliberative democracy and consensual politics at the national level. This chapter first takes a look at the reasons why the CCP prefers deliberative democracy, not electoral democracy. Next, the chapter examines the unique system of political consultation as a way to institutionalize the deliberative democracy. Finally, it makes three case studies on the deliberation process in making three important national laws, namely, the marriage law, the property right law, and labor contract law.

Chapter 5 turns to the development of deliberative democracy at the local and community level. As the market-oriented economic reform has transformed local communities from work unit based to residential neighborhood based ones, local governance relies more and more on community support for its decisions on urban development. This paper will take a closer look at three cases of citizen reactive participation in urban development projects. The reactive participation is a form of civil participation that is a reaction of community people to the elite or closed decision-making process, usually dominated by the state.

Theodore Lowi argued that policies determine politics.[52] Part three examines policy changes in recent years aimed at promoting the new politics of equity. Chapter 6 studies the regulatory policy in the area of environmental protection. This chapter examines the dynamics of the politics of environmental regulation in China. More specifically, it examines how laws and regulations, such as "command and control" regulation, environmental pricing reform, and environmental rating system, can be used to reduce the social and environmental costs of economic growth, and how the environmental economy and public involvement can help reduce negative externalities of economic activities. It will first examine the political logic of the regulatory reform in the area of environmental protection. Then a detailed analysis of the regulatory changes taking place in recent years will be presented.

Chapter 7 will first examine two transitions of labor policy since 1949, since both have had an important bearing on the status of Chinese labor's political power, social prestige, and economic interests. The first transition took place around 1949 when wage laborers were turned into a ruling class. The second transition has taken place since the 1980s when workers began to lose their previously acquired political and economic rights, and were forced to accept the terms and conditions of the market economy. Next, we will examine recent changes in labor policy under the new equity-oriented reform regime. More specifically we will analyze the efforts made by the state to improve China's labor standards through labor-friendly social legislation, and the active role the official trade unions have played in protecting labor rights in recent years.

Chapter 8 will examine policy initiatives launched in recent decades, and assess their successes and failures. Section one provides some background information on the health-related reforms. Section two examines some key components of the new health-care system. Section three assesses the new rural cooperative health care scheme and its impact on extending access to health care in rural areas. Section four will look at the new comprehensive proposal for health care reform under deliberation.

The final chapter will summarize major findings of this book. The importance of developing a comprehensive theory of political legitimacy is far from accomplished. This book provides some empirical evidence on the validity of this analytic framework. However, like any other theory, the theory of political legitimacy proposed in chapter one can be further modification and tested empirically by more case studies.

I also strongly believe that the Chinese view of political legitimacy is ubiquitous. People in different political environment may focus on a particular aspect of the issue of political legitimacy. But a two- or three-dimensional view of political legitimacy can be seen everywhere in the world. The notion that only liberal democracy provides for real political legitimacy is simply far from the truth. I hope this study of Chinese political legitimacy will shed some new lights on the issue of political legitimacy.

Notes

1. Joshua Cooper Ramo, *The Beijing Consensus: Notes on the New Physics of Chinese Power* (London: Foreign Policy Center, 2004). Many Chinese scholars have kept cool to the notion of "Beijing Consensus." They believe that China's economic and political development is still unfolding, and it is too early to call it a Chinese model. Some still prefer to call it "socialism with Chinese characteristics." See Xu Zhiyuan, "Cong Zhongguo Tese dao Zongguo Moshi [From Chinese Characteristics to Chinese Model]," an article published by China Elections and Governance.org, http://chinaelections.org/NewsInfo.asp?NewsID=171367 (accessed March 11, 2010).

2. *Ibid.*, 5.

3. John Naisbitt and Doris Naisbitt: *China's Megatrend: the 8 Pillars of a New Society (Zhonghuo Da Qushi)*(Beijing: Zhonghua Gongshanglian Chubanshe, 2009).

4. Jie Chen, *Popular Political Support in Urban China* (Washington DC: Woodrow Wilson Center; Stanford, CA: Stanford University Press, 2004).

5. Daniel A Bell, *Beyond Liberal Democracy: Political Thinking for an East Asian Context* (Princeton, NJ: Princeton University Press, 2006).

6. Samuel P. Huntington, *Political Order in Changing Societies* (New Haven, CT: Yale University Press, 2006).

7. Arthur M. Okun, *Equity and Efficiency: the Big Tradeoff* (Washington, D.C.: The Brookings Institution, 1975).

8. Similar views are also shared by John Rawls. According to him, while the market can assure efficiency, it is incapable of achieving equity, and effort to achieve equity will result in some loss of efficiency. See John Rawls, *A Theory of Justice* (Cambridge, MA: Harvard University Press, 1999), revised edition. Other studies, however, challenge the underlying assumption that there is a coefficient on a single inequality statistics in the growth regression. According to Sarah Voitchovsky, income inequality at the top end of the distribution is positively associated with growth, while inequality at the lower end shows that the distribution is negatively related to subsequence growth. Consequently, she argues that redistributive polities such as progressive taxation and social welfare are likely to facilitate growth through their impact on low-income families, but will hinder growth for the high-income families. See Sarah Voitchovsky, "Does the Profile of Income Inequality Matter for Economic Growth? Distinguishing Between the Effects of Inequality in Different Parts of the Income Distribution," *Journal of Economic Growth*, 10, (2005), 290.

9. Alexander Hamilton, James Madison, and John Jay, *Federalist Papers* (New York: Penguin Classics, 1987), Essay No. 51.

10. Samuel P. Huntington, *op cit*, 28.

11. Giovanni Andrea Cornia and Julius Court, *Inequality, Growth and Poverty in the Era of Liberalization and Globalization*, policy brief, no. 4, World Institute for Development Economic Institute, the United Nations University.

12. George Lakoff, *Moral Politics: What Conservatives Know that Liberals Don't* (Chicago: University of Chicago Press, 1996).

13. Morris, Zelditch, Jr., "Theories of Legitimacy" in John T. Jost, Brenda Major, ed., *The Psychology of Legitimacy* (New York, NY: Cambridge University Press, 2001).

14. Aristotle, *Politics* (Sioux Falls, SD: NuVision Publications, 2009).

15. Thomas Hobbes, *Leviathan,* ed. by Edwin Curley (Indianapolis, IN: Hackett Pub Co, 1994); John Locke, *Second Treatise of Civil Government* (Amherst, NY: Prometheus Books, 1986); Jean-Jacque Rousseau, *On the Social Contract,* Dover Thrift ed. (Mineola, NY: Dover Publications, 2003).

16. Talcott Parsons, "Authority, Legitimation, and Political Action" in C. J. Fredrich, ed., *Authority* (Cambridge, MA: Harvard University Press, 1958); Seymour Martin Lipset, "Some Social Requisites of Democracy: Economic Development and Political Legitimacy," *American Political Science Review* 53 (1959): 69-105.

17. Ronald Rogowski, *Rational Legitimacy: a Theory of Political Support* (Princeton, NJ: Princeton University Press, 1974).

18. David Easton, *A Framework for Political Analysis* (Englewood Cliffs, NJ.: Printice-Hall, Inc., 1965), 230.

19. Niccolò Machiavelli, *The Prince* (New York: NY: Oxford University Press, 2005); Karl Marx and Frederick Engels, *The German Ideology,* in *Karl Marx, Frederick Engles: Collected Works* (New York, NY: International Publishers, 1976), Vol, 5: 19-539.

20. Max Weber, *Economy and Society,* ed. by G. Roth and C. Wittich (Berkeley, CA: University of California Press, 1968); Jügen Habermas, *Legitimation Crisis,* trans. by T. McCarthy (Boston, MA: Beacon Press, 1975).

21. The concepts of legitimacy and justification have been discussed extensively. For example, John Rawls used the concept justification extensively in his book *A Theory of Justice* (Cambridge, MA: Harvard University Press, 1971). A. John Simmons argues that a state justified is not necessarily a state legitimized. See A. John Simmons "Justification and Legitimacy," *Ethics* 109 (July 1999): 739-771. I believe legitimacy consists of at least two dimensions: original (moral) justification and utilitarian (interest-based) justification. There could be a third justification, namely, procedural justification. Samuel P. Huntington used this concept in his book *The Third Wave: Democratization in the Late Twentieth Century* (Norman, OK: University of Oklahoma Press, 1993). Carl Schmitt believes that legality can also be an important dimension of legitimacy, see Carl Schmitt, *Legality and Legitimacy,* trans and ed. by Jeffrey Seitzer (Durham, NC: Duke University Press, 2004). Chinese traditional political theory was weak in these two dimensions.

22. Mandate of Heaven comes from "Pangenshang," *Book of History.*

23. *Ren Zheng* comes from "Liang Huiwangshangg," *Mencius.* A contemporary discussion of rule by virtue is available in Kang Xiaoguang's book *Renzheng: Zhongguo zhengzhi fazhan de disnatiao daolu (Rule by Virtue: The Third Way of Chinese Political Development)* (Singapore: Global Publishing, 2005).

24. *Minben* comes from "Wuzi zhi ge," *Book of History.*

25. *Tianxia weigong* comes from *"Liyun,"* *Book of Rites.*

26. Jacques Benigne Bossuet, *Political Treatise,* in J. H. Robinson, ed. *Readings in European History,* 2 vols. (Boston: Ginn, 1906), Vol. 2, 273-277.

27. Max Weber, *Vocation Lectures,* edited by David Owen and Tracey B. Strong (Indianapolis, IN, Hackett Publishing Co., 2004).

28. Confucius, *Analects,* trans. D.C. Lau (New York: Penguin, 1979).

29. *Datong* comes from "Liyun," *Book of Rites.*

30. *Junzi* was used in *Book of Poems*

31. Ding Xiaoping, *Political Wisdom in Ancient China* (Hongzhou, Zhejiang: Zhejiang Daxue Chubanshe[Zhejiang University Press], 2005); Li Cunshan, "Rujia de Renben yu Renquan (Renben and Human Rights in Confucianism)," *Yuandao* 7, no. 18 (2003), http://www.yuandao.com/zazhi/7ji/rjdmbyrq.html (accessed August 14, 2003).

32. *Mencius*: IV A:9 , cited in *Sources of Chinese Tradition*, vol. 1, eds. WM Theodore de Bary, et al. (New York: Columbia University Press, 1960), 93.

33. Mencius, *Mencius,* trans. D.C. Lau (Harmondsworth and New York: Penguin, 1970).

34. *Book of Rites*, "The Convenience of Rites."

35. *Mencius*, Book 3a sec. 4, trans. by D.C. Lau (London,1970), cited in Schrecker, *Chinese Revolution,* 23.

36. Jeremy Bentham, *An Introduction to the Principles of Morals and Legislation* (New York: Hafner Publishing Co., 1948[1789]), I. Yan Jinfen's book *Utilitarianism in Chinese Thought* (Quebec: World Heritage Press, 1998) provides a detailed discussion of Chinese utilitarianism and neo-utilitarianism.

37. Donald Bishop, *Chinese Thoughts: An Introduction* (Columbia, MO: South Asia Books, 2001), 60.

38. The original quote was "天下顺治在民富，天下和静在民乐," and it is from Wang Tingxiang's *Shenyan*.

39. According to *Book of History*, the three most important elements in good governance are cultivating rulers' virtue, utilizing people's talents, and enriching people's livelihood" (正德、利用、厚生谓之三事).

40. Roger T. Ames, *The Art of Rulership: A Study of Ancient Chinese Political Thought* (Albany: State University of New York Press, 1994), 156.

41. The original wards was "不富无以养民情," from " Dalue," *Xunzi,*

42. *Liu fu* or 六府 referrs to six types of wealth. They are: water, fire, metal, wood, earth, and grain. Together with *san shi* 三事, it is called in *Shangshu* (*Book of History*) as "nine functions (九功)." *Liu fu* was later changed to *wu wing* (五行), which implies a natural balance of the five essential material elements of the universe. The ruler's job is to maintain an adequate supply of these elements. Ancient political thinkers believed that any distortion of the five elements would result in chaos.

43. Qiu Jun, *Daxue Yanyi Bu* 大学衍义补 in Sun Wen-xue, "A Study of Qiu Jun's Financial Ideas of Nurturing People," *Research on Financial and Economic Issues,* no. 7, 2005.

44. Lucian W. Pye, *The Mandarin and the Cadre* (Ann Arbor, MI: University of Michigan Press, 1988), 165.

45. According to Guanzhong, "[government] should take from the rich and give it to the poor" (《管子·揆度》 "富而能夺，贫而能与."《晏子春秋. 外篇第七》 "权有无, 均贫富").

46. This original quote was "家给人足，天下大治" from "A Letter to the Renzong Emperor" by Wang Anshi, once a premier of the Northern Song Dynasty 1058, http://www.confucianism.com.cn/wenxue/Show.asp?id=8619 (accessed on January 2, 2010).

47. Mao Conghu, "On Utility Study," *Huadong Shifan Daxue Xuebao* [Journal of East China Normal University], 2 (1989).

48. Abraham H. Maslow, "A Theory of Human Motivation," *Psychological Review* 50, no. 4 (1943): 370-96.

49. Ted Robert Gurr, *Why Men Rebel* (Princeton, NJ: Princeton University Press, 1971).

50. Seymour Martin Lipset, *Political Man* (Baltimore, MD: John Hopkins University Press, 1981).

51. Samuel P. Huntington: *Third Wave: Democratization in the Twentieth Century* (Norman, OK: University of Oklahoma Press, 1991).

52. Theorode J. Lowi, "Four Systems of Policy, Politics and Choice," *Public Administration Review* 32, no. 4 (July/August 1972), 288.

Chapter 2
A New Governing Philosophy

The study of political value orientation is a key part of political culture study. Kluckhohn and Strodtbeck's value orientation theory suggests that all human societies must answer a limited number of universal problems. Some of the common problems we are facing include questions about human relations with time, nature, self, and each other.[1] China is no exception. Every generation of CCP leaders must respond to the same kinds of problems derived from these relationships, albeit in a very different set of political and economic environment.

The values and norms each generation develops are reflections of their own answers to these difficult problems. We expect continuity as well as changes in the generational value orientations. The value orientation of Chinese political elite formed during the reform era is largely pragmatic and utilitarian in nature. This realistic and materialistic mindset produced a period of very impressive economic growth in China. Nevertheless, the decades of single-minded pursuit of growth has also contributed greatly to social disharmony and environmental degradation. The endorsement of the values of economic efficiency, free market competition and profit maximization also led to income polarization and inequality. The market approach has begun to show its limits in many areas. Without some kind of non-market remedies, China is inevitably falling into multiple crises; all are rooted in the distortion of human relations with nature, self, and each other.

Chinese reform has been elite-driven. The value orientation of Chinese political elites is known to have profound impact on Chinese society due to the strong position of the party and the state.[2] This is in line with Arent Lijphart's classification of political culture into a political culture of mass and a political culture of elites.[3] Another explanation for the strong role of the political elite is that the elite have the ability to manipulate public opinion by political framing and propaganda. Through a monopolistic control over mass media, the framing party can effectively control the discussion and perception of an important issue, such as political legitimacy.[4]

In this chapter, we will analyze the value-orientation of the political elite who have governed China since the beginning of the economic reform in 1978. We will first examine the efficiency-enhancing politics conducted during the eras of Deng Xiaoping and Jiang Zemin. Then we will discuss the value orientation of the post-Deng-Jiang era and the key elements of the emerging governing philosophy.

Politics of Efficiency and Its Pitfalls

China's economic reform since 1978 is a process of gradual marketization. The policies made by the reformers bear a resemblance to many of the action plans called for by the "Washington Consensus," a set of policy recommendations made by neo-liberalist economist John Williamson in 1989. He advocated, among other things, the redirection of public spending from welfare subsidies, liberalization of trade and foreign direct investment, and privatization of state enterprises.[5]

Between 1978 and 2002, all reforms, including agriculture, industries, education and health care, were designed to strengthen the role of the market in the decision-making process and to make public sectors more productive and more cost-effective. From the endorsement of a "commodity economy" in 1984 to the backing of a "market economy" in 1992, China took measured yet decisive steps to move away from the planned economy China was accustomed to in previous decades. After the 15th CCP Congress, China further extended market reforms from the enterprise system and property ownership system to the systems of income distribution, finance, public utilities, telecommunications, insurance, education, mass media, and health care. Market suddenly became a silver bullet for all problems China was facing, and efficiency became the highest goal to be pursued at all costs. Reformers utilized all kinds of market mechanisms used in the West to facilitate the transition to a market economy. Many liberal economists all of a sudden found a paradise for the ideas and changes they have championed for years. Many Western liberal economists came to China to offer assistance in establishing market institutions and regulations, and many of them were busy providing lectures and advice to Chinese students and government officials. The efficiency-first mentality was also translated into political value orientation, and the technocratic and authoritarian style of governance is preferred to ensure social stability and to minimize political quarrels and political cost.

The result of the decades-long market reform is uneven. As China's economic system is liberalized almost completely, new social classes and stratifications emerged, and traditional social relations of all kinds are under stress. Meanwhile, Chinese society is also depoliticized. "Getting rich" becomes a prevailing mentality among citizens and is glorified by mass media. The worship of money quickly replaced the worship of charismatic leaders. No doubt, profit-seeking mentality helps boost China's economic efficiency and prosperity. However, the unrestricted pursuit of money and profit also weakens China's traditional values and demoralizes or corrupts players in the market places, including politicians, bureaucrats, businessperson, professional, and cultural elite.

Political leaders formulated a governing philosophy during the formative years of the reform that set them apart from the value orientation of the revolutionary generation. Pragmatism, "efficiency first," and "socialism with Chinese characteristics" are the three main components of this new governing philosophy.

Pragmatism

The ideology of pragmatism served as a guiding principle of initial economic reform: whatever works to improve China's economic performance will have an appeal to policy makers, regardless its ideological label. Deng Xiaoping was a strong believer of pragmatism. In 1962, when discussing a new contract responsibility system for agricultural production, Deng Xiaoping reportedly made the following remarks at a meeting of the CCP Central Secretariat: "no matter whether it is a yellow cat or a black cat, whatever method works . . . we should use that method." Over the years, the yellow cat became a white one, and the wording of Deng's Cat Theory becomes "It doesn't matter if it is a white cat or a black cat, as long as it catches mice, it is a good cat." [6]

Deng's pragmatic philosophy bears resemblance with pragmatism originated from the writing of Charles S. Peirce and John Dewey, even though we were not sure if Deng had ever read any of their books.[7] Pragmatism developed by Peirce and Dewey is characterized by their insistence on consequences, utility, and practicality as vital components of truth. Ontologically speaking, it objects to the view that human concepts and intellect alone accurately represent reality, and therefore stands in opposition to both formalist and rationalist schools of philosophy.[8]

The Chinese pragmatism originated from the debate over the criteria for truth in 1978. A well-known national newspaper, *Guangming Daily,* published an editorial on the subject which provoked an immediate attack from the Maoists. Deng Xiaoping personally backed the editorial and used it as a way to break away from the personality cult of Mao Zedong.[9] Like Peirce, Deng believed that no question was significant unless results of answering it had practical consequences. "The adjective preferred by technocratic leaders and administrators," Centeno wrote, "is 'programmatic,' indicating that they will follow Deng Xiaoping's oft-quoted advice to concentrate on the quality, not the color, of the cat."[10] Deng promoted professional elite to replace the revolutionary old guards. He was hostile to populism and egalitarianism, and was determined to end all forms of political campaigns and mass movements.

"Efficiency First"

The transition from a command economy to a market one has proven to be painful and is full of twists and turns. The official endorsement of "efficiency first" principle took place in the third plenary session of the 14th CCP Congress in 1993. The official document adopted contained the phrase of "giving priority to efficiency with secondary consideration to fairness."[11] The 16th Party Congress further clarified the concept. The report passed by the congress stated, "Priority will be given to efficiency in the primary distribution, and fairness should be the focus of redistribution."[12]

How do the decision makers in *Zhong Nanhai* manage to accomplish the process without causing a major disruption to the economy? The answer may lie in how the developmental mentality is justified. In order to move away from the

egalitarian mentality of the old socialist system, Deng and his supporters carefully articulated the doctrine of "efficiency first, and equity second" (*Xiaoyi
youxian, jiangu gongping*), a doctrine the CCP formally adopted in 1993.[13]

Deng believed that it was impossible to let everyone or every region of the
country develop at the same pace or at the same time. The best strategy, according to him, was to adopt an uneven development strategy to let some individuals
get rich first, and to let the some areas develop first.[14] The precondition of this
asymmetric approach was that these developments must not lower the standard
of living of the rest of the population. Although Deng Xiaoping was not an
economist, many of his ideas are identical with some of the important principles
of neoclassic utilitarian economic approach.[15] This notion of asymmetric development is surprisingly similar to the so-called Pareto improvement or Pareto
efficiency.

Pareto efficiency was an idea proposed by the Italian economist Vilfredo
Pareto (1848-1923) and has since become an important concept in the study of
economics. A change from one allocation to another that can make at least one
individual better off without making any other individual worse off is called a
Pareto improvement. An allocation is defined as Pareto efficient or Pareto optimal when no further Pareto improvements can be made. A Pareto efficient outcome may be very inequitable, but it is efficient if at least one person is made
better off and nobody is made worse off.[16]

Secondly, Deng Xiaoping also believed that although some people would
benefit more than others would initially, everyone would eventually benefit
since the overall benefits of the reform will exceed the overall cost, and those
who are better off first will compensate those who have fallen behind. This can
be done through government regulations that will obligate the rich areas to help
the poor areas, and distributive and redistributive policies to help the disadvantaged groups. In the end, everyone will be better off.[17]

Figure 2.1 A Model of Utility-Based Legitimacy

This idea is similar to what economists called Kaldor-Hicks efficiency. According to Nicholas Kaldors (1908-1986) and John Hicks (1904-1989), economic improvement cannot guarantee that nobody will become worse off, and that
the extent the Pareto improvement can apply is very limited.[18] They believe that
this problem can be solved through compensation, i.e., beneficiaries can virtual-
ly make the Pareto improvement by compensating victims for a loss. Under
Kaldor-Hicks efficiency, an outcome is more efficient if those that are made

better off could in theory compensate those that are made worse off, and consequently, Pareto optimal outcome can still be achieved.[19]

The practice of compensating potential losers underscores why China has been able to transform its command economy into a functional market economy without causing a major social and economic breakdown. It is not a secret that the reformers simply "buy" their way out. Social stability or "peace and unity" is an overwhelming concern of the reformers. Therefore, deliberate efforts have been made to tighten political control. The politics of efficiency would not have worked had there been no authoritarian control. But at the same time, different schemes of compensations, concessions, or side payments are routinely made to minimize resistance from those whose interests may be hurt by the new reform measures.

One example of such a compensation scheme is the generous bonus offered to the revolutionary old guards. In order to replace the revolutionary elite, reformers had to make substantial "side payments" to the old guards which included, among many other things, bonuses and guaranteed security in housing and health care. According to the current official rule, a provincial level cadre does not pay premiums to his or her retirement, yet his or her retirement income can be ten times more than regular pensioners can get. Another example is the price reform on agricultural products such as food at the beginning of the reform. To prevent social unrest, the government had to give most, if not all, urban residents monthly cash subsidies to make sure their purchasing power was not lowered. Similarly, in order to privatize the residential housing, all occupants of public housing were provided with subsidies and bonuses to purchase them. This strategy has worked very well.

"Socialism with Chinese Characters"

In 1982, Deng Xiaoping mentioned the words "socialism with Chinese characteristics" for the first time. However, it was not given any specific meaning and definition. He was only keenly aware that China was at the "primitive stage of socialism," and would remain in this stage for quite some time.[20] As the worldwide communist movement began to crumble after the troubled political reform in the Soviet Union, the need for developing a different kind of socialism was ever stronger. Nevertheless, it was not until the "June 4 Incident" that the CCP was really in a panic mode.

Jiang Zemin and his group came to power amid the most serious political crisis PRC had ever faced. Through his tenure as the Party Secretary, he struggled with the task of rebuilding the public confidence in the party and the state, speed up the economic transition to the market economy. Although Deng Xiaoping discouraged theoretical debates, Jiang found that he had no choice but to exhort and step up efforts to redefine socialism in order to save it from becoming an endangered species.

Many believed that China's socialist system established in the Mao era was a variant form of state socialism.[21] What Jiang and his fellow comrades did was to reinvent a new version of socialism that was compatible with the market economy.[22] Market socialism as a political idea was not entirely new. It first emerged in the 1930s. Friedrick von Hayek proposed to incorporate market into the state planning process.[23] Oskar Lange suggested a total market price for consumer goods and semi-regulated industrial pricing by Central Planning Bureau (CPB).[24] Yugoslavia was the first socialist country that implemented a market-oriented reform and a system of self-government by workers since the 1950s. However, all early experiments with market socialism failed because of the continued political control over production decisions and the lack of competition.[25]

China's long march towards the market economy was full of vicissitudes. It took nearly eighteen years for the neoliberal reformers to finalize a blueprint for a market economy. As early as 1979, Deng Xiaoping proposed that a socialist planned economy can be supplemented by a market economy.[26] From 1979 to 1998, China's attitude toward the market changed several times. Initially, the market was only given some minimum attention. Socialism was understood as primarily a planned economy where the market was allowed to have a limited role to play. At the second stage, the planned economy was replaced with the concept of a commodity economy. In 1987, Deng Xiaoping for the first time emphasized that state planning should no longer be the primary mechanism for the economy. Instead, both the market and planning should be treated as useful tools for promoting the development of the productive forces. By 1992, at last, the concept of commodity economy was replaced by the concept of a socialist market economy. In November 1993, the CCP adopted a resolution that for the first time discussed in details about building a market economy. [27]

As reform progressed, reformers began to touch upon some key questions of state socialism: What is public ownership? How can it be realized in an economically backward country like China? The well-known Chinese liberal economist Li Youwei has argued strongly for restructuring the existing form of public ownership through socialization. He points out that the complete public ownership envisioned by Engels is not realistic in a developing country such as China. The only form of public ownership that is compatible with the primitive stage of socialism is what he calls the social ownership. He suggests that the socialization of the means of production at the current stage can only be realized by promoting social ownership instead of state ownership. By social ownership, he means a system of producer stock ownership which is different from capitalist minority private ownership. In other words, it is what Marx called the "reestablishment of individual ownership"–turning the proletariat into a property-owning working class at first.[28] Li is not the first one to promote the concept of stock socialism. Wang Yu, a Chinese professor, proposed a similar concept in 1994. He suggested that stock ownership by individual workers should be the main form of public ownership.[29]

In the speech made to the 15th Party Congress, Jiang Zemin also expressed a similar view over the issue of public ownership. He reiterated that Chinese socialism is still in its infancy. He called for a diversification of ownership while maintaining the dominant state-ownership. Public ownership, Jiang claimed, can be supplemented by other forms of public and private ownerships, such as stock-cooperative ownership.

The Pitfalls

One of the major fallacies of the efficiency-driven developmental strategy is that it shrinks the complex demands of the people to the simple needs of food, shelter, and wealth. For a poor country, this approach has its merit. However, after China's per capita GDP went beyond US$3,000, people's needs became much more diversified. Many new social elites demand more political freedom and more opportunities to participate in political process. The failure to incorporate these new groups of social and political elite also led to the weakening of the regime's original justification and malfunctioning of in the corporatist state that had so successfully incorporated various groups of elites during the formative years of economic reform.

Drawing on the lessons of the 1980s, the 1990s was characterized as an era of alliance between political elite and economic elite. Chinese society was largely depoliticized. There was a gold rush throughout the nation to make money and to accumulate personal wealth. Nevertheless, the public administration was politicized with various political elites using political power to benefit themselves.[30] The 15th Congress of the CCP reiterated the primitive nature of China's socialism and endorsed a plan to privatize small- and medium-sized public-owned businesses and to establish modern enterprise system for the large-size state-owned companies. This reform made many new business entrepreneurs and created an entirely different set of new political elites. According to Richard Baum and Alexei Shevchenko, there are four groups of new elites being born in China; namely, *developmental, entrepreneurial, clientelist,* and *predatory* groups. The *developmental* group is made of political elite who help create a business-friendly environment such as suppressed labor rights and preferential tax treatment. The *entrepreneurial* group consists of political elite who participate in economic activities directly. The *clientelist* group also refers to rent-seeking political elite who trade power for personal interests. The *predatory* group is made of political elite who demand economic profits directly from business elite.[31] Together, the political elite groups formed an alliance with business elite.

Ironically, Jiang Zemin openly supported admitting the business elite into the CCP as a way of political incorporation. As a result, by 2003, more than one-third of private business owners were CCP members, and many joined the party to take advantage of the new policy.[32] To abduct them politically into the corporatist political system, many of them also were selected to serve in various government institutions. By 2007, there were a total of 1,361 private business owners serving as people's deputies in national or provincial people's congress or members of the national and provincial Chinese People's Political Consultation Conferences (CPPCCs).[33]

In a liberal democracy, political power is marketized in terms of allowing interest group competition for political favors and campaign contributions from big businesses. However, there is no legitimate channel for interest group competitions in China and the lack of transparency in the decision making process has resulted in frequent under-the-table deals. In a market economy, if there is no proper regulation, big businesses can acquire unfair advantage, resulting in monopoly and unfair competition. In politics, it is the same. If the rent-seeking politicians formed an alliance with big businesses, it too can lead to political monopoly of power and corruption.

Indeed, rent-seeking and corruption are two main forms of political marketization in China. The new social classes use their new-found wealth to buy their ways in the system and to bribe government officials. Many public officials also use their political power to make personal gains. There are several forms of rent-seeking practices in China. One is the administrative rent-seeking; i.e., use administrative interference to guarantee the interests of certain groups. Another one is the legislative rent-seeking. Several government departments or agencies fight for the right to draft key legislation, such as the Law of Transportation, and the Anti-trust Law. Each department is trying to protect or maximize its own interests, as the legislation regarding the provision of collecting gasoline taxes to replace various transportation surcharges and fees.[34]

One direct result of the rent-seeking is the marginalization of the disadvantaged groups. While the Chinese economy has grown into a much bigger cake, not everyone is able to keep their fair share. It is believed that less than 30 percent of citizens now control the majority of the 22 trillion on personal savings (in RMB, 2008).[35] Between 1996 and 2005, the income distribution for the average worker dropped from 70.5 percent to 59.4 percent.[36] At the same time, the number of Chinese who entered the world's richest people's club has increased at a phenomenon rate. According to Hurun Wealth Report 2009, China has 825,000 individuals with personal wealth of more than 10 million *yuan* (US$ 1.46 million) and 51,000 individuals with more than 100 million *yuan*. In 2004, there were only three billionaires in China. However, in 2009, that number increased to 130.[37] This kind of income polarization has produced what experts have called the "Latin Americanization of China." As some scholars noted, China has entered into a "cloven society,"

> The new rich and powerful now live in walled, guarded villas and modern apartment complexes, enjoying vast differences in wealth, power, and rights from the swelling ranks of the rural poor and urban dispossessed. The latter are composed of millions of migrant workers living in shantytowns, alongside the growing numbers of urban unemployed and low-income residents who are being forcibly removed from the city center to make way for new real estate development.[38]

One interesting observation can be made about the lack of political reform. When it comes down to depriving the people's "iron rice bowl," the bureaucrats act swiftly and decisively. However, when the reforms such as the use of public vehicles and disclosure of official incomes are concerned, the bureaucrats have resisted, and no progress has been made. Clearly, the alliance between the political elite and the new social economic elite has innate legitimacy deficiency. The new politics of equity will help break the alliance and promote a fair representation of all political forces in the political process.

A New Social Contract

When Hu Jintao and Wen Jiabao took over the top leadership positions in China in 2002, the new administration faced many serious challenges, such as the SARS epidemic, rampant corruption, widening income disparities, and sharp increases in the number of social unrests. The achievement-based legitimacy that the reformers have relied on is running thin as more and more people feel the pain of the so-called relative deprivation. Health care, education, and housing are becoming three new "mountains" for most ordinary people. The need for social justice and equity is stronger than ever.[39]

Since 2002, the new leaders in Beijing have quietly engaged in some serious soul-searching and reevaluation of China's recent developmental strategy and governing philosophy. Conscious efforts were made to solicit new ideas and recommendations among Chinese elite domestically as well as overseas.[40] The party scholars were also busy in inventing a new consensus-based theory to supplement the somewhat ambiguous Theory of "Three Represents" proposed by former party leader Jiang Zemin. Soon the "Scientific Development Perspective" was pronounced by Hu Jintao. Intensive inner-party reeducation as well as a public campaign was launched to propagate the new value orientation of the new administration. Finally, in the 17th CCP Congress held in 2007, the new theory was codified as the new party guiding principle, parallel to Deng Xiaoping Theory, and the Theory of "Three Represents."

In addition to the need of strengthening the political legitimacy of the party-state, there are a number of other reasons as to why this is happening. First of all, there is a need for new ideas and policies whenever there is a transition of power taking place in the CCP's recent history. According to the CCP's own account, Hu and Wen represent the fourth generation of party leaders. As one of the unwritten rules of the CCP, each generation must develop its own independent thinking and policies that are at least new and non-conventional compared to the previous generation. CCP Chairman Hua Guofeng, though endorsed by the deceased former paramount leader Mao, was not considered a "generation" since he did not have his own independent thinking and any real contributions to the party's theory and policies. Therefore, he was only considered as a transitional leader.[41] Deng Xiaoping made his mark by throwing out Mao's revolutionary ideology and adopting a more pragmatic one. He was considered the leadership core of the second generation. Deng's successor, Jiang Zemin, also tried very hard to come up with some new ideas and new policies of his own. Even with some dismay displayed over his performance by the paramount leader, Deng Xiaoping, during his tour of southern China in 1992, Jiang managed to secure his position as the leadership core of the third generation by formally endorsing the market economy and by proposing a set of new guiding principles for the party.[42]

After nearly a decade in waiting, Hu Jintao officially took over CCP's number one post at the 16th CCP Congress held in 2002. This was the first time in the CCP's history that an orderly and peaceful transition of power had ever occurred, though it actually took nearly two years for the transition to complete. Hu subsequently became President of the People's Republic of China (PRC 2003), and Chairman of the CCP's Central Military Committee (2004). In order to consolidate his power, Hu Jintao was eager to come up with some theoretical innovations in order to secure his place in history. To do so, he organized multiple working groups that consisted of scholars and top leaders to reexamine past successes and failures, and to come up with something new in developmental theories, strategies and policies. Meanwhile, beginning in 2004, the "third major debate about reform" generated some urgency about a systematic review of past reforms and the future direction over the fate of market-oriented reform. Hong Kong economist Lang Xianping openly attacked the reform of the state-run enterprises.[43] In 2005, a research report published by the State Council's Development Research Center declared the health care reform to be unsuccessful and denounced commercialization and marketization to be the wrong direction.

Between 2002 and 2009, Hu and his think tankers captured the media headlines by pumping out one new concept after another. A new set of political values has been carefully spelled out and reiterated through official speeches and the government-controlled media. At the heart of this new round of value reorientation is the so-called "Scientific Development Perspective." This new theory is obviously not the work of one person; instead, it represents a new group consensus of the fourth generation of political elite. The new theory calls for a balanced approach towards economic development and human development and economic growth and social justice. Keenly aware of the deficiencies in the efficiency-oriented developmental strategy, the new thinking embraces a people-centered and environmentally-friendlier approach. While the central political issue for the decades of efficiency-driven economic growth was how to develop, the new issue to be addressed by the new governing elite is who will benefit from the reform and what are the purposes of the development. In the process, Hu and his followers have abandoned the single-minded approach toward development; they want to devote more energy and resources to social and human developments and to make China's development a sustainable one. The march toward market socialism has already consumed much of the political capital the CCP has acquired in its revolutionary era; it must now seek new grounds for justification to stay in power. Deng Xiaoping once reminded his comrades that the essence of socialist appeal lay in the prosperity of all people, not just a few.[44] How to obtain this goal, without sacrificing efficiency, will be the main challenge ahead.

Anyone who has followed Chinese media closely in the past few years will be amazed by the dazzling display of new political phrases and jargon that have appeared in headlines. Using the most popular Chinese Internet search engine, the words that appeared most frequently in the Internet sites include "Scientific Development Perspective" (68 million pages), "put the people first" (49.9 million references), and "harmonious society" (47.8 million), far exceed the old lexicon such as "Three Represents" (24 million), Deng Xiaoping Theory (22.1 million), Mao Zedong Thought (10.9 million).[45] Let us look at each of the new official lexicons.

"Putting People First"

One typical way to formulate a new public consensus is by borrowing from political wisdoms of the past. In September 2001, the CCP adopted the instrumental view of legitimation and proposed a new concept called *"yi ren wei ben"* in a document calling for strengthening citizens' character education.[46] Two years later, the term was mentioned again in another official document that called for the perfection of Chinese market economy with a focus on social and human development.[47] However, there is no detailed elaboration of what this new concept means. On the surface, it is a rejection of the value orientation of *"yi wu wei ben"* which permeated throughout Chinese society during the 1990s. However, since *men ben* was a traditional idea of political legitimacy, it is apparent that Hu Jingtao is using a traditional metaphor to justify his value orientation. Its essence is to take an instrumental approach toward strengthening CCP's political legitimacy. It is hoped that by the policy of benefiting, enriching and nurturing people, citizens will approve CCP's right to govern. On March 10, 2004, CCP General Secretary Hu Jintao made the first clear definition of the concept. According to him,

> Adherence to *"yi ren wen ben"* means that the human development to its fullest potential shall be made an end in itself; the designing and promotion of development must be based on the fundamental interests of the people; the increasing material and cultural demands of the people must be met continuously; and the economic, political and cultural rights of the people must be guaranteed; and the fruits of the development must be shared by all people.[48]

In communist lexicon, people are always affiliated with class attributes. Mao specifically defined people as those who support the communist party and the socialism. Anyone else is typically classified as class enemies. Hu's usage of people is more closely associated with the concept of a natural man or humankind, not a class-based man.[49] It is in this way that a harmonious relationship between man and nature are emphasized. The use of natural men instead of the class-based concept of *ren min* has clearly broken away from the orthodox Marxist tradition. Although the meaning of the new concept remains unsettled, *yi ren wei ben* has now formally become a part of governing philosophy of the fourth generation of CCP leaders. It redefined the objective of the development and shifted the Deng-Jiang's economic-center approach. Economic development is no longer a developmental goal in itself; rather, the human development is considered more important than material accumulation.

Scientific Development Perspective

The second major conceptual innovation of the new leaders was the idea of new developmental perspective. After the SARS crisis, the CCP suggested that economic reform must make some major adjustment. This consensus was reflected in the "Decision on a Number of Issued Related to the Improvement of Market

Economy." The key concept developed in this document is "comprehensive development" which was interpreted as a "coordinated, balanced, and sustainable economic, social and human development."[50] Although Hu Jintao used the word "scientific development" in his speech made to the Third Plenary Session of the 16th CCP Congress that adopted the decision, the official usage was first elaborated by Hu in his speech made in the National Conference on Population, Natural Resources and Environment.[51]

Hu pointed out that the new concept represents the CCP's new vision of development and should become the guiding principles for the party for the new century. Human comprehensive development is the ultimate goal of the development. The development should include not just economic development, but political and cultural development as well. The balanced development of five areas was specifically mentioned: rural development, regional development, social and human development, sustainable development, and peaceful development. Lastly, the sustainable development emphasizes the harmonious relationship between man and nature, and the balance between population, resource and environment. One notable change in the official metaphor was the change in the popular expression of "fast and sound development" to "sound and fast development," indicating the quality of the growth is now more important than the speed.

Harmonious Society

The concept first appeared vaguely in Jiang Zemin's Report to the 16th CCP Congress in 2002 which mentioned "social harmony" as one of the six goals of the society of "small comfort." But it left much undefined. In the 4th Plenary Session of the 16th CCP Congress held between September 16 and 19, 2004, "building socialist harmonious society" was used as one of the five governing capability the CCP intended to acquire.[52] In February 19, 2005, Hu Jintao made his comment on this new concept. He described what a harmonious society should look like: democracy and rule of law, equality and justice, honor and love, full of vitality, stability and order, and environmental protection. The Central Committee of the CCP held a special session to discuss the building of the harmonious society in October 2006 and adopted "the Decision on Several Critical Issues related to Building Socialist Harmonious Society."[53] In his report to the 17th Party Congress, Hu moved away from the "efficiency first" principle and proposed for the first time that fairness should also be given priority in the primary distribution.

Those three new concepts constituted the core values in the new government philosophy of the fourth generation of party leaders. They are powerful

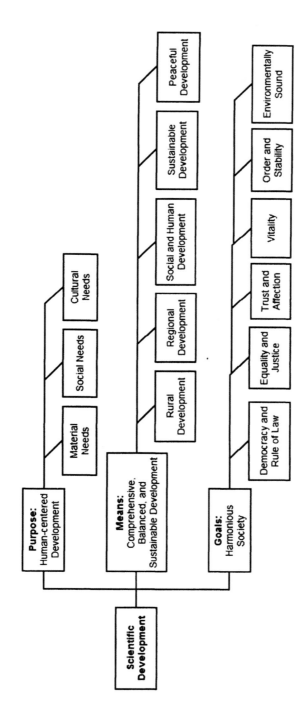

Figure 2.2 A Concept Map of the Scientific Development Perspective

conceptual metaphors used for positive political framing (see Figure 2.1).[54] Positive political framing is a process of control over the individual's perception of meanings through the use of carefully chosen metaphors as if the values presented by these metaphors are only viable options and the alternative will be risky and unpleasant. The framing makers define how a discussion is confined so that only certain interpretations can be accepted, and all others will be ruled out.[55] No one can challenge that since the opposition is being framed as inhuman, unscientific, and non harmonious. The metaphor describing people as the foundation of a state put morality into politics, and served as a useful legitimizing scheme. The conceptual metaphor describing development as a scientific undertaking put an indictment on all previous development model. The notion of harmonious society moved away from Marx's class struggle theory. Overall, the new government philosophy of this administration is very comprehensive, well elaborated, and extremely popular. They are also more than rhetorical.

All of the key values developed have significant policy implication. If the Deng Xiaoping's reform is a major breakthrough, the new view of the scientific development represents an asserted effort to rationalize the reform and move the country ahead.

A Return to Chinese Traditional Humanism

The first thing an observer of Chinese politics may notice is the similarity between the latest call for people-centered development and the traditional Chinese *min ben* idea which first appeared in *Book of History* written roughly during the Warring State Period (475-22 BC).[56] It later became a main tenet in Chinese traditional governing philosophy throughout various dynasties in Chinese history. It was used to regulate the relationship between rulers and people and to strengthen a ruler's political legitimacy. The traditional concept *ben* is often translated into "foundation of the state." However, from the political science perspective, it simply refers to the roots or sources of political legitimacy. The employment of this ancient metaphor is clearly a part of the atavism that is so prevalent in China today. With the fading influence of Maoism, political tradition has suddenly becomes a source of inspiration. From gigantic status of ancient ancestors erected everywhere to elaborate ceremonies held to pay respect to some historical figures such as Emperors Yan and Yuang and Confucius, one can discern this trend. The rediscovery of the Confucian "*men ben*" idea has two meanings: one is to find a more popular metaphor to strengthen the CCP's popular roots; and two, also most importantly, to redefine China's developmental strategy.

Although some Chinese propagandists want you to believe that the *men ben* idea is the latest theoretical innovation the current political elite made to Marxist ideology, many scholars quickly point out that the new governing philosophy is nothing but a restored version of the traditional *min ben* idea. Although some scholars in China have tried to distinguish *yi ren wei ben* and *yi min wei ben*,[57] many others believe that "men" and "ren" in Ancient Chinese are us

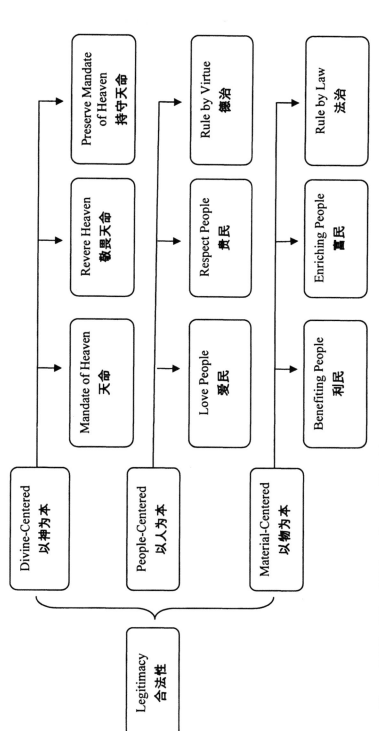

Figure 2.3 Traditional Chinese System of Legitimation

Interchangeably in ancient time, and there is no substantial difference between
the ancient usage of *ren ben* and *min ben*.[58] After all, it is the earliest expression
of humanism in China.

Humanism has always been a core value in Chinese traditional understanding of political legitimacy. It has been translated into various Chinese words. As
part of a three-tiered system of political legitimacy, it differs very much from
divine-based legitimacy and material-based legitimacy (see Figure 2.3). The
divine-based legitimacy emphasizes the mandate of heaven or God, which is a
characteristic of much of the medieval European and Japanese history. Although
Chinese traditionally believed in the existence of heaven, there is no love of God
in Chinese tradition other than being respectful to him.[59] As a distinctive feature
of Chinese traditional political theories, Chinese traditionally emphasized the
unity between heaven and the people. In this sense, the idea of Mandate of Heaven is often interpreted as mandate of the people. The material-based legitimacy
is essentially eudemonic in nature. It is based on a ruler's legitimacy on the satisfactory of people's material needs. Therefore, it is primarily achievement-
driven.

Nevertheless, Confucian understanding of humanism, which became a dominant governing philosophy since the Han Dynasty, is limited to humanitarianism in nature. It believed that human beings are precious, and should be treated
as such by rulers.[60] Human beings' basic needs must be satisfied. Although there
is some level of popular consent with this kind of governing philosophy, the
consent is only a tacit one. The Mandate of Heaven is quite often interpreted as
mandate of the people. According to this view, a ruler, who has the Mandate of
Heaven, possesses the quality of virtue, shows respect to his subjects, follows
the rules of the ancestors, and tries to win the hearts and minds of the people,
will be considered a just and legitimate one. A just ruler will strengthen his legitimacy by promoting policies that will benefit the people, not himself, by ensuring relatively equal distribution of these benefits, and by allowing the people to
do what they do best. This way of thinking has influenced every Chinese government and its rulers throughout history.[61] Yet, the Confucian humanism does
not embrace individual freedom and equality. It is paternalistic and hierarchical
in nature.

To invoke a historical metaphor as part of new value orientation is a smart
choice since the idea is already deeply rooted in Chinese political culture. However, there is an inherent risk in embracing the ancient governing philosophy
without some serious criticism. Chinese traditional humanism, no matter how
appealing it may sound, is an ideology for authoritarianism.[62] The ruler is not
going to share power with the people. The hierarchical ethical virtue implied in
Confucianism is inherently unequal. The working class is to be used but not to
be taught how to make decision.[63] *Ren ben* calls for a government
for the people, but not by the people. It differs from the modern ideology of democracy that calls for the active participation of the decision-making process,
and the modern notion of human development, which calls for realization of its
full potential under conditions of liberty and equality. Traditional *men ben* ideas
such as *zhong min, ai min, li min, hou min* and *ji min* can help make benevolent

rulers, it does not give people the power to make rulers accountable. People's silence may be a sign of tacit consent, but there is no way to express their explicit consent or discontent with the ruler.

The revival of people-centered value orientation sends a signal for a possible convergence of the materialist and humanist socialist movements. The scientific socialism, which derives largely from the writings of Marx, Engel, Lenin and Stalin, has competed with democratic socialism, which derives its key doctrines largely from Prudon, Lassall, and Bernstein, since the mid-nineteenth century. By emphasizing humanism and harmonious society, Hu Jintao has gone further beyond Marx's analytical framework of class struggle and class-based dictatorship.

Embracement of Humanist Marxism?

For over half a century, Marxist ideology has served as the new Mandate of Heaven for the communist revolutionaries throughout the world. The key tenets of this revolutionary movement include proletarian dictatorship, class struggle, and public ownership of means of production. It leaves little room for class cooperation, democracy, and humanism. Chinese leaders like Mao Zedong endorsed the use of "revolutionary humanitarianism," but the concept of people has a class connotation. Only people or the working class, not the class enemies, shall be the master of the society.

However, the result of the nearly three decades of reform has created a pluralistic society. Most people now are property owners in one way or another. The traditional definition of proletarian dictatorship has apparently encountered its biggest challenges. The blue-collar industrial workers that Marx considered to be the main social force for communist revolution have now shrunk in size. Knowledge workers in service industry will soon surpass the number of traditional industrial workers. New occupations and professions mushroomed in contemporary China. The CCP has now formally opened its door to capitalist and other small business owners to join its party ranks.

One of the CCP's recent initiatives was to set up a "Research and Implementation Project of Marxist Basic Theory."[64] A new Academy of Marxist Studies was established in 2004. The government allocated a generous amount of funds to support theoretical researches, re-translate Marxist classics, authorize new textbook revisions and publications, and offer training to young Marxist scholars. There is a new wave of publications on socialist and Marxist studies. One of the key concerns is how to incorporate humanism into Marxism. Three main points stand out:

More Attention Given to the Thoughts of Young Marx

Cong Dachuan, a mainland Chinese scholar, believes that historical materialism, which is the cornerstone of capitalism, is not the core value of Marxist philosophy; instead, the "practical humanism" developed in his *Economic and Philosophical Manuscripts of 1844* represents his true value orientation. Professor

Cong has published over a hundred articles on this subject. The following is what he has found: Based on Marx's theory of alienation, when a laborer is disenfranchised by his own labor, he becomes a commodity or a slave of the capitalists, and loses his human status and dignity. Rather than being the purpose of all material development, capitalist development turned human beings into a tool for surplus values. Communism is a rejection of material-worship and money-worship capitalism, and its goal is to create an association of free productive individuals that are liberated from alienation and returned to their natural and social agency and subjectivity.[65]

Major Effort to Distinguish Radical Marxism from His Later Writing

In an article written by Xie Tao, a former vice president of Renmin University of China, he declared that only democratic socialism could save China. He pointed out that Marx and Engels made major revisions to their earlier theory when they wrote the third volume of *Capital* and many other works; they endorsed stockownership as a way of realizing public ownership, and supported democracy and peaceful evolution. He believed that all the major reform policies adopted in the reform era resembled what the democratic socialists have championed for years. In order to avoid being labeled as "revisionism," the CCP used the phrase of "socialism with Chinese characteristics." Xie believes that the constitutional amendment to include the "theory of three represents" and the protection of private property marked the beginning of democratic socialism in China.[66]

More Emphasis on the New Phase of Modern Economy

Xu Congzheng, another Marxist scholar, also points out that human development is not simply political freedom; it is the economic freedom that will allow individuals to realize their full potentials. Additionally, in classical economies, capital is the key to surplus values. However, in today's knowledge-based economy, human intelligence and technology advancement are the sources of surplus values. The study of Marxist theory, according to Xu, must be reoriented from the study of the role of capital and production relationships to the study of the role of men and the comprehensive development of individuals.[67]

There is no consensus as to how to classify China's new vision of socialism. Most of the new thinking discussed above has faced relentless attacks from the left, especially Xie's article. To avoid theoretical division within the party, Hu Jiintao made a quick response by making a speech on adherence to building the socialism with Chinese characteristics.[68] It appears that the political elite in Beijing do not feel comfortable with the notion of democratic socialism. The most likely scenario is a gradual convergence of the major theory and practices of scientific and democratic socialism. China's democratic socialism, if it is ever developed, will be somewhat different from European democratic socialism.[69]

Conclusions

The governing philosophy of the fourth generation represents a major departure from orthodox Marxist class theory. It challenged the material-based governing philosophy, and tried to restore the traditional Chinese governing principle of people-first and the humanist Marxism. The "Scientific Development Perspective" is more than just official masking; it represents a paradigm change in Chinese developmental state. If the Deng Xiaoping Theory served as a basis of social cohesion for the first thirty years of reform, this new governing philosophy will provide some new moral and utilitarian justifications for the political leaders in China and a basis of a new consensus in the second phase of China's reform and social transformation. The politics of equity has just begun.

Will the equity-enhancing mentality augment the legitimacy of the Leninist party? Will the emphasis on humanistic values compromise economic efficiency? Is the new value orientation permanent or temporary shift? These questions will be examined in the next few chapters.

Notes

1. F. R. Kluckhohn, and F. L. Strodtbeck, *Variations in Value Orientations* (Evanston, Ill.: Row, Peterson, 1961).

2. Daniel A. Bell, *Beyond Liberal Democracy: Political Thinking for an East Asian Context* (Princeton, NJ: Princeton University Press, 2006), 152-162.

3. Arend Lijphart, *Democracy in Plural Societies: A Comparative Exploration* (New Haven, CT: Yale University Press, 1977).

4. Erving Goffman, *Frame Analysis: An Essay on the Organization of Experience* (Cambridge: Harvard University Press, 1974).

5 John Williamson, "What Washington Means by Policy Reform," in John Williamson ed.: *Latin American Readjustment: How Much has Happened* (Washington DC: Institute for International Economics 1989).

6 "The Background on Deng's Remark on Good Cat [Deng Xiaoping Haomao Lun Chutai Qianhou]" http://www.dxp.org.cn/ShowArticle.asp?ArticleID=2791(accessed February 2, 2006).

7. The Peirce Edition Project, *The Essential Peirce* (1983-1913) (Bloomington, IN: Indiana University Press, 1998); Larry A. Hickman and Thomas M. Alexander, *The Essential Dewey* (Indiana: Indiana University Press, 1999).

8. John Dewey, *How We Think* (Lexington, MA: D.C. Heath, 1910), Reprinted (Buffalo, NY: Prometheus Books, 1991).

9. Hu Fuming, "Practice is the Only Criteria for Verifying Truth," *Guangming Daily*, May 11, 1978, http://www.epicbook.com/history/practice.html (accessed August 10, 2006).

10. Miguel Angel Centeno, "The New Leviathan: the Dynamics and Limits of Technocracy," *Theories and Society* 22, no. 3 (June 1993): 307-335.

11. The CCP, "Decisions on a Number of Issues Relating to Establishing a Socialist Market Economy," http://www.china.com.cn/chinese/archive/131747.htm (accessed February 2, 2006).

12 . Jian Zeming, "Report to the 16th Party Congress," http://news.xinhuanet.com/ (accessed February 2, 2006).

13. CCP, "Decisions on a Number of Crucial Issues Relating to Establishing a Socialist Market Economy," *op.cit.*

14. Deng Xiaoping, "There is no Fundamental Contradiction between Socialism and Market Economy," *Selected Works of Deng Xiaoping*, Vol. 3, October 23, 1985, http://gd.cnread.net/cnread1/zzzp/d/dengxiaoping/3/048.htm (accessed August 10, 2006).

15. Julian Le Grand, *Equity and Choice: an Essay in Economics and Applied Philosophy* (London and New York: HarperCollins, 1991).

16. Amartya Sen, "Markets and Freedom: Achievements and Limitations of the Market Mechanism in Promoting Individual Freedoms," *Oxford Economic Papers* 45, no. 4 (1973): 519-541.

17. Deng Xiaoping, "Summary of Speeches Made during the Southern Inspection Tour of Wuhan, Shenzhen, Zhuhai and Shanghai," *Selected Works of Deng Xiaoping*, Vol. 3, http://gd.cnread.net/cnread1/zzzp/d/dengxiaoping/3/118.htm (accessed August 10, 2006).

18. Yue Tianmin, *Zhengzhi Hefaxing Wenti Yanjiu [A Study of Political Legitimacy]*(Beijing, Zhongguo Shehui Kecue Chubanshe, 2006), 314.

19. Nicholas Kaldor, "Welfare Propositions in Economics and Interpersonal Comparisons of Utility," *Economic Journal*, 49, no. 195 (1939): 549–552; John Hicks, "The Foundations of Welfare Economics." *Economic Journal*, 49, no. 196 (1939): 696–712.

20. Wu Guoyou, "Shehui Shuyi de Kexue Lunduan Shi Ruhe Zuochue de [How the Judgment of Socialist Primitive Stage is Made], *People's Daily*, June 30, 2001.

21. A. Y. So and X. Yu , "From State Socialism to State Developmentalism: the Changing Pattern of Classes and Class Conflict in China," paper presented at the annual meeting of the American Sociological Association, Atlanta Hilton Hotel, Atlanta, GA, http://www.allacademic.com/meta/p107772_index.html (accessed December 6, 2009).

22. Sujian Guo, *The Political economy of Asian Transition from Communism* (Burlington, VT: Ashgate, 2006), ch. 6. See also Le-Yin Zhang, "Market Socialism Revisited: the Case of Chinese State-Owned Enterprises," *Issues and Studies* 42, no. 3 (September 2006): 1-46.

23. Friedrick von Hayek, "The Nature and History of the Problem," in *Collectivist Economic Planning,* ed., Friedrick von. Hayek (London: George Routledge and Son, 1987).

24. Oskar Longe, "On the Economic Theory of Socialism," in *On the Economic Theory of Socialism*, ed., B. Lippincott (Minneapolis: University of Minnesota Press, 1956).

25. John E. Roemer, *A Future for Socialism* (Cambridge, MA: Harvard University Press, 1994).

26. Deng Xiaoping, "Shehui Zhuyi Ye Keyi Gao Shichang Jingji [Socialist Counties Can also Implement Market Economy]," *Selected Work of Deng Xiaoping*, Vol. 2, 236. http://web.peopledaily.com.cn/deng/ (accessed on January 7, 2010).

27. *Renming Ribao* (Overseas Edition), "Zhong Gong Shi Yi Jie San Zhong Quan Hui Yi Lai Da Shi Ji" (Major Events since the Third Plenum of the Eleventh Party Congress of the CCP), December 16, 1998.

28. Li Youwei, "*Guanyu Suoyoushi Ruogan Wenti De Sikao*" [Some Thoughts on the Issues of Ownership], *China and the World*, no. 8 (1997).

29. Cao Yiping and Song Jun, "Laodongzhe Geren Gufen Suoyouzhi Yin Shi Gongyouzhi De Zhuyao Xingshi" (Stock Ownership by Individual Workers Should be The Main Form of Public Ownership), *Xinhua Wenzhai* (August 1994).

30. Kang Xiaoguang, "Zailun 'xinzheng xina zhengzhi' ('The Administralization of Politics' Revisited)," in Kang Xiaohuang, *Renzheng: Zhongguo Zhengzhi Fazhan de Disantiao Daolu* [Rule of Ethics: the Third Way of Political Development in China] (Singapore: Global Publishing, 2005).

31. Richard Baum and Alexei Chevchenko, "The State of State" in Merle Goldman and Roderick MacFarquhar, ed, *The Paradox of China's Post-Mao Reforms* (Cambridge, MA: Harvard University Press, 1999), 333-360.

32. "More and More Capitalists Have Jointed the CCP,"A Global Network for Chinese Professionals, http://www.networkchinese.com/region/china/yrueo.html (accessed January 12, 2010).

33. Jiang Kaiqiu and Guan Xinjiang, "Zhengque Bawo Za Xinde Shehui Jieceng Fazhan Dangyuan de Wenti [Proper Handling of the Party Member Recruitment among Members of the New Social Stratus], http://www.allzg.com/n41895c79.aspx (accessed January 8, 2007).

34. It took more than ten years to implement the gasoline tax as required by the Laws on Transportation. The legislative process over the Anti-trust Law also invited some competition among the National Development and Reform Commission, the Department of Commerce, and State Commission for Industry and Commerce. See http://news.xinhuanet.com/fortune/2005-01/11/content_2442715.htm (accessed February 9, 2007).

35. NBS, *China Statistical Yearbook* (2008), http://www.stats.gov.cn/ (accessed February 9, 2007).

36 . "Widening Income Disparities Will affect Economic Development," http://en.secretchina.com/finance_business/3275.html (accessed February 9, 2007).

37 . *Hurun Wealth Report, 2009*, http://www.hurun.net/listreleaseen374.aspx (accessed December 10, 2007).

38. George J. Gilboy and Eric Heginbotham, "Latin Americanization of China?" *Current History* (September 2004):256-261.

39. Long Hua, *Hu-Wen Zhiguo Jiemi* [the Secret of Hu-Wen Governance] (Hong Hong: Xinhua Caiyin Chubanshe, 2005).

40. The author attended one of such consultation meetings in Washington D.C. organized by Chinese Ambassador to the United States Mr. Zhou Wenzhong.

41. "Inside Stories of Hua Guofeng's Resignation: Chen Yun Asked Him to Yield to Others," Phoenix TV, December 23, 2008, http://news.ifeng.com/history/1/jishi/200812/ (accessed February 9, 2007).

42. A theory proposed by Jiang Zemin in 2000. The theory calls for the CCP to broaden its social basis and to be a representative of the developmental needs of advanced productive forces, the direction of advanced culture, and the interests of the whole people. This theory was enshrined as the guiding principle of the CCP in 2002.

43. Lang Xianping, "Zai 'Guotui Minjin' Shengyan Zhong Kuanghuan de Greencool Capital Limited" (The Fiesta of Greencool Capital Limited in Taking over State Enterprises), sina.com, Aug. 16, 2004, http://finance.sina.com.cn/t/20040816/ (accessed February 9, 2007).

44. Deng Xiaoping, *Selected Works of Deng Xiaoping* (Beijing, People's Publishing House, 1993), 109, 110-111.

45. The search was conducted on February 17, 2010.

46. CCP Central Committee, "Implementation Outline for Building Public Ethics," Oct. 24, 2001, http://www.chinanews.com.cn (accessed on March 7, 2008).

47. CCP Central Committee. "The Decisions on a Number of Issues relating to the Improvement of Socialist Market Economy)," adopted by the Third Plenary Session of the 16th Party Congress in October 14, 2003, http://www.people.com.cn (accessed February 9, 2007).

48. Hu Jintao, "Speech Made to the National Conference on the Work of Population, Natural Resources and Environment," March 10, 2004, http://www.people.com.cn/GB/shizheng/1024/2427943.html (accessed June 3, 2008).

49. Bai Guicai, "Men Benwei Yu Menben Sixian (People-first Principle and Men Ben Idea)," http://www.chinavalue.net/Blog/BlogThread.aspx?EntryID=135429 (accessed June 3, 2008).

50 .CCP Central Committee, "The Decisions on a Number of Issues relating to the Improvement of Socialist Market Economy," http://cpc.people.com.cn/ (accessed June 3, 2008).

51. Li Junru, "Kexue Fazhanguan Tichu de Shidai Beijing [Historical Background of the Formation of the Scientific Development Perspective]" http://www.chinaelections.org/NewsInfo.asp?NewsID=47561; Hu Jintao, "Speech to the National Forum on Population, Resources and Environmental Protection," March 10, 2004, http://www.people.com.cn/GB/shizheng/1024/2427943.html (accessed May 21, 2008).

52. Li Peilin, "Goujian Shehui Zhuyi Hexie Shehui Tichu de Guocheng [The Formation Process of the Scientific Development Perspective]," http://www.southcn.com/nflr/llzhuanti/hexie/hxlw/200504150397.htm (accessed June 3, 2008).

53. CCP Central Committee, "Decision on Certain Important Issues Relating to the Building a Socialist Harmonious Society," October 8-11, 2006. http://cpc.people.com.cn/GB/64093/64094/4932424.html (accessed June 3, 2008).

54. Snow, D. A., Rochford, E. B., Worden, S. K., and Benford, R. D., "Frame Alignment Processes, Micromobilization, and Movement Participation," *American Sociological Review* 51, (1986): 464–481.

55. Jeffrey Feldman, *Framing the Debate: Famous Presidential Speeches and How Progressives Can Use Them to Control the Conversation (and Win Elections)* (Brooklyn, NY: Ig Publishing, 2007).

56. *Book of History*, 《尚书·夏书·五子之歌》"民可近, 不可下. 民为邦本, 本固邦宁" ("People can be loved, but not to be looked down because people are the foundation of the state. The state will only become stably if the foundation is strong.").

57. Feng Guang, "Yi Ren Wei Ben Yu Yi Min Wei Ben Qubue de Tantao (A Study of the Differences between the Idea of Putting People First and Putting the Governed First)," *Lilun Qianyan (Theoretical Frontline)* 18 (2005): 36-37.

58. These quotes came from some Chinese classics which is hard to translate. So I will quote Chinese original text in the next few citations: 《管子·霸言》: "夫霸王之所始也，以人为本，本理则国固，本乱则国危。"

59. In *Book of History*, there are statement about "敬天" (respect heaven) and "畏天" (fearful of heaven), but one cannot find "爱天" (love god or heaven).

60. *Book of Filet Piety*,"天地之性 (生) 人为贵."

61. Baogang Guo, "Political Legitimacy in China's Transition," *Journal of Chinese Political Studies* 8, no. 1-2 (2003):1-16.

62. *Book of Rites,* "Ziyi": "民以君为心，君以民为体…君以民存，亦以民亡."

63 *Analects,* "Taibo": "民可使由之，不可使知之"

64. CCP Central Committee, "Decision on Further Development of Philosophy and Social Sciences," March 20, 2004, http://news.xinhuanet.com/newscenter/2004-03/20/content_1375777.htm (accessed May 2, 2008).

65. Cong Dachuan and Sun Yong, "Qian Tan Yi Wu Wei Ben de Fazhan Guan He "Yi Ren Wei Ben' de Fazhan Guan" (Comparing the Human-based and Material-based Developmental Perspectives," *Journal of Baoji University of Arts and Sciences* 26, no. 3 (2006): 5-10.

66. Xie Tao, "Only Democratic Socialism Can Save China."

67. Xu Congzhen, "Comprehensive Human Development: the Creative Development in Marx's Economic Theory," *Guangming Daily,* July 4, 2007, http://myy.cass.cn/file/2007070628039.html (accessed August 17, 2008).

68. Hu Jintao, "A Speech Made at the CCP Party School," *People's Daily.* June 26, 2007.

69. Wu Jiaxiang, "Two Kinds of Democratic Socialism," *Guancha* [Observer], July 1, 2007, http://www. guancha.org/ (accessed August. 17, 2008).

Chapter 3
The Emergence of a New Political Elite

Many political scientists have taken notice of cyclical changes among political elite in China. Lowell Dittmer's elite factionalist model provides some insight over the zigzag of the reform and retrenchment that have accompanied throughout the reform era.[1] However, critics of this theory point out that this model follows broadly the "two-line struggle" model used by the CCP, and that the significance of this type of factional politics may become less important as ideologies have become chief dividers among political elite.[2] Furthermore, factional politics does not capture the generation changes that are more permanent than merely factional disagreement within the same generation of political leaders.

John H. Kautsky's modernization theory provides another useful analytical framework. According to Kautsky, there existed two types of modernizers in developing countries: the revolutionary modernizers and the managerial modernizers. The formers consisted of "professional men, highly educated, and with cosmopolitan perspectives." They are generally lawyers, journalists and teachers, students of humanities and social sciences, philosophers, novelists and poets, and "they are men with a vision of the future." The revolutionary modernizers are concerned more about drawing its support from political ideology and charismatic leadership, the technocratic modernizers rely more on rationalizing rules, laws, and institutionalization.[3] Kautsky believes that a successful modernization depends on the replacement of the former with the latter. Many of the earlier studies of Chinese elite mobility focused exclusively on the "red" and "expert" career paths of the elite.[4] Some empirical studies have confirmed Kautsky's observation.[5]

Kautsky's analytical framework is instrumental in distinguishing the revolutionary leaders from the managerial ones. Nevertheless, it still falls short in the dynamic dimension. The problem with Kautsky's classification is that it does not address the issue of vibrant changes in elite formation and the cyclical pattern of elite circulation. A crucial question we have to ask is what happens after the professional replaces the revolutionary. Will the humanist elite ever have a place again in the elite circulation process? Another point we may challenge is Kautsky's observation that elite with humanist and social science background does not have to be revolutionary, and the scientific managers can be equally revolutionary in their approach to social economic transformation. What set them apart, in my view, are their own priorities and the historical conditions they are living in. Therefore, the traditional division of "red" and "expert" or "revolutionary" and "professional" can be very superficial. The real difference is that the humanist-populist elite like the revolutionary old guards in China con-

43

cerned are the issues of harmony, equity and fairness, while the scientific-business elite are accustomed to scientific and rational thinking and reasoning.[6] In real politics, it may take two to tangle, and it is always better off if both groups can work together.

The theory suggested in Chapter 1 assumes that the circulation of political elite is largely the rotation of political powers between two generations of political elite: those who are efficiency-oriented and those who are equity-oriented. Because of the efficiency-equity trade-off, the politics will constantly involve the two forces to correct and balance each other. One of the key assumptions of this book is that the emerging politics of equity will require and be facilitated by a group of new political elite. The elite groups who have occupied the center stage of Chinese politics since the 1980s have made their impressive marks on China's economic development, but their training and value-orientation have limited their ability to solve the emerging problems of lack of human, social and political developments. They are destined to be replaced or supplemented by a new generation of political elite whose training and value orientation may be better suited to the new challenges facing China today.[7]

In the following discussion, we will first examine the rise of the generation of technocrats in the reform era. Next, we will study the elite changes during the era of Jiang Zemin and Hu Jingtao. Finally, we will take a closer look at the "lost generation" who will ascend to power in the upcoming 18th CCP Congress.

The Generation of Revolutionary Modernizers

Before analyzing the generation changes, we must redefine the term "generation" since it is frequently misused. The use of the concept "generation" is normally related to sociological science that found its roots in the works of Karl Mannheim.[8] In sociology, the concept of generation is a subjective rather than an objective experience of time. A group of elite who share a similar historical experience during the formative years forms a common link.

However, for the Chinese, the term *dai* means something very different. When Deng Xiaoping made himself the core of the second generation and Jiang Zeming the core of the third generation in 1989, he made the concept of generation akin to the term "reign" or "era" applied to certain rulers in dynasties. One generation really means one reigning emperor. As Michel Bonnin points out,

> The main problem with Deng's categorization is not its historical inexactitude, but the fact that it was later developed by people who tried to take it as a general presentation of political generations in China. In doing so, they confuse the term "generation" used by Deng and the meaning this term has in social sciences. They use this division into four generations *as if* it coincided with genuine generations. This kind of mixture can only contradict historical accuracy and the sociological theory of generations.[9]

To make sense of the generational transition, we use the term generation to describe a group of elite who share common historical experiences rather than the reign of a supreme leader. The generational change is more related a change in the historical experience, even though the leader's name can still be used to represent the same generation.

We believe the CCP has had two broadly defined generations of political elite (instead of three or four) so far. The first generation can be referred to as the generation of revolutionary modernizers or mobilizers. The second one is the managerial technocrats with engineering backgrounds. The first generation includes leaders like Mao Zedong, Liu Shaoqi, and Zhou Enlai. In an even broader sense, the first generation also includes communist pioneers such as Li Dazhao and Chen Duxiu, and they are the first tier. The founders of the PRC such as Mao Zedong, Zhu De, Zhou Enlai and Deng Xiaoping can be treated as the second tier. The two tiers of the first generation lasted from the 1920s to about the 1970s. They are the generation of revolution.

The revolution modernizers governed China from the founding of the CCP to the end of the Cultural Revolution in 1976. It has the longest time span, and many eras embodied by one or a few paramount leaders. There are obviously many eras during the first generation. Li Dazhao and Chen Duxiu represent the first era of communism in China, followed by Li Lisan, Wang Min, and Mao Zedong. Influenced by the Bolshevik Revolution in Russia, the earlier revolutionary elite launched a communist revolution to eradicate capitalism and feudalism from China. The top leaders tended to be students of humanities and social sciences. They were lawyers, teachers, journalists, and writers (see Table 3.1). However, most of the rank-and-file members of this generation had little formal education. Most of them fought in battles and wars and had impressive military credentials. Before 1981, only one-third of Politburo members had a formal college education.[10] Inspired by Marxist ideas of social equality and a utopian future and motivated simply by their desire to have a good life, the revolutionary old guards followed the few educated intellectuals who conspired to bring Soviet-style of communism to China.

Revolutions can provide legitimacy for the revolutionary party. As discussed in Chapter 1, the Marxist scientific socialism and dialectic materialism prescribed powerful mandates and original justifications for the change. This type of legitimacy was poorly understood historically. Chiang Kai-shek, the leader of the KMT, probably never fully understood why the communist rebellion had such a powerful appeal to many Chinese, especially the young and the poor. The same problem existed among many Western observers. For example, some Western scholars characterized the Maoist era as one of the brutal and totalitarian regimes and lacking any political legitimacy. If so, how could the regime stay in power for so long? It was true the communists exercised many forms of coercion to silence their opponents, but the majority of the working class people did regard the new government as a legitimate one. For a long time, the CCP relied primarily on revolution itself as a ground for

Table 3.1 Credentials of First-Generation CCP Leaders

Name		Education	Profession	Position
Chen Duxiu	(1879-1942)	Waseda University, Japan	Journalist, professor	Leader of New Cultural Movement, "Commander-General of the May Fourth Movement"; co-founder of the CCP
Li Dazhao	(1889-1927)	Waseda University, Japan, major in politics	Professor of economics and library director of Beijing University	Co-founder of the CCP
Mao Zedong	(1893-1976)	Hunan No. 1 Normal College	Poet, journalist, career politician	Co-founder of the CCP, Party Chairman
Dong Biwu	(1886-1975)	University of Japan (private), major in law	Legal scholar	Co-founder of the CCP
Zhou Enlai	(1898-1976)	Nankai University, studied overseas in France	Professional revolution-ary	Premier
Liu Shaoqi	(1898-1969)	Moscow Communist Workers' University	Leader of labor move-ment	President of the PRC
Deng Xiaoping	(1904-1997)	Studied overseas in France and Moscow Sun Yat-sen University in the USSR	Party activist	Chief architecture of China's reform
Zhu De	(1886-1976)	Chengdu Advanced Normal College, Studied overseas in Germany and Moscow Communist Workers' University in the USSR	Commander-general of the Red Army	

political legitimacy.[11] While Marxist ideology provided them with the original justification, their utilitarian justification was largely based on radical programs designed to eradicate social and economic inequality. Mao himself also relied heavily on personality cults to supplement the CCP's political legitimacy.

After the 1949 Communist Revolution, communist ideology was carefully articulated to replace the traditional idea of Mandate of Heaven. The official ideology was crucial to the institutionalization of the CCP's legitimacy. "Without the ideology," wrote Peter Moody, "the Party would have no claim to legitimacy."[12] The theories of historical materialism, class struggle, and scientific socialism provided necessary moral justification for the new party-state. Communists believe that they have a historical mission to put an end to capitalism and feudalism. They are destined to transform the existing society of injustice into an entirely new one. "The socialist system," wrote Mao, "will eventually replace the capitalist system; this is an objective law independent of man's will."[13] According to the theory of scientific socialism, the industrial working class, organized and conscious, is certain to overthrow capitalism and to create a society of abundance with universal brotherhood and true freedom.[14] The Russian leader Lenin insisted that an elite-based communist party must be established to serve as a vanguard of the industrial working class, which, in itself, was also a pivotal social force of a historical transformation. Once in power, according to Lenin, the Communists would not share power with anybody, and they must establish a one-party rule on behalf of the proletariat.[15]

Since revolution and the revolutionary ideology served as the basis of original justification, the implementation of such type of legitimacy required a total politicization of Chinese society. This was accomplished through the establishment of a "unified leadership," the use of personality cult, and mass mobilization and the elimination of private sphere.

Based on the Leninist party theory, the CCP established a "unified leadership" (*yi yuan hua*), and a party-state, after taking power in 1949. According to a decision made in 1949 by the CCP Central Committee, the party committees, instead of government agencies, were the highest decisions-making bodies in all work units, and decisions made by these committees must be obeyed and carried out unconditionally by all government agencies, military units, and mass organizations. This arrangement was at first meant to be a temporary measure to facilitate the command of the revolutionary forces. However, after taking over power, the unified leadership was extended to all aspects of society, and was regularly strengthened under the influence of the party radicals. Party committees were established in every governmental organization to put into action about the party leadership.[16]

In addition to the appeal of the ideology, the CCP also relied heavily on personality cult to enhance its public appeal. The Chinese communist revolution took place in an economically backward peasant society. Good emperors were traditionally peasants' only hope. Personality cult was a mutual choice between the peasant masses and the Party. All of the founding communist leaders became new god-like figures. Mao, in particular, was enshrined as the never-setting sun and a godly savior of the Chinese people. During the Cultural Revolution, the worship of Mao reached its peak. Mao's own writings became infallible and

were a source of all wisdom. As a god-like figure, Mao's words became the ultimate truth. People would march on the street fanatically to celebrate Mao's
latest speeches or directives. When Mao died in 1976, his successor Hua Guofeng had no choice but to rely on Mao's personal note of approval to convince
the public that Mao had chosen him to be his successor.

The revolutionary elite led by Mao mastered the "mass line" to generate social support. Mao was a strong believer of the traditional *min ben* idea. He became a master of the "mass line"–a term used by Mao meaning that all decisions
must be "from the masses and to the masses." Mao, however, did not like spontaneous popular actions. He believed that people must be organized and controlled. For that reason, the Chinese Communists embraced a form of state corporatism to put all mass organizations under the tight control of the CCP and the
party-state. Mao justified the party's control by saying that "without the efforts
of the Chinese Communist Party, without the Chinese Communists as the mains-
tay of the Chinese people, China can never achieve independence and liberation,
or industrialization and the modernization of her agriculture."[17] Workers, wom-
en, and youth were organized into monopolistic organizations and became a part
of an extended network of social and political control. Political socialization,
political education and political campaigns are part of daily citizen life. As a
result, the private sphere no longer existed, civil society disappeared, and social
life became completely politicized.[18]

Overall, the Maoist era was dependent on the following utilitarian justifications for legitimacy: national independence, liberation, modernity, social and
economic equality, and fraternity.[19] Nationalist pride was especially important to
the CCP's claim to power. China was unified for the first time since the collapse
of the Qing Dynasty. No Chinese political force had been able to achieve this
objective since China's humiliating defeat in the Opium War (1839-1842). Later
on, Mao's tough stand against the United States, the Soviet Union, and India
reinforced China's national pride and made Mao himself a true national hero.

The persuasive power of national liberation was also applied in domestic
politics. The Communists promised a new beginning, a government of the
people – a government that would care for the interests of the common people.
Mao wrote,

> We should pay close attention to the well-being of the masses, from the prob-
> lems of land and labor to those of fuel, rice, cooking oil and salt. . . . All such
> problems concerning the well-being of the masses should be placed on our
> agenda. We should discuss them, adopt and carry out decisions and check up
> on the results. We should help the masses to realize that we represent their in-
> terests and that our lives are intimately bound up with theirs. We should help
> them to proceed from these things to an understanding of the higher tasks
> which we have put forward, the tasks of the revolutionary war, so that they will
> support the revolution and spread it throughout the country, and respond to our
> political appeals and fight to the end for victory in the revolution. [20]

He promised that in the new republic people would truly become the master
of the society, enjoying a wide range of democratic rights that have never seen
before in Chinese history. The feeling of being "liberated" held by workers and

peasants translated into enormous support for the regime.[21] The gratitude and affection people showed towards their new leaders provided the strongest moral capital for the new government.

Mao understood that the only way communism would appeal to ordinary people was to bring a better life to them.[22] In a number of areas, the progress made was evident. Women, for instance, were now treated as "one half of the sky" and were promised equal pay for equal work. Women's participation in the work forces reached 49 percent in the 1960s, much higher than the world average of 34.5 percent. Chinese women made about 80 percent of men's income, while at the same time in the United States, women only made about 60-70 percent of what men made in spite of the passage of the Equal Pay Act in 1963.[23]

Through land distribution and land reform, the CCP solved one of the major sources of inequality in China, land ownership. Land reform fulfilled the dream of millions of peasants. From 1950 to 1952, over 60 million acres of farmland were confiscated from property owners and redistributed free to over 300 million poor peasants.[24] However, the privatization of lands did not last long. The collectivization of agricultural lands soon followed. The establishment of People's Communes created a communal land system similar to those used during the early period of the Tang dynasty (618-907 AD). The collective farms soon proved to be inefficient, but they provided economic equality and social security for poor villagers. Nonetheless, even during the Maoist era, inequality persisted. According to a document written during the Cultural Revolution, many former urban business owners, intellectuals, artists, and state and party leaders received much higher salaries than did the ordinary workers. Some artists received a salary as high as 2,000 RMB (US$240) a month, an astonishing figure if it were compared with the monthly wages of 30-50 RMB(US$4-6) that a worker usually received.[25] These gaps were eventually eliminated by the radicals during the Cultural Revolution. The pursuit of economic equality turned into extreme egalitarianism at that time.

With a goal to emulate the Soviet-style of state socialism, China took only a few short years to eradicate all private ownership and completed the initial stage of socialist transformation. Many state-owned factories were built during the periods of the first and second Five-Year Plans. Millions of farmers joined industrial labor forces. In 1949, there were only eight million workers in the state-owned enterprises. By 1981, this number had jumped to 83.7 million.[26] The state abolished the wage labor system and installed a scheme of workplace democratic management system. Workers were mostly complacent about their improved economic status and showed strong support for the communist regime.[27]

The magnitude of the radical social, political, and economic changes the new government engineered was truly unprecedented in Chinese history. Between 1952 and 1974, China's industrial output increased ten times, and agricultural output increased three times. China quickly became a major military power with a strategic nuclear force.[28] Even without a Western-style democratic election, a free market economy, and the rule of law, the CCP could still govern without serious internal challenges. It survived even the most difficult years, such as in the aftermath of the Great Leap Forward and the Cultural Revolution.

However, the rigid command economy and the endless political-style economic campaigns caused economic stagnation by the end of the 1970s. The widespread shortage of consumer goods forced the government to set up a strict rationing system. Evidence from an analysis of the changes in the Engel Index showed very little improvement in people's standard of living between 1957 and 1981.[29] The revolution-based legitimacy was running out of steam. The Communist political legitimacy suffered the first major crisis in 1976 when people were not even allowed to mourn the death of Zhou Enlai, a highly respected premier, a moderate leader, and a proponent of China's continued modernization and economic development.

The Generation of Technocrats

A series of historical events disrupted the reign of the revolutionary elite unexpectedly. The deaths of Zhou Enlai, Zhu De, and Mao Zedong in 1976, the arrest of the "Gang of Four," and the termination of the disastrous "Cultural Revolution" put an end to the era of political turbulence in China. The termination of the Cultural Revolution marked the beginning of an era of meritocracy and technocracy.

Technocracy appears to be an unavoidable stage of modernization. William Henry Smith, a Californian engineer, invented the word "technocracy" in 1919 to describe "the rule of the people made effective through the agency of their servants, the scientists and engineers."[30] In his influential book on the efficiency movement in the United States, John Jordan traces the significant influence on American politics of a most unlikely hero: the professional engineer.[31] During the American progressive era, the efficiency movement flourished and permeated into all aspects of the management of the economy, society and government. President Herbert Hoover, a trained mining engineer, believed that there were technical solutions to all social and economic problems. Other well-known Americans such as Frederick Taylor, John Dewey, Thorstein Veblen, Lewis Mumford, Walter Lippmann, Charles Beard, and John D. Rockefeller were associated with the movement. In the former Soviet Union, there was a similar period of *tekhnokratizatsiia* of the party apparatus between the 1950s and the 1970s. This process began with the third generation of Soviet leaders led by Nikita Khrushchev but reached its peak during the fourth generation led by an industrial engineer Leonid Brezhnev.[32]

Technocracy is based on the assumption that the elite should rule on behalf of the people and perform society's essential tasks more efficiently. Experts often serve as policy entrepreneurs and govern "for the people" based on scientific and natural laws. The best technical and managerial solutions are deemed more important than what perceived as the common sense by ordinary people. They claim domination over the modernization process simply by the "application of instrumentally rational techniques."[33] Technocracy is inherently elitist and authoritarian in nature, and its political legitimacy is based on scientism and a presumed pragmatism.[34]

Ironically, leaders like Deng Xiaoping, Hu Yaobang and Zhao Ziyang are the third and fourth tiers of the revolutionary generation. They served as facilitators to bring about an era of technocracy. In this sense, they are all transitional figures. Deng's successors like Jiang Zemin, Zhu Rongji, Li Peng, Hu Jintao, Wen Jiabao and Wu Bangguo are all engineers and managerial technocrats. They are part of the second generation of China's political elite.

Deng Xiaoping and Hu Yaobang were instrumental in promoting cadres with scientific and engineer backgrounds. For a while, Deng was busy purging the radical revolutionary elite and restoring the old revolutionary guards to power. However, Deng soon began to promote younger cadres to various leadership positions. He first created the CCP Central Advisory Committee and persuaded most of the revolutionary elite to be in semi-retirement and to serve only in this honorary committee. Between 1980 and 1986, of the more than 1.4 million senior cadres recruited before 1949, most of them have little college education, and were put into full retirement with very generous fringe benefits offered as an incentive. Meanwhile, over 469,000 college-educated younger cadres were promoted to leadership positions above the county level.[35] This elite turnover is believed by some to be the largest peaceful elite transition in human history.[36]

Between the 12th to 16th Party Congresses (1982-2002), politicians with engineering or natural science background established its stronghold within the CCP and the state apparatus. According to Cheng Li's study, by 1988, 73.8 percent of China's 160 cabinet-level ministers and vice ministers were engineers or had natural science backgrounds. Those with economic and social science backgrounds made up only 16.8 percent of the total, and humanities 7.5 percent. Among the 166 mayors surveyed, 74.6 percent had engineering and natural science backgrounds, 12.6 percent had economics and social science backgrounds, and only 12.6 percent were in humanities.[37] At the top, the transition to technocratic rule reached its peak in the 16th CCP Congress. Among the 25 members of the Politburo, 18 of them were engineers or had a science background. All nine members of the standing committee were engineers or had a scientific background.

The political legitimacy of this generation of technocrats is largely based on two things: the achievement of the economic reforms and the de-politicization the Chinese society. Concerns over equality were replaced with concerns over efficiency. The objectives of enriching people and benefiting people provide the utilitarian basis of political legitimacy of this generation.

The new generation of college-trained young political leaders at different levels was busy promoting the GDP growth rate and launching new construction projects. Indeed, Chinese people have enjoyed unprecedented prosperity and improvements in their standard of living. Many are complacent with what they have: more deposable incomes, private-owned apartments and vehicles, and the luxury of having more and more leisure time for traveling. The embracement of the free market economy was a return to an efficiency-driven economy. Economic growth was achieved largely through the improvement of efficiency. Rural population became more productive with the introduction of the household responsibility system. The new enterprise system improved industrial productivity significantly.

The efficiency-driven development has also resulted in a large number of unemployed in urban areas. Millions of surplus farm laborers freed after the dismantlement of the collective farms poured into urban areas seeking jobs. The new entrepreneurs, professionals, and many officials became rich first. Nevertheless, millions have fallen into the new urban poor. Political leaders whose training is limited to science and engineering created many of the problems China is facing today. Although technocracy is an important step towards acquiring what Max Weber has termed a rational-legal basis of political legitimacy, the lack of popular sovereignty and an innate tendency towards an oligarchic rule will eventually weaken the justification of bureaucratic technocracy.

The establishment of the technocracy took nearly ten years to complete. Between 1976 and 1989, Hua Guofeng, Hu Yaobang, and Zhao Ziyang headed the CCP one after another. All three were part of the revolutionary generation who ascended to power due to their revolutionary credentials. However, Deng Xiaoping masterminded the downfall of each of these younger leaders. Meanwhile, the CCP consciously promoted scientific cadres such as Jiang Zemin, Li Peng, and Zhu Rongji.

Jiang Zemin stepped in as the new CCP General Secretary amid the 1989 crisis. The Coming of the Jiang marked an end to the rule of the revolutionary generation, and the coming era of the generation of orthodox. Unlike their predecessors, this generation received formal education either prior to the founding of the PRC or right after that. They had little or no revolutionary credentials and had to build their career path from the bottom up. Their rapid ascendance to power was due largely to the policies of reform and opening-up. Jiang Zemin and his colleagues Li Peng and Zhu Rongji eventually became the officially sanctioned core of this generation.

Leaders in this group share many similarities with the first generation, but tended to embrace some elements of the market system. They were heavily influenced by orthodox communist ideologies, and some even studied in the former Soviet Union. They were often labeled as the "socialist generation" or "orthodox generation."[38] Because of the underdevelopment of humanities and social sciences during this period of time, very few people with humanities and social science backgrounds were included in this group.

Without charismatic personality, strong revolutionary credentials, or an impressive record of personal achievements, Jiang did not enjoy the same level of respect and unquestionable authority. He must now earn people's respect through his own efforts. With Deng still behind the curtain in his first term, Jiang continued to take a hard-line towards political reforms. However, he moved swiftly to liberalize the economy. Under his leadership, a full-scale urban reform program was launched, and some major breakthroughs were made. Most small and medium-sized enterprises were sold, merged or shutdown. Stock ownership was used to diversify business property rights. The state's share of the overall economy declined quickly. The private and foreign owned companies mushroomed. The total foreign direct investments exceeded US$400 billion. The average growth rate was about 9 percent for a decade. China avoided the financial crisis of East Asia in the late 1990s.

The sustained economic growth brought significant improvement to people's living standard. China's population in poverty went down from 20 percent in 1981 to about 5 percent in 1997, and average per capita GDP in the same period increased from US$200 to US$750. The Engel Index in the urban areas dropped from 57.5 percent to 37.9 percent between 1978 and 2001, and in the rural areas, the Index changed from 67.7 to 47.8.[39]

The return of Hong Kong and Macao as well as being awarded the right to host the 2008 Olympic Game by the International Olympic Committee (IOC) also increased prestige of this new group of political leaders. These successes seemed to have strengthened the regime's legitimacy. According to a survey of Beijing residents conducted by Chen Jie et al. in 1995, the regime enjoyed a moderately high level of affective support (citizen's evaluation of governmental legitimacy), and this provided a reservoir of diffused support that the system could draw upon in the future.[40] Another survey of Beijing residents in 1995 also found no apparent public pressure for democracy.[41]

Another thing that also helped to boost the regime's legitimacy was the de-politicization of society and the restoration of a private sphere. Chinese leaders followed the classical teaching of Machiavelli and formulated policies designed to discourage mass political activism and channel the masses' energy into private pursuits.[42] In discussing the legitimation system in advanced capitalism, Jürgen Habermas wrote,

> In the structurally depoliticizing public realm, the need for legitimation is reduced to two residual requirements: The first, civil privatism—that is, political abstinence combined with an orientation to career, leisure, and consumption. . . . Secondly, the structural de-politicization itself requires justification, which is supplied either by democratic elite theories (which go back to Schumpeter and Max Weber) or by technocratic system theories (which go back to the institutionalism of the twenties).[43]

This analysis can be applied to Chinese politics during the reform era as well. De-politicization took place in art, literature, education, sports, media, economy, agriculture, social status, and urban and village life. On January 28, 1979, the government decided to remove the political identity of former landlords, rich peasants, anti-revolutionary, and bad elements, and liberated 4.4 million people and granted them equal treatment, and over 20 million people benefited indirectly from the removal of the political classification.[44] The last one removed from this classification system was in 1982. This policy helped to remove the political system of class struggle. In the same year, over 700,000 former small business owners were declassified from capitalists to working class, and 450,000 former employees of the nationalist government who were mistreated even though they surrendered to the Communists in the liberation war between 1946 and 1949. Intellectuals were no longer treated as "the stinky ninth rank," and old cadres were no longer labeled as "capitalist roaders." By 1980, over a half-million or 99 percent of so-called "rightists" who were given the political "hat" in 1958 was liberated and declassified.[45] All of these efforts helped to end political stratification of the society, and paved the way for political equality and facilitated the development of a civil society.

Furthermore, people had more and more freedom in their social and private lives. The work units were no longer part of the political and social web of control. People were free to quit their jobs and find new ones. An additional day of weekends and the long national holidays gave people more and more leisure time. Domestic and international tourism are booming. China has in fact entered into a consumer society. Automobiles have gradually entered into families of ordinary people Personal enjoyment and private life became more colorful and diversified. Most people are concerned nowadays about how to make money, own an apartment, purchase a car, travel overseas, and send kids to good schools. Politics is the last thing on most people's mind.

Nevertheless, the economic success had its toll. Among many other things, the growing economic inequality was the most troubling one. According to Chinese official statistics, China's *Gini* Coefficient, an internationally accepted measurement of the degree of inequality in the distribution of income in a given society, rose from a low level of 0.33 in 1980, to 0.40 in 1994, and 0.49 in 2006. Even though the number is skewed somewhat by the differences derived from the historical separation of urban and rural areas, China has joined these countries which have the worst records of unequal distribution of wealth.[46] After a decade of agricultural recovery, thanks mainly to the household responsibility system, peasants have been once again left behind. Over 90 million rural peasants have now become migrant workers, floating between cities to search for odd jobs or seasonal employment. To reduce the employment pressure, the government has called for the acceleration of the urbanization process and the reform of the household registration system.

During the Jiang era, the CCP's original justification for political legitimacy continued to erode. Official corruption got worse and worse. The exposure of corruption cases involving high-ranking officials, such as Cheng Kejie, the former vice-chairman of the Standing Committee of the NPC, Li Jiating, the former governor of Yunnan, and Chen Liangyu, former Mayor of Shanghai, did little to repair the damages that had already been done to the image of the Party.

The relationship between the CCP and the industrial workers has also been strained. The very foundation of the communist regime is based on an unwritten social contract: the Party gets the social support it needs to stay in power, and the working class in turn is protected by the socialist welfare system. At the end of Jiang's tenure, this contract had become a laughing stock. The equal relationship between enterprise cadres and workers was gone; the wage labor system came alive. Over 50 million workers of state-owned factories were either laid-off or forced into early retirement.[47] According to Feng Tongqing, the relationship between workers and enterprise management "is now based primarily on an exchange of economic interests rather than on cooperative comradeship or collectivity."[48] In private enterprises, violations of workers' rights became a serious problem. In some worst cases, intimidation, physical violence, corporal punishment, and restriction of workers' freedom were widespread.[49] The number of labor disputes increased from 28,000 in 1992 to 181,000 in 2002.[50] The government agencies at the local levels are weak in enforcing its own labor standard laws, but are harsh on labor activists who dare to organize strikes or independent unions.[51]

Jiang realized that in order for the CCP to survive in this environment of growing social antagonism and tension, the Party must accelerate the process of transforming itself from a revolutionary party to a ruling party. The "Theory of Three Represents" that he proposed before his semi-retirement in 2002 is part of the ideological reconstruction of the CCP's official ideology. The theory intends to broaden the party's social support and boost the party's image as a party of all people. With his strong lobbying effort, the 16th Party Congress officially adopted the new theory as a part of the party's new mission statement in 2002. However, what was most discussed about this new theory was the acceptance of private entrepreneurs to become party members. The theory helps justify the fact that one-third of the two million plus private business are actually owned by CCP members. These "red capitalists" employ over 7 million workers and control an estimated 600 billion RMB capital assets.[52] Nevertheless, their overall number is still very small. It is unclear whether their presence within the party will make any difference.

The so-called fourth generation in this chapter is considered part of the generation of Technocrats. The backgrounds of Hu Jintao and his politburo members are identical to Jiang's team: they are all engineers. The only difference is that they all received their formal education after the founding of the PRC, and were products of the new education system. They managed to finish their college educations, but the Cultural Revolution disrupted their professional and political career paths. This group ascended to power officially in 2002.

This group is also a transitional one. As we discussed in Chapter 2, this group of political elite has favored extensively value reorientation. Although being part of technocrats, they began to realize the limits of the efficiency-first strategy. Deliberate efforts have been made to promote non-engineers into political services. The governing philosophy laid out by Hu Jintao continues to emphasize scientific development. The reform in the electoral system, household registration system, social security, and human rights was painstakingly slow. Hu has raised public expectations when he came into office in 2002. How much he can deliver remains to be seen.

In sum, the basis for the party-state's legitimacy during the Deng-Jiang era significantly differs from the Maoist era. While in the Maoist era, the CCP relied on the revolution as a basis for legitimacy, Jiang era relied primarily on rationalization as a basis for legitimacy. As scientists and engineers, technocrats see human miseries are technical problems that can be resolved through economic development and material accumulation.[53] They lack true comprehension of the political nature of these problems, and consequently, have not given adequate attention to political, social and human developments. In the end, they cannot escape from the dilemma of modernization: the efficiency-equity trade-off. As the efficiency-maximizing politics has compromised equity and justice, a new politics and a new generation of political leaders are needed to correct the problems and to rebalance the equilibrium.

The Rise of the "Lost Generation"

Michael Bonin's study of the "lost generation" gives a very good starting point this emerging group of China's new political elite. The so-called "lost generation" refers to the "generation of educated youth" (*zhiqing*), who were born between 1947 and 1960. Most of them spent between two to twelve years in the countryside. As Bonin noted,

> The "lost generation" did not lose only its illusions and beliefs but also the opportunity to develop its intellectual and professional capacities and this loss is still more or less affecting the lives of most of its members today.[54]

The biggest leadership change at the national level at the 17th CCP Congress was the election of Xi Jinping and Li Keqiang. Xi is likely to succeed Hu Jingtao as the next CCP General Secretary, and Li may be a candidate for the next Premier in a few years. Their promotion kicks out a new transition of power in the upcoming 18th CCP Congress. Both Xi and Li hold doctoral degrees, the highest level of education ever held by a national leader since 1949. Both of them were "educated youth" that were sent to the countryside during the Cultural Revolution. Both joined the CCP in the 1970s and served as village party secretaries. Paradoxically, both of them were beneficiaries of the inner party patron-client relations. Xi is the son of Xi Zhongxun, one of the former high-ranking party leaders, and worked for Geng Biao, one of Xi Zhongxun's subordinates, before he was promoted to provincial level leaders. Li was born to a low-ranking party official's family in Anhui. He had opportunities to work closely with Hu Jintao as a young cadre in the Central Committee of the Communist Youth League (CYL), and is consider part of the CYL faction.

The 17th CCP Congress represented a major departure from the two decades of rule by engineer-turned politicians. The election of the group of the "lost generation" to the central party committee paved the way for a major elite change in the 18th Party Congress. This time, the Qinghua graduates will no longer dominate the key posts of the central government. Instead, we expect most senior leaders will have a non-engineer background. Many rising stars in the "lost generation" have backgrounds in social sciences, economics, business, and humanities. Xi Jinping and Li Yuanchao have a graduate degree in law. Li Keqiang received a Ph.D. in economics. Wang Qishan has a college degree in history and a professional title of senior economist. Bo Xilai has a master's degree in journalism, and Wang Huning has a bachelor's degree in political science and a master's degree in law.[55]

Many China observers have tried to identify those who will be the next generation of national leaders in 2012. Table 3.2 is a quick survey of these likely contenders. What distinguishes this group from the previous one is that most of them were sent to the countryside during the Cultural Revolution. Many witnessed first-hand the kind of poverty the rural peasants had to endure. Although the Cultural Revolution disrupted their lives and career paths, they all managed to continue their education and acquired a college education. Many of them have long time working experience at the grass-roots level and had gone through some of the toughest challenging times during their tenure as local or provincial leaders. Many of them had gained popularity among the local people. The basis of their political legitimacy is their economic and social achievements, unlike their predecessors who focused their attentions on improving economic efficiency and economic growth. When Xi Jinping served in the top party position in Zhejiang, he helped to sustain growth rates averaging 14 percent per year. Li Keqing helped Henan Province raise its national GDP rank from 24th in the 1990s to 18th place in 2004.

This group also served as firefighters to fix the mounting social and economic issues resulting from the untamed growth of the 1980s and 1990s. For example, Xi Jinping was appointed as the Party Secretary of Shanghai in the aftermath of the corruption scandals of Chen Liangyu. Wang Qishang was hastily sent to Beijing to deal with the SARS crisis in 2003 after the sudden dismissal of Beijing Mayor Meng Xuenong. Bo Xilai was forced to launch an anti-mobster in Chonqing in 2008 and cracked 32,771 criminal cases, and executed or arrested 9,512 people in eighty days.[56] Li Yuanchao barely survived the "Tieben Steel Mill Project Scandal,"[57] and Li Keqing suffered tremendous loss of political capital in Henan due to the AIDS scandal.[58] This group was keenly aware that they were under pressure to break new ground and lead a new direction in China's prolonged reform. They were extremely vulnerable and are under much more pressure than their predecessors were. When Wang Yang was appointed as Guangdong's new party chief, he vowed to open up a new "blood-filled" pathway to further the reform.

One unique feature of this "lost generation" is that many of them are returning overseas students. The number of foreign-educated returnees increased from 20 on the 16th Central Committee to 36 on the 17th Central Committee. Zhu Min, a newly appointed vice-governor of the People's Bank received his master's degree from Princeton University and a doctorate from Johns Hopkins University. Wan Gang, the Minister of Science and Technology, received his doctoral degree at Technical University of Clausthal, Germany. Yi Gang, the new Bureau Chief of the State Administration of Foreign Exchanges, received his doctoral degree in economics from the University of Illinois, and worked as a tenured professor of economics at the University of Indiana. These foreign-educated political elite are all carefully screened, and they will not be able to "rock the boat" as some Western politicians would like to see. However, since they have lived in Western democracy, they may have favorable attitudes toward political freedom and political democracy. They can potentially serve as the catalyst for change.

If the "lost generation" was mostly born in the 1950s, the younger cadres born in the 1960s have also entered into the political horizon. They have the identical environment in their early lives as those born in the 1950s. Most of them joined the "educated youth" and were sent to the countryside to be re-educated by peasants. Their early education was distorted and interrupted. Many of them were not good at math, chemistry or physics since their education did not value these, but social sciences and humanities were their strong points. Unlike the youth who grew up in the 1970s and 1980s, the 1960s lived in a poor, albeit egalitarian society, idealism and passion occupy the central stage of their world outlook. They were thirsty for knowledge but were not very materialistic. This background may lay the foundation for their value orientation once they become the leaders of China.

Table 3.2 The "Lost Generation"

Names	Cultural Revolution	Education	Local Work Experience
Xi Jinping	"Educated Youth"	BA in Political Education, PhD in Law	Hebei, Fujian, Zhejiang, Shanghai
Li Keqiang	"Educated Youth"	BA in Economics, PhD in Economics	Henan, Liaoning
Bo Xilai	"Reeducation"	BA in History MA in Journalism	Dalian, Liaoning, Chongqing
Wang Qishan	"Educated Youth"	BA in History	Guangdong, Hainan, Beijing
Li Yuanchao		BS in Mathematics, PhD in Law.	Shanghai, Nanking, Jiangsu
Wang Yang		BA in Economics MS in Management	Anhui, Chongqing, Guangdong
Zhang Dejiang	"Educated Youth"	BS in Economics	Jilin, Zhejiang
Yuan Chunqing		BS in Management, PhD in Management	Shaanxi
Zhao Leji	"Educated Youth"	BA in Philosophy, Master's Degree in Economics	Qinghai, Shaanxi
Lu Zhangong	"Educated Youth"	BS in Civil Engineering	Zhejiang, Hebei, Fujian and Henan
Ling Jihua	"Educated Youth"	BS in Management, Master's in Business Management	No local experience
Wang Huning		BA in Political Science, MA in Law (International Relations)	Shanghai

Many of them now have ministerial or vice-ministerial-level appointments. Zhou Qiang, governor of Hunan province, was born in 1960. He received his master's degree in law. Sun Zhengcai, born in 1963, received a doctoral degree in agriculture. He served as the Minister of Agriculture in 2008 and is currently the Party Secretary of Jilin Province. Hu Cunhua, born in 1963, was a graduate of Beijing University. He worked for many years in Tibet. His toughest challenge was the "Sanlu Poisoned Milk Power Incident" when he served as the provisional governor of Hebei province.[59] Now he is the Party Secretary of Inner Mongolia. For his frontier experiences, some have speculated that he can be a possible candidate to succeed Xi Jinping in the future. Nur Bekri, a Uyghur cadre, was born in 1961, now serves as the vice-chairman of the Xinjiang Autonomous Region. He was a professor of political science before he was promoted to Urumqi Mayor's position. He was known for cleaning up Urumqi's pollution problem and being an active promoter of bilingual education among Uyghur's student population. Xia Yong, born in 1961, has a doctoral degree in law, now serves as the Director of National Administration for the Protection of State Secrets. He wrote extensively on human rights and tried to build a new *men ben* theory that will lay the philosophical foundation of "new civil rights" in the Chinese context.[60] Pan Yue, born in 1960, has a Ph.D. in history and currently serves as the Vice-Minister of the Department of Environmental Protection. His report, published in 2002, called for transforming the CCP from a revolutionary party to a ruling party, was considered the most influential proposal for political reform.[61] He launched the environmental storms when he assumed the leadership role in the nation environmental protection agency and captured world attention.

Conclusions

As we discussed in Chapter 1, the revolutionary generation had a strong basis of original justification building upon the revolution itself and on personal charisma. The Engineer-technocrats based their legitimacy primarily on utilitarian justification derived from economic reforms and performance-based achievements. The "lost generation" will have to develop a new basis of legitimacy. The equity-enhancing objectives, such as achieving social justice, more equitable economic distribution, strong rule of law, and a more democratic decision-making process, may be their only hope.

Notes

1. Lowell Dittmer and Yu-shan Wu, "Leadership Coalitions and Economic Transformation in Reform China: Revisiting the Political Business Cycle" in *Domestic Politics in Transition: China's Deep Reform,* edited by Lowell Dittmer and Guoli Liu (Lanham, MD: Roman and Littlefield, 2006).

2. Shaun Breslin, "Do Leaders Matters? Chinese Politics, Leadership Transitions and the 17th Party Congress," *Contemporary Politics* 14, no. 2 (June 2008): 215-231.

3. John H. Kautsky, "Revolutionary and Managerial Elites in Modernizing Regimes," *Comparative Politics* 1, no. 4 (July 1969): 441-453.

4. C. Johnson, *Changes in Communist Systems* (Stanford: Stanford University Press, 1970); A. Walder, "Career Mobility and the Communist Political Order," *American Sociological Review* 60, no. 3 (June 1995): 309-328.

5. B. Anderson, "Social Stratification in the Soviet Union," *Studies in Comparative Communism* 8, (1975): 397-412; E. Bailes, *Technology and Society under Lenin and Stalin* (Princeton: Princeton University Press, 1978).

6. In Chinese, people sometime use the phrase *like siwei* (scientific reasoning) and *wenke siwei* (humanist reasoning) to illustrate their differences. While scientific reasoning focuses on order and natural law, humanistic reasoning emphasizes harmony and unity.

7. Cheng Li and Lynn White, "The Thirteenth Central Committee of the Chinese Communist Party: From Mobilizers to Managers," *Asian Survey* 28, no. 4 (April, 1988): 371-399.

8. Karl Mannheim, "The Problem of Generations" in *Essays on the Sociology of Knowledge by Karl Mannheim,* edited by P. Kecskemeti (New York: Routledge and Kegan Paul, 1952).

9. Michel Bonnin, "The Lost 'Generation': Its Definition and Its Role in Today's Chinese Elite Politics," *Social Research* 73, no. 1 (Spring 2006): 257.

10. Xiaowei Zhang, "Elite Transformation and Recruitment in Post-Mao China" *Journal of Political and Military Sociology* 36 (Summer 1998), 45, Table 1.

11. Ralph Thaxton, *China Turned Rightside Up: Revolutionary Legitimacy in the Peasant World* (Yale, NJ: Yale University Press, 1983).

12. Peter R. Moody, *Tradition and Modernization in China and Japan* (Belmont, CA: Wadsworth, 1995), 172.

13. Mao Tse-tung, "Speech at the Meeting of the Supreme Soviet of the USSR in Celebration of the 40th Anniversary of the Great October Socialist Revolution" (November 6, 1957), *Selected Works of Mao Tse-tung,* vol. III.

14. Karl Marx and Frederick Engels, *The Communist Manifesto* (New York: International Publisher, 1948). Ian Shapiro, *The Moral Foundation of Power* (New Haven: Yale University press, 2003), Ch. 4. George Brunner, "Legitimacy Doctrine and Legitimation Procedures in Eastern European Systems," in T. H. Rigby and Ferenc Feher, eds., *Political Legitimacy in Communist States* (New York: St. Martin's Press, 1982).

15. *Completed Works of Lenin,* Vol. 29, 489-490, cited in Xie Qingkui, *et al., Zhongguo Zhengfu Tizhi Fenxi* [A Study of the Chinese System of Government] (Beijing: China Radia and Televison Press, 1995),16-17.

16. *Ibid.,* 222-225.

17. Mao Tse-tung, "On Coalition Government," *Selected Works,* Vol. III.

18. Tang Jing, "'Excessive Politics' in China's Society in the Early Part of New China and Consequences," *Taiyaun ShifanXxueyuan Xuebao (Journal of Taiyuan Normal College [Social Science Edition])* 6, no. 2 (2007).

19. Zhong Yang, "Legitimacy Crisis and Legitimation in China," *Journal of Contemporary Asia* 1, no. 1 (1996), 205.

20. Mao Tse-tung, "Be Concerned with the Well-Being of the Masses, Pay Attention to Methods of Work" (January 27, 1934), *Selected Works,* Vol. I, 149.

21. Ralph E. Thaxton, *op cit.*

22. Mao Tse-tung, "Speech at the Supreme State Conference (January 25, 1956)," *Selected Works of Mao Tse-tung,* Vol. III.

23. Hao Tiechuan, "Quanli Shixian de Chaxu Geju (Variations in the Realization of Citizen Rights)," *China Social Sciences* 5 (1999), 121.

24. Immanuel C. Y. Hsü, *The Rise of Modern China,* 5th ed. (Oxford: Oxford University Press, 1995), 653.

25. Chinese Online Military Forum, "Document Revealed the Problem of Social and Economic Inequality," http://www.cmilitary.com/forums/general/messages/276256.html (accessed on August 12, 2003).

26. CCP Secretariat and ACFL, *The Condition of the Working Class in China* (Beijing, Central Party School Publishing House, 1983), trans. *by International Journal of Political Economy* 25, no. 1 (Spring 1995).

27. Baogang Guo, "From Master to Wage Labor: Chinese Workers at the Turn of the New Millennium," *American Reviews of China Studies* 1, no.1 (2000): 111-128.

28. Yue Dongxiao, "Riben de Qinlue Yu Lueduo Shi Zhongguo Pinqong de Zhijie Yuanyin (The Invasion and Exploitation by Japan is a Direct Cause of China's Poverty)," *Muzi Shumu*, http://shuwu.com/ar/chinese/112730.shtml (accessed September 14, 2003).

29. *Ibid.*

30. Barry Jones, *Sleepers, Wake! Technology and the Future of Work* (Oxford University Press, 1995), 214.

31. John Jordan, *Machine-age Ideology: Social Engineering and American Liberalism, 1911-1939* (Chapel Hill, NC: University of North Carolina Press, 1994).

32. Evan Mawdsley and Stephen White, *The Soviet Elite from Lenin to Gorbachev: The Central Committee and Its Members, 1917-1991* (Oxford: Oxford University Press, 2000).

33. Miguel Angel Centeno, "The New Leviathan: the Dynamics and Limits of Technocracy," *Theory and Society* 33, no. 3 (June 1993), 314.

34. See a more detailed discussion in my chapter "Beyond Technocracy: China's Quest for Legitimacy in the Era of Hu Jintao," in *China in the Twentieth-First Century: Challenges and Opportunities*, ed. by Shiping Hua and Sujian Guo (New York: Palgrave, 2007).

35. Hong Yung Lee, *From Revolutionary Cadres to Technocrats in Socialist China* (Berkeley, CA: University of California Press, 1991).

36. Cheng Li, *China's Leaders: the New Generation* (Lanham, Maryland: Roman and Littlefield Publisher, 2001), 34.

37. *Ibid.*, 41.

38. Michael Bonin, *op cit.*, 258.

39. Kong Lingzhi, "Food Consumption and the Health Status of Chinese People," International 5 a Day Symposium in Berlin (January 15, 2003), a PowerPoint presentation; the author is an official from the Department of Disease Control, Ministry of Health, P.R.C., http://www.5aday.com/berlin/powerpoint/food_consumption/800/index.html (accessed September 14, 2003).

40. Chen Jie, Yang Zhong, Jan Hillard, and John Scheb, "Assessing Political Support in China: Citizen's Evaluation of Governmental Effectiveness and Legitimacy, *Journal of Contemporary China* 6, no. 16 (November 1997): 551-566. See also Chen Jie, *Popular Political Support in Urban China* (Stanford: Stanford University Press, 2004).

41. Daniel V. Dowd, Allan Carson, and Shen Mingming, "The Prospects for Democratization in China: Evidence from 1995 Beijing Area Study," *Journal of Contemporary China* 8, no. 22 (1999): 365-380.

42. Niccolo Machiavelli. *Prince* (Chicago: University of Chicago Press, 2003).

43. Jurgen Habermas, *Legitimation Crisis* (Boston: Beacon Press, 1973), 37.

44. *People's Daily*, January 30, 1979.

45. *People's Daily*, January 2, 1979.

46. Gene H. Chang, "Cause and Cure of China's Widening Income Disparity," *China Economic Review* 13 (2002): 335-340.

47. Baogang Guo, "From Master to Wage Labor," *American Reviews of China Studies* 1, no. 1 (2000), 116.

48. Feng Tonqing, *Zhongguo Gongren de Minyun [the Fate of Chinese Workers]* (Beijing: Shehui Kexue Wenxian Chubanshe, 2002), 7.

49. Anita Chan, *China's Workers under Assault: the Exploration of Labor in a Globalizing Economy* (Armonk, NY: M.E. Sharp, 2001); see also Anita Chan, "Labor Stan-

dards and Human Rights: the Case of Chinese Workers under Market Socialism," *Human Rights Quarterly* 20, no. 4 (1998): 886-904; Baogang Guo, "From Master to Wage Labor," *op cit.*

50. Ministry of Labor and Social Security, PRC, *China's Annual Labor and Social Security Statistics Summary Reports* (1992, 2002), http://www.molss.gov.cn (accessed August 13, 2003).

51. Report of the Committee on Freedom of Association, International Labor Organization (ILO), *Violations of the Right to Organize and Trade Unionists' Basic Civil Liberties, Detention of Trade Unionists and Harassment of Family Members,* Report No. 316, Case No. 1930, Vol. LXXXI, 1998, Series B, No. 2, 1998.

52. According to the official survey, 10 percent of private business owners also indicated a desire to apply for party membership. See United Front Department of the CCP, et al., *The Fifth National Survey of China's Private Businesses (2002),* http://www.china.com.cn/chinese/zhuanti/282715.htm (accessed August 14, 2003).

53. David E. Apter, *The Politics of Modernization* (Chicago: University of Chicago Press, 1965), 327.

54. Michael Bonin, *op cit.,* 250.

55. Cheng Li, "China's Leadership, Fifth Generation," Brookings Institution, http://www.brookings.edu/articles/2007/12_china_li.aspx (accessed August 13, 2003).

56. Liang Jing, "Bo's Anti-Mob Campaign in Chongqing Challenges Hu's Rule by Empty Rhetoric" *China Digital Times,* Oct. 20, 2009.

57.   http://www.chinaacc.com/new/63/73/146/2006/2/yi9425426512822600267680.htm (accessed on February 21, 2010).

58. "China's AIDS Villages Steps out of Shadow," *People's Daily,* Nov. 10, 2005.

59. BBC, "The Number of Children Effected by the *Sanlu* Poisoned Milk Power has raised to 6000," September 17, 2008. http://news.bbc.co.uk/ (accessed February 21, 2010).

60. Xia Yong, *The Philosophy of Civil Rights in the Context of China* (Beijing: Sanlian Shudian, 2004).

61. Pan Yue, "Some Considerations about Transforming the Revolutionary Party to a Governing One," http://www.360doc.com/content/060627/03/2311_143743.html (accessed August 13, 2003); Xiyin, *Zhongguo Haoceng Wendan* (Zhejiang Renmin Chubanshe), quoted from http://lz.book.sohu.com/chapter-9401-3-1.html (accessed August 13, 2003).

Chapter 4
Toward a Deliberative State

A quick review of recent literature on China's democratization would reveal a great number of studies that use the introduction of elections at the national and provincial levels as a sign of political reforms in China. To their disappointment, these types of electoral reforms have never appeared on the horizon. While China has carried out direct elections of people's deputies to county-level people's congresses for three decades, there is no timetable for the introduction of popular election at the provincial level. Even if it indeed takes place in the near future, it may take another two or three decades to perfect it before a popular national election of the National People's Congress (NPC) can be put on the agenda. It is still far from certain that the CCP will be willing to accept the outcome of elections such as being defeated at the polls. After all, China is still a party-state with a constitutional guarantee of the ruling party status of the CCP. The development of electoral democracy will continue to be slow-paced. Small-scale changes are permissible, as long as they are either non-threatening or manageable.

Against this political environment, a practical approach to advance China's political reform may lie in the promotion of good governance rather than electoral reform. In this chapter and the chapter that follows, we will examine the unconventional pathway of political reform, i.e., broadening political participation through establishing a deliberative state. Since the crisis of participation, an inevitable by-product of modernization, cannot be resolved through electoral reform now, promoting civil participation in the governmental decision-making process by the various social groups, large or small, may be a variable option to foster democratic governance. It will help bring down the state-dominated corporatist state and move China into a societal corporatist state.[1]

In recent years, some scholars in the West have turned their attention to a different form of democracy that does not focus exclusively on the selection of the ruling elite; it focuses, instead, on citizens' ability to participate directly in the decision-making process. Some call this form of democracy deliberative democracy, while others call it discursive democracy.[2] While the theory of electoral democracy emphasizes the role of elections and voting as the central ingredients of a true democracy, deliberative democracy theorists believe that legitimate decision-making can only rise from public participation and deliberation.

Chinese political elite and scholars have shown growing interest in deliberative democracy. Li Junru, an influential party scholar, insists that China is not new to this type of democracy, and he believes that China can simply strengthen the existing mechanisms of deliberative consultation to serve as a breakthrough point for China's political reform, together with the implementation of inner-party democracy.[3] However, clearly there are some important distinctions between the CPPCC system and the deliberative democracy advocated by the critics of liberal representative democracy in the West. It is true that the CPPCC shares some elements of deliberative democracy, but significant changes have to be made in order to qualify the system as a true form of deliberative democracy.[4]

This chapter will first examine the logic for China's embracing deliberative democracy. Next, the chapter will study the role of the CPPCC in implementing the legislative deliberation. Finally, the chapter will focus on a number of case studies to show public participation in the new legislative deliberation process.

The Logic of Deliberative Democracy

To treat deliberative democracy as an alternative method of delivering democratic values, one has to view democratic politics as a multi-dimensional process. Some scholars believe that democratic politics contains multiple components. Many agree that the ability of citizens to participate directly or indirectly in the public policy decision-making process is of critical importance. Political transparency that allows people the right to free access to all necessary, unbiased, and uncensored information in order to make informed decisions is also indispensible for sound public policies.[5] The realization of these and other equally important objectives will be a slow process and may be difficult to obtain all at once.

Citizen participation in the policymaking process can provide procedural justice for political governance. According to Jügen Habermas, democratic legalism based on election and rational choice can only create legitimation "when, only when, grounds can be provided to show that certain formal procedures fulfill material claims to justice understand institutional boundary conditions."[6] Procedural justice can be achieved through inviting concerned groups to take part in the decision making process. Liberal democracy assumes the citizens' interests are in constant conflict, and the conflict can only be resolved through electoral representation, interest competition, and majority rule. Therefore, liberal democracy is a form of "adversarial democracy." Advocates of deliberative democracy assume citizens have common interests, and their differences can resolved based on their shared common interests, complete information, and mutual respect. Consensus building and collaboration is possible when discussion and deliberation are open and fair. While electoral democracy tries to minimize the involvement of the people in the decision-making process, deliberative democracy invites people back and put them in the central stage of the governing process.

Deliberative democracy, in a broader sense, is a form of managed democracy. Participation is controlled and orderly. If used properly, it can be less risky than a spontaneous electoral democracy. Liberal democracy can produce instability and bear a high cost to developing nations whose priority is predominantly political stability and economic development. Too often liberal democracy is promoted in countries that are clearly lacking social and economic support for such a system. As a result, many of these countries were dragged into long-term political chaos and economic mischief. Rational-choice theory lets us believe that reforms are always a balancing act between costs and benefits. Some scholars who have observed electoral democracy in many countries have become critical of liberal democracy. They conclude that several main features of liberal democracy, such as majority rule and elite rule, are fundamentally undemocratic. For them, democracy should be participatory. Jane Mansbridge believes that "a democracy based solely on the cold facts of national conflict will encourage selfishness based on perceiving others as opponents and discourage reasoned discussion among people of good will."[7]

Political leaders in Beijing have consistently shown a negative attitude toward liberal democracy. This negative view is based on the belief that liberal democracy will bring about political instability.[8] Obviously, the other undesirable political consequence is the possibility of an electoral defeat of the CCP in polling places, a result that is unthinkable to the ruling elite. The leaders are always afraid that what happened in the former Soviet Union could also happen in China. In 1990, when the former Soviet Union eliminated the constitutional guarantee of one-party rule, the communists were forced to compete with over twenty-plus political parties. They lost the election and the Russian Communist Party has become an opposition party since then. This painful lesson serves as a constant reminder to the Chinese leaders about the danger of adopting liberal democracy.[9] The "color revolutions" taking place in Central Asia in the early 2000s have made the leaders in Beijing even more cautious about electoral reforms.

However, the Chinese leaders cannot afford to postpone political reform indefinitely either. According to Chinese scholar Lin Shangli, China's challenge today is the contradiction between the one-party rule and an increasingly pluralistic society, and any solution to the challenge must retain the stability and continuation of the one-party system, i.e., not to challenge the CCP's leadership.[10] This is a true dilemma in China's political development.

China's political structure may also have a decisive impact on the sequence of political changes. According to some scholars, there exists a core-peripheral power structure in the unitary system, which the Chinese communist state inherited from the past. The communist core resembles the imperial power of the past. It is inviolable and autonomous. Changes are most likely taking place at the peripheral level. The core may translate the change to the national level if it feels comfortable with the change. Therefore, for the changes to take place, it has to be incremental and controllable.[11] One can apply this analysis in China's reform in the last thirty years. Changes like household responsibility system and village election all began at the grassroots level and in the so-called peripheral area.

Historically, China seems to have bad luck in its quest for electoral democracy. China had struggled for over a century towards the goal of establishing a representative democracy. From demanding democracy from the emperor in the late Qing dynasty to parliamentary democracy under the Northern warlords, from Nationalists' National Participation Conference (*Can Zheng Hui*) to the creation of Political Consultation Conference after the WWI, the democratic institutions were replaced by dictatorships every time.[12] The founding of the People's Republic of China did raise some hope for a representative democracy. In the Joint Platform issued by the first CPPCC in 1949, Article 12 stated that the popular election of the people's deputies should be carried out at all elections of the People's Congress at all levels. However, even until today, this exists on paper only. Gradually, the new NPCs became rubber stamps of the CCP. All civic organizations were organized and incorporated into a network of political control. No autonomy was granted to any of these organizations. No opposition to the party rule was tolerated.

After the death of Mao, the transformation of the totalitarian state began. The liberalization of economic life led to enhanced economic freedom for individual citizens. The ruling elite cannot and is no longer interested in exercising total control of all aspects of the society anymore. The restoration of democratic parties and key state-controlled interest groups has re-institutionalized formal political participation by various social elite within the CPPCC system.[13] However, opposition outside the system is still strictly forbidden. Today, China looks a lot like a corporatist state. There is one monopolistic group for every segment of the population. Most of these organizations are licensed and sponsored by the state. Some even perform many administrative duties on behalf of the state.

These days, one reads a lot of news about mass incidents taking place in China. Despite the sheer number of these unrests, there is no imminent danger of a general crisis in government; instead, what we have seen is a crisis of governance. The government, at least at the national level, still enjoys a relatively high level of public support, and its political legitimacy is still strong due to its successful economic reforms.[14] However, with the growing number of people joining the middle class and rapid diversification of economic and social interests of society, social inequality has become a major issue.

There are two types of governance crises in China today: traditional and non-traditional. Both serve as powerful forces for political openness. The traditional crisis refers mainly to the lack of communication channels for citizens to participate in the decision-making processes that have a direct impact on their day-to-day lives. The non-traditional crises were created by the Internet and communication revolution, while instant communication has made government control extremely difficult, and lack of timely response can cost the government greatly.

The lack of proper channels for citizen participation in public decision-making has contributed significantly to the manifested frustration and mistrust by various groups of people. The sieges and attacks on government buildings and a police headquarter on June 28, 2008, by thousands of local residents in Weng'an County of Guizhou province, highlighted the extent of this kind of frustration. The provincial Governor, Shi Zongyuan, acknowledged openly that the incident was an accumulation of discontents people had over the years. Another interesting development recently was the latest directive from the central government to reduce and stop citizens from travelling to Beijing to seek grievance redresses through the system of *xinfang* (or submitting grievance letters in person to public officials).

The spread of the Internet poses a different kind of challenge. By the mid-2010, about 400 million Chinese had Internet access. The Internet connects people regardless of where one lives. It is open and interactive. People are for the first time equal with one another, including the government, in information sharing. However, the content distributed is not necessarily true. Internet opens new channels for citizen activism. A call for action transmitted via the Internet or instant message can cause a riot on the street. Participation via the net is equal, spontaneous, and voluntary. In a number of recent mass protests, community organizers simply used text messaging or Internet chat rooms to share information and organize the boycotts or protests. Electronic activism is also on the rise. People bring protests to the Internet though the use of on-line petitions, e-mail spamming, virtual attacks on government sites, and posting banner videos and photos on the net. This kind of activism creates the *wang min* ("netizens") and new tools that can support the online vigilantes, such as using the Internet to conduct *renrou sousuo* ("human flesh search") to find and expose people who appear in the media or public that "netizens" consider puzzling or suspicious. However, the Internet can create its own problems. The phenomenon of "digital divide" actually causes unequal representation of the public among the population. [15]

The Chinese government has fought an up-hill battle to extend censorship to this new frontier. It is reported that in order to influence public opinion, the CCP has secretly trained a million Internet Commentators whose job is to post pro-government messages and report its "questionable" contents to the authorities. They are nicknamed as *wu mao dang* ("fifty-cent party") since the first known person hired by the government to post on the net had the user name "fifty cents." This is certainly a wrong approach for managing the issue and has not gone well with these tech-savvy "netizens."

How to create more channels for citizen participation? How to facilitate and manage net-based participation? How to institutionalize an orderly civic participation in the emerging civil society without rocking the power core? The use of deliberative democracy or participatory politics may hold the key to these questions. According to Robert A. Dahl, the emergence of participatory politics is a function of the cost of suppression and the cost of the tolerance. If the cost of suppression is too great, the state may become more tolerant of opposition's voice. [16] The cost of suppression as demonstrated in the June 4 crackdown is so high that future leaders will be reluctant to repeat the nightmare of having to confront students and civilians with tanks and armed soldiers. In the Wen'an case, the cost of arbitrary use of police forces was so high, the authority suddenly realized that they must find a way to let citizens express their grievances, or else it would become another "artificial lake of blocked speeches" (*yan sai hu*).

Building good governance has always had an important place in Chinese political theory. The "way of governance" (*zhi dao*) is always more important-than the "way of politics" (*zheng dao*). [17] While Taoism emphasized laissez-faire policy, legalism focused on rule by law. As the dominant governing philosophy, Confucianism always emphasized the rule of virtue. In Chinese interpretation, electoral democracy focuses on building a good government; deliberative democracy focuses on good governance.[18] Since the choice of the form of government is not an option, citizens can do little to change the corporatist nature of the state. Any players in Chinese politics must cooperate with the state in order to have a realistic chance for making changes.

Good governance involves cooperation between the state and the citizens. Deliberative democracy moves away from the totalitarian top-down control of the society by the state, and brings the state and the citizens closer to each other through open dialogs and debates. The goal is to ensure fairness and justice of the governing process. Its essence is to substitute politics with public administration. The party, the state or government officials still stay in the dominant positions, and are the recognized authority in decision making. Individuals or a group of citizens can have a direct dialog with authorities to influence the policy outcome. The process of decision-making is no longer closed, and citizens can voice their opinion legally.

Though we may not expect that the adoption of deliberative democracy will change the corporatist nature of the state, it may help transform the existing authoritarian corporatist state to a new societal corporatist state. In the post-WWII era, many industrializing economies in East Asia (China, Taiwan, South Korea) and Latin American countries (Brazil, Peru, Argentina) adopted state corporatism in which the state subordinated civic groups in order to prevent social conflicts that may arise from the economic modernization process. The industrialized economies such as northern Europe (Finland, Sweden, Austria, Norway, Iceland, Ireland, and the Netherlands) and south Europe (Spain and Portugal) adopted a soft version of corporatism or "societal corporatism."[19]

The nature of Chinese party-state shared many similarities with state corporatism during this time. The party-state established or controlled a vast network of social and political groups that represent all major social groups of the society. The All China Federation of Trade Unions (ACFTU) had a membership of 100 million people. The All China Women's Organization (ACWO) had over 1 million local chapters. The Chinese Communist Youth League (CCYL), which had 74 million members, also controlled three other youth organizations: the All China Federation of Student Organizations (ACFS), United Society of Chinese Youth (USCY), and the Chinese Communist Pioneers Organization (CCPO). The ACFS represented 80 million graduate, college and high school students. The CCPO had a membership of 130 million.

The so-called "democratic" party was organized in the same fashion. According to an official memorandum issued in 1996, each party was supposed to recruit its members from a reassigned group. For example, *Zhigongdang* would only recruit members from returned oversees students and their family members. *Minjian* was asked to recruit members only from business leaders, and *Minmeng* recruited members only from cultural, educational and scientific elite.[20] One thing in common for most of these organizations was that they had become a part of the administrative state and did not possess the essential ingredients of civil organizations such as autonomy and financial independence.

However, in recent years, the number of civil organizations has mushroomed (see Table 4.1). In 2007, there were about 357 thousand registered civil organizations in China. Some put the number of registered and unregistered civil organizations to 8 million.[21] Although the state attempts to incorporate new organizations through a licensing and regulating process, it is, however, increasingly unwilling to do so directly. In January 2008, the Ministry of Civil Affairs (MCA) organized a semi-official Association for Promotion of Chinese Civil Organization (APCCO). It intended to make it an intermediate organization to help the Ministry manage the civil organizations.

Table 4.1 The Growth of Chinese Civil Organizations (units: tens of thousands)

Type	2000	2001	2002	2003	2004	2005	2006	2007
Social Organizations	13.1	12.9	13.3	14.2	15.3	17.1	19.2	21.2
Private, non-profit organizations	2.3	8.2	11.1	12.4	13.5	14.8	16.1	17.4
Growth rate (%)	-4.6	-1.6	3.1	6.8	7.7	11.8	12.3	10.4

Sources: MCA, *Chinese Civil Affairs Development Annual Report*, 2007.

It is also apparent that the central government is determined to begin another round of administrative reforms aimed at changing the role of the government in ten years. This implies a great opportunity for the government to shift its focus from controlling and restricting to promoting and regulating social organizations, especially in utilizing the civil organizations to help build a self-regulatory society, which has been promoted as an important element in "building socialist democracy" in China. In a study of Chinese civil society, Gordon White et al. reveals that Chinese civil organizations exhibit elements of both civil society and corporatism. On the one hand, civil organizations remain tightly controlled by the state though leadership selection, finance, and registration. One the other hand, more and more groups now manifest some level of autonomy and financial independence.[22]

True deliberative democracy demands the engaged parties to be equal. In light of the existence of a corporatist and administrative state, it is realistic to expect this kind of equal dialog to occur anytime soon in China. The primary deliberation will be in the form of state-citizen dialogs, public hearings, and public opinions. And the most likely venue for the deliberation to take place is either within the existing framework of people's congresses or Chinese people's consultative conferences, or at the local administrative policy making process.[23]

According to Lin Shangli, deliberative democracy can be implemented in four areas: citizen legislative deliberation, administrative deliberation, consultative deliberation, and citizen deliberation of coordination.[24]

The discussion of deliberative democracy has gained some momentum within China thanks to the role of some of the CCP scholars like Li Junru. Deliberative democracy has been officially recognized as one of the major directions in China's political reform. Various schemes of political deliberation have already been developed. In this chapter we will take a look at some of the positive changes taking place in the systems of CPPCCs and NPCs.

CPPCCS and the System of Political Consultation

As a corporatist state, China's political system is unified under the CCP's leadership. Any attempt to build a deliberative democracy must engage in dialogs with the CCP. A key test to deliberative politics is if the CCP is willing to engage these dialogs on an equal basis with other social groups.

Citizen participation has always been one of the primary sources of political legitimacy of the CCP. Legal participations are traditionally conducted in two ways. One is mass mobilization, and the other, the system of CPPCCs. During Mao's era, mass line and mass mobilization were used frequently to generate public support for the state. Mao's famous quote "from the masses, to the masses" speaks for the essence of this populist leadership style. It requires the party and the government to find out the conditions of people, learning about and participating in their struggles, gathering ideas from them, and creating a plan of action based on these ideas and concerns of the people. However, this kind of participation is non-voluntary, not free, and not equal, and in many cases, even non-voluntary. This type of participation accumulated into the disastrous Cultural Revolution and has been subsequently discontinued by the CCP.

The transformation of the Chinese economy and the anti-rightist campaign literally shattered Chinese civil society. With the establishment of the one-party rule, no autonomous organization is allowed to exist outside of state control any more. The CCP's Department of United Front Works is in charge of establishing and maintaining a large system of United Front as an important strategy in its alliance-building effort. According to the CCP's own account, there are currently over 100 million people broadly defined as "targets of the United Front."[25] They include members of "democratic" parties, non-patrician elite and top intelligentsias, former KMT patriots, former business leaders, minority and religious leaders, returned overseas Chinese, and Chinese in Hong Kong, Macau, Taiwan and other countries.

Revival of the CPPCC System

The chief organ of legislative deliberation and consultation is the system of CPPCCs, which represent group interest instead of individual and local interests. The first CPPCC was held on September 20, 1949. Eleven non-communist parties participated in the conference. After some consolidation, only eight parties were presented in the conference. Initially, it was a legislative body; however, with the establishment of the NPC, the CPPCC was deprived of its legislative function, and became solely a consultative body. Before 1966, there were 1,171 CPPCCs at all levels, and 101 thousands deputies served in these bodies. The united government gradually became a party-state. The party system also seemed to be frozen once and for all: no more and no less, and there were always these eight parties on the CCP side, and they were supposed to be partners with the CCP. No new party was even allowed to register, either cooperative with the CCP or in opposition with is. Between 1966 and 1978, the CPPCC stopped working altogether due to the outbreak of the Cultural Revolution. Because of the change, Western observers never took this system of consultation seriously since it was considered merely a window-dressing for democracy.

The economic reform started in 1978 gave a new life to the CPPCCs. The system was restored, but to a large extent, it remained insignificant in the decision-making process. In recent years, the system was gradually strengthened. By 2000, there were 3,117 CPPCCs at all levels, and 539,490 people served as delegates to these CPPCCs.[26] The CCP took about one-third of all the seats, the remaining seats were allocated to other political parties, important social groups, and different social sectors. According to one official account, there were 50,000 proposals raised by CPPCC members in the past fifty-plus years.[27]

In 1982, the CCP added "democratic supervision" as a new function of the CPPCC, along with democratic consultation. In 1994, CPPCC Chairman Li Ruihuan put the participatory governance into the Constitution of the CPPCC.[28] In January 1989, the NPPCC adopted basic rules on democratic consultation and supervision.[29] It limited the consultation items to major issues such as legislation, budget, party and state leadership nominees, provincial boundary changes, diplomacy, unification and other issues related to people's lives. The CCP reestablished the Central Socialist Academy to serve as a party school for all "democratic parties" and non-party elite. It is responsible for training leaders of "democratic" parties, and deputies selected by the "democratic" parties to the CPPCCs. It requires that Marxism, Leninism and Mao Zedong Thoughts must be part of the overall curriculum. From these requirements, one can easily detect corporatist influence.

During the 1989 political turmoil in Beijing, many members of the CPPCC or members of "democratic" parties and "mass" groups showed sympathy to the student demonstrators, and some even got involved in organizing demonstration activities. When the dusts settled, the CCP moved on to tighten its control over this system. In order for the continued cooperation between the CCP and the "democratic" parties, the CCP warned that all parties must accept the CCP's leadership, and stick to the "four cardinal principles,"[30] and only under these conditions the "democratic parties" will be granted a role of "participating parties."[31] This document also warned that any organization that was considered to be deviating from the "four cardinal principles" would be suspended. This tough stand revealed the inferior and unequal status of these so-called "democratic parties."

In recent years, the rhetoric to build deliberative democracy has suddenly given a new life to the CPPCC. The intention of the CCP is clear: it wants to transform the CPPCC into functional corporatist political institutions in which a substantial level of deliberation, supervision, and discussion can be conducted. All of these are also part of the effort for building a socialist harmonious society. The CCP issued three key documents between 2005 and 2006 to define the official version of the new deliberative system between the CCP and other political parties and other political elite. In 2005, the CCP issued a document on strengthening the CCP's system of multi-party cooperation and deliberative democracy. The use of deliberative decision-making was to become a mandatory requirement for all major party and state decisions. It proposed two types of deliberative mechanism. One was the consultation between the CCP and the other "democratic parties." The other was the political consultation between the CCP and other "democratic parties" delegates to the CPPCC. In February 2006, the CCP issued another document on strengthening the work of the CPPCC. For the first time, it declared that electoral democracy and deliberative democracy are both important forms of "socialist democracy." It also stated that deliberative democracy is consistent with Chinese traditional culture and constitutes a Chinese characteristic in democratic decision-making.[32] In the same year, the CCP also called for strengthening the institutions, standards and procedures of the deliberative system within the CPPCC.[33] Chen Suyu, a member of the CPPCC, proposed that deliberative democracy must contain four elements: participation, listening, deliberation, and compromise.[34]

Because the CPPCC is not a legislative body and does not have legislative power, it has been traditionally an institution for "empty talk." Some members don't even show up for the meeting. In recent years, there has been some improvement. The number of proposals for policy changes has risen steadily. In the 9th CPPCC meeting (1998-2003), delegates offered 17,722 piece of proposals. In the 10th CPPCC meeting, a total of 23,000 proposals were submitted.

The institutionalization, routinization and standardization with the system of the consultation also improved over the years. Each year, the CCP committees at various levels would come up with a list of issues that they would like to consult with the CPPCCs. Democratic parties would have opportunities to engage in detailed research on these issues, and make inspection tours, if necessary. Then each party would present its views in CPPCC meetings as a group. The CCP must provide feedback to the suggestions and recommendations made. There are currently four type of consultation:

- *Policy Consultation*: includes major policy decisions to solve major issues such as reform measures or economic plans.
- *Legislative Consultation*: includes some important legislative drafts, but not all legislation.
- *Personnel Consultation*: includes major nominations of key leaders, usually done before their elections.
- *Project Consultation*: includes projects that are significant, such as the Three Gorge Project, the Water Diversion Project to divert water from the south to the north.

Case Studies: The Local CPPCC in the City of Zhengzhou

To see how local CPPCC works, we did some case studies on the activities of the CPPCC in Zhengzhou, the capital city of Henan province, with a population over seven million (2007). In 1980, it only had 150 members. It is now expanded to 566 delegates (2009) representing 28 different groups or fields. We found that the CPPCC has become relatively active in recent years in the city's decision-making process. Between 2004 and 2008, delegates submitted 3,868 proposals, conducted 500 inspection tours, and made 2,500 policy recommendations to the city government. Between 2007 and 2009, the CPPCC submitted 130 research reports.[35]

Table 4.2 Zhengzhou CPPCC Proposals

Year	Proposals	Accepted	Imple-mented	Rate of Im-plementation	Satisfac-tion Rate
2006	1,010	920	712	73.4%	95.6%
2005	803	746	621	83.4%	96.2%
2004	820	796	--	--	94.0%

Sources: *Zhengzhou Yearbook*, (Zhengzhou, Zhengzhou Yearbook Press), 2005-2007.

Do the CPPCC consultation and supervision activities make any differences? Are there any deliberations going on with these proposals? The following are some of the cases we come across.

Case 1
In 2006, Zhengzhou CPPCC called upon two face-to-face decision meetings (*xian chang banli hui*) with related city officials. In discussing the proposal on "no arbitrary alteration of residential sub-divisional plan," deputies were unhappy about the lack of public knowledge of the city planning process. The City Planning Office adopted four measures proposed by the deputies. From March 1, 2006, all proposed city plans will be made public either before the approval or after the approval. In this case, the CPPCC members acted as a facilitator for dialogs between city residents and city officials.

Case 2
When some deputies raised the issue of health insurance for the retirees of the previous state-owned companies in 2006, the deputy mayor, who is in charge of this issue, directed the related city office to simply allocate 50 million *yuan* from the city budget to cover 43,000 retirees from 98 state-owned enterprises who had trouble receiving their pension

payments. The Ministry of Labor and Social Security praised the city's action publicly in the national conferences. Although no deliberation was made in this case, the recommendation did benefit a large group of retirees. The CPPCC members served as entrepreneurs championing the interests of the elderly.

Case 3
In November, 2006, the city government organized a group of CPPCC members from the national, provincial and county levels to inspect high priority projects. This group of deputies held 32 meetings with the project leaders, visited 42 construction sites, and eventually came up with 82 suggestions. This case highlights the important role of the CPPCC as a supervisory body over the administrative agencies.[36]

Overall, the existing practice of political consultation does possess some level of deliberation. The CPPCC members can play a significant role in some of the key decisions relating to policies, legislations and personal nominations. Members of the CPPCC did extensive researches on a given task before going to these consultation sessions. However, the current system of political consultation has several fatal defects that will severely compromise its effectiveness.

It has no teeth. The CPPCC is not a decision-making organ; it is merely an advisory body. Its opinion is not legally binding on the government. Its members do not have the same level of protection over their speeches. This is not to say that the CPPCC is totally powerless. As long as they are allowed to voice their opinions, they are influential. The CPPCCs were responsible for many pieces of new legislation and administrative regulations or decisions. Had the CPPCC been given the same legal status of its Western equivalency, such as the Senate in the U.S. or the House of Chancellors in Japan, its deliberative role would have been significantly strengthened.

The legitimacy of the selection process. The selection of the deputies to the CPPCC is also problematic. Members are nominated instead of elected. The CCP still has to approve the all nominations. The allocation of the delegates reflects the proportionality of two dozens of social groups, but the actual allocation can be arbitrary. Most members still consider the membership to be merely an honor, a sense of elite status, or a form of public reorganization.

It has become bureaucratized. The CPPCC is also considered a part of the state apparatus, and are staffed and financed by public budgets. The cadres of the deputies and leaders are considered state cadres; enjoying the same benefits as state leaders in the same levels. Many of the leaders of the CPPCC are actually former state leaders; they are assigned to these positions prior to their retirement.

Inadequate resource Although the CCP has realized the importance of the CPPCC as an indispensable asset for legitimizing its decisions, it does not allocate resources in the same way as it does to itself. Figures 4.1 and 4.2 suggest that the CCP had the overwhelming advantage in budget allocations between 2001 and 2006. The number of staff hired also reflected the same trend. The city's CCP organization employed over 3,200 individuals, which was 22 percent more than the budget appropriated, and four times more than the combined number of employees of the CPPCC, "democratic parties" and various government sponsored social organizations.

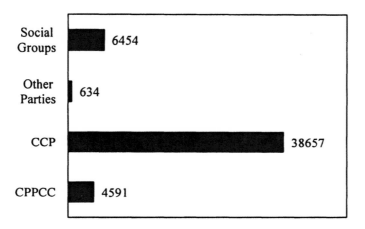

Figure 4.1 Zhengzhou City Budget Allocation (2001-2006)   (units: percentage)

Sources: *Zhengzhou Yearbook*, 2001-2007 (Zhengzhou: Zhengzhou Yearbook Press).

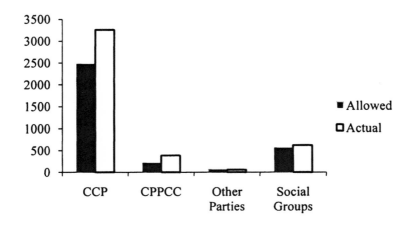

Figure 4.2 Zhengzhou City Government Employees (2006)   (units: people)

Sources: *Zhengzhou Yearbook, 2007* (Zhengzhou: Zhengzhou Yearbook Press, 2008).

Legitimacy of "democratic" parties is in question. The CCP's second mechanism is the consultation with non-communist parties. These parties are licensed patriotic political, social, religious, economic, or popular organizations who joined the CCP in 1949 to form the new government. Some of their leaders are often CCP members as well. As Figures 4.1 and 4.2 show, the state is the source of their funding, legitimacy, and personal well-being.

The NPC and Open-Door Legislation

The NPC is the legislative body in China. China has a unicameral system in which the legislative branch is made of a single house. The NPC meets once a year for less than two weeks. The NPC deputies serve a five-year term and have no term limit. There are nearly 3,000 members. The NPC's Standing Committee, which consists of about 160 members (2009), is given most of the legislative power.

In recent years, the NPC has experimented with various schemes of open legislation in order to promote public deliberation. One such mechanism is to publish many pieces of controversial legislative proposals, and collect feedback from various groups. This practice was first used in 1954 when the newly drafted Constitution was published for public comments. The Constitution of 1982 was also based on public comments. The first legislative proposal published for public comments was a public land management law in 1999. Between 1999 and 2008, sixteen legislative drafts were made public to seek public input.[37] In this section we will examines two pieces of legislation and study the roles of two national interest groups in the legislative process.

Marriage Law

In 1999, the 1st Session of the 9th NPC decided to revise the Marriage Law of 1980. Legal scholars quickly presented a proposal to the NPC in April 2000. The initial draft was discussed twice by the NPC on January 11, 2001 and soon the proposed bill was made public. In the three-month period for the public comments, nearly 4,000 written opinions were sent to the NPC. Media carried many discussions that were more open on various issues relating to the marriage law. The level of public participation in the deliberation process was truly unprecedented.

Some people wanted to maintain the integrity of family and pushed very hard on imposing penalties for extra marital affairs. Business owners wanted to legalize the use of premarital agreements to protect their assets in case of a divorce. Married women wanted to receive divorce settlements that would be favorable to them if their husbands were found engaging in infidelity, adultery and polygamy. Young people preferred to have more free choices in their life styles and wanted to make cohabitation more acceptable and divorce easier to obtain. The debates reflected a clash of various social interests and moral values. The key question was to what extent marriage law should incorporate the ever-changing social norms and individual morality.

The Marriage Law of 1980 permits divorce to be granted based on no-fault or breakdown of mutual affection. Surprisingly, majority opinions voiced recommended an elimination of the no-fault divorce clause in order to protect families and save marriages. Thankfully, the NPC's Legislative Affairs Committee did not adopt this recommendation.[38] On the issue of extra marital affairs, some supported criminalization of the phenomena of "*er nai*" or mistress as well as adultery, while others refused to use legal means to deal with the issue of immorality.

In the debate, the All China Women's Federation (ACFW) played an important role. The ACFW was founded on April 3, 1949. Its mission was to protect women's rights and interests. However, the ACFW was described as a typical monopolistic corporatist organization that claimed to be the sole voice of all women in China. Historically, it served primarily as a periphery organization of the CCP. In recent years, the ACFW started to focus more of their attention on the protection of women's legal rights and economic interests. For instance, it played an important role in protecting women's interests in the establishment the rural family responsibility system and village elections.

During the public comment period, the ACWF was mobilized to add more protection for women and children. The ACWF used two strategies to influence the revision process. First, it did an extensive national-wide survey and investigation on what women wanted to change. Based on the opinion poll and discussions, the ACWF suggested five areas to be changed: polygamy, family violence, family property protection, visitation rights for divorced parents, and invalid marriages. It then chose to use both formal and informal ways to exert its influence. It not only submitted a number of recommendation materials to the NPC's Legislative Affairs Committee, the key decision making body, but also lobbied female legislators in the NPC. They utilized their position as the only representative group for women to communicate effectively with key legislators. Most of their proposals were adopted.

Unlike the conflict model, the ACWF played the role as an interest aggregator. It did not seek to compete with other social groups, but instead, it played the power game to offset the interest difference. The ACWF skillfully utilized its monopolistic position to instigate a successful revision process that was in favor of women. [39]

Property Rights Law

After thirteen years of debate and extensive deliberation, the NPC finally passed China's first Property Rights Law on March 16, 2007. Only fifty-two votes were cast against the new law. The overwhelming major of the deputies supported it. This represented a major victory for China's market reform. It codified the protection of both individual and public properties.

To achieve this level of consensus was not easy. Not until 2002 was the first draft of the bill was submitted to the NPC for consideration. In the subsequent years, the NPC discussed the bill eight times, unprecedented in the NPC's history. On July 10, 2005, the NPC decided to publish the draft and invite public to comment on the proposed bill. Within forty days, the NPC received 11,514 comments. The NPC held 100 deliberation meetings and legislative hearings over the controversial issues related to the bill. Gong Xiantian, a professor at Beijing University wrote an open letter in September and challenged the constitutionality of the bill. He argued against the provision to grant equal protection for private and public property, and believed that the protection of public property should be the key to socialism.[40] Many people posted messages on Beijing University's BBS to support his position. This action literally put the legislation process on hold for ten months. The NPC's Legislative Work Committee sent four committee members to meet with him in person to discuss his opposition. In December, 148 liberal legal scholars wrote a letter to the CCP Central Committee and asked the CCP to support the drafted property bill. Before the NPC considered the fifth version of the bill, the opposition reached its climax. Gong was joined by 718 leftist political elite and intellectuals and sent another opposition letter to each of the nine Politburo members and 170 members of the NPC standing committee.

However, the NPC decided to speed up the deliberation process, and considered the draft for the sixth and seventh time in six months. More letters from both sides were sent to the NPC either to promote or block the legislation. In order to secure passage of the bill, the NPC sent the eighth version to all NPC members prior to the annual meeting. Many standing committee members were sent to each province to help NPC deputies to understand the legislation and to minimize potential resistance. The CCP's Central Committee sent a directive to urge all NPC deputies to unify their thoughts and secure the passage of the legislation. Gang and his supporters did not give up. They posted another open letter fifteen days before the scheduled NPC vote. This time over 3,000 people signed the open letter.[41] Despite the objection, the NPC managed to pass the new legislation with little oppositions from NPC members.

Conclusions

In this chapter, we explored the logic for developing a structure of deliberative democracy in China, and examined various forms of legislative deliberation within the framework of the NPC and the CPPCC. The conclusion derived from these discussions is that there has been some progress in opening up the legislative process and in legislative deliberations at both the national and local levels. We also see certain level of civic activism in state-society relations. However, China clearly has a long way to go to build a system of political deliberation. The major obstacle to building a functional deliberative democracy is the strong state and the unequal relations among parties engaged in the discussion. Deliberation is still conducted in the form of political consultation, which is a primitive stage of deliberative democracy. In the next chapter, we will turn our attention to citizen activism and deliberation at the local public administration.

Notes

1. Howard Wiarda, *Corporatism and Comparative Politics: the Other Great "Ism"* (Amonk, NY: M.E. Sharp, 1997); Philippe Schmitter, "Still the Century of Corporatism?" *Review of Politics* 85 (January 1974): 85-131.

2. Joseph Bessette, "Deliberative Democracy: The Majority Principle in Republican Government," in *How Democratic is the Constitution?* (Washington, D.C., AEI Press, 1980):102–116. John Dryzek, *Discursive Democracy: Politics, Policy and Political Science* (Cambridge University Press, 1994); Baogang He, *Democratic Theory: Dilemma and Approach* (Beijing, Law Press, 2008).

3. Li Junru "Chinese Should not be so Humbled about Democracy," http://politics.people.com.cn/GB/1026/4624705.html (accessed June 18, 2008).

4. Jin Anping, Yao Chuanming, "Xieshang Minzhu Buying Wudu [Deliberative Democracy should not be Misinterpreted]," *Zhongguo Renming Zhengxie Lilun Yanjiuhui Huikan (Journal of Association on the Study of the Theory of Chinese Political Consultation), no. 3 (2007).

5. Yu Keping, "Zhengzhi Xue de Gongli [the Laws of Politics]," *Jiangsu Social Sciences*, no. 5 (2003): 6-62.

6. Jürgen Habermas, *Legitimation Crisis*, trans. by Thomas McCarthy (Boston, MA: Beacon Press, 1973), 99.

7. Jane Mansbridge, "Unitary and Adversary: the Two Forms of Democracy," *In Context*, no. 7 (Autumn 1984), 10.

8. Samuel Huntington, *Political Order in Changing Societies* (New Haven, CT: Yale University Press, 2006).

9. Xu Juezai, "Guowai Zhengdan Zhizheng Fangshi Chutan [Preliminary Study of the Models of Governance of the Ruling Parties]," *Political Science: Reprints of Journal and Newspaper Articles by Renmin University of China* 2 (2004), 49.

10. Lin Shangli, "Xieshang Zhengzhi yu Zhongguo de Zhengzhi Xingtai [Deliberative Democracy and China's Political System]," *People's Consultation Conference Newspaper*, September 21, 2000.

11. Xu Yong "Neihe-Bianceng: Ke Kong de Fangquanshi Gaige [The Core-Peripheral structure: the Manageable Reform of the Decentralization]," *Dongfang*, Feburay 2002, 13-18.

12. Xu Zongmian and Zhang Yigong, *Jin Dai Zhong Guo Dui Min Zhu de Zhui Qiu* [The Pursuit of Democracy in China's Modern Time] (Hefei, Anhui People's Publisher, 1996).

13. Juan J. Linz, "Opposition in and under an Authoritarian Regime: the Case of Spain," in Robert A. Dahl. ed., *Regimes and Oppositions* (New Haven: Yale University Press, 1973).

14. Jie Chen, *Popular Political Support in Urban China* (Stanford, CA: Stanford University Press, 2004).

15 Liu Wen, "Wangluo Shidai Zhengzhi Canyu de Nanti ji Duice [The dilemma and solution to the issue of political participation in the era of Internet]," *Zhongzhou Xuekan* [Academic Journal of Central Plain] 6 (2003):14-18.

16. Robert A. Dahl, *Polyarchy: Participation and Opposition* (New York: Harper and Collins, 1971), 13-14.

17. Jin Yaoji, *Xingzheng Xina Zhengzhi–Xianggand de Zhengzhi Moshi [Politics by administration–the Hong Kong Model in Chinese Politics and Culture]* (Oxford: Oxford University Press, 1997): 21-45.

18. Jia Jianfang, "Zhuangui zhong de Zhongguo Zhengzhi Zouxiang: Shanzhi yu zengliang Minzhu [The political trend during the transition: good governance and quan-

titative-enhancing democracy], *Kexue Shehui Zhuyi* [Scientific Socialism], no. 1 (2004): 3-7.

19. Howard Wiarda, *Corporatism and Comparative Politics: The other Great "Ism,"* (Armonk, NY: M.E. Sharpe, 1997). Phillippe Schmitter, "Still the Century of Corporatism?" *Review of Politics* 36 (1979):35-131.

20. "Memorandum of the Meeting on Issues Related to Organizational Development of the Democratic Parties," cited in *Wu Meihua, Dangdai Zhongguo de Duodangheczuo Zhidu* [The Contemporary Multiparty Cooperative System] (Beijing: CCP Historical Record Press, 2005), 250.

21. Yu Keping, "Zhongguo Gongmin Shehui Rugan Wenti de Yanjiu [An Inquiry on a number of Issues Relating to the Civil Society in China], http://www.chinanpo.gov.cn/ (accessed June 28, 2008).

22. Gordon White, Jude Howell and Shang Xiaoyuan, *In Search of Civil Society: Market Reform and Social Changes in Contemporary China* (Oxford, Clarendon Press, 1996), 126.

23. Baogang He, *Ibid.*, 248.

24. Lin Shangli, "Citizen Deliberation and the Development of Grassroots Democracy in China," *Academic Monthly (China)* 39, no. 9 (2007): 13-20.

25. CCP Department of United Front Works, "The United Front will be Important and Existed for a Long Time under the New Era," http://www.zytzb.org.cn/zytzbwz/theory/lilun/200804/t20080430_373773.htm (accessed June 25, 2008).

26. Wu Meihua, *Dandai Zhongguo de Duodanghezuo Zhigu [The Contemporary Chinese Multiparty Cooperative System]*(Beijing, CCP Party History Press, 2003), 124.

27. People's Daily, "Backgrounder: Role of the CPPCC a Key to State," *People's Daily*, March 3, 2004, http://english.peopledaily.com.cn/200403/ (accessed June 25, 2008).

28. Wu, *op cit.*, 125.

29. NPPCC, "Provincial Rules on Political Consultation and Supervision," January 27, 1989, http://www.hsxzx.gov.cn/Article/ShowArticle.asp?ArticleID=85 (accessed June 25, 2008).

30. These principles were proposed by Deng Xiaoping in 1979, which incude upholding "socialist path," "people's democratic dictatorship," "leadership of the CCP," and "Marxist-Leninist-Mao Zedong thoughts."

31. CCP Central Committee, "Opinions on Adherence and Improvement of the Multiparty Cooperation and Political Consultation under the CCP's Leadership," Dec. 30, 1989, http://news.xinhuanet.com/ziliao/2005-02/21/content_2600060.htm (accessed June 25, 2008).

32. CCP Central Committee, "Opinions on Strengthening the Work of the CPPCC," http://www.cnjxol.com/xwzx/gnxw/content/2006-03/01/content_29373.htm (accessed June 25, 2008).

33 CCP Central Committee, "Opinions on Strengthening and Enlarging the United Front in the New Century," http://news.xinhuanet.com/politics/2006-11/28/content_5403323.htm (accessed February 12, 2009).

34. Chen Suyu, "Strengthening Deliberative Democracy and Promote Social Harmony," speech made at 5th Plenary Session of the 10th CPPCC Meeting, March 3, 2007.

35. All data used in this study were taken from Zhengzhou CPPCC's website, http://www.zzzxy.gov.cn/ (accessed February 12, 2009).

36. All cases are from *Zhengzhou Yearbook*, 2005-2007 (Zhengzhou: Zhengzhou Yearbook Press).

37. "Zhongguo 'Kaimen Lifa' Shi Ruhe Chengwei Changtai de?" [How has the 'Open Legislation' Become a Standard Practice], http://www.law-lib.com/fzdt/newshtml/szpl/20080422085217.htm (accessed December 17, 2009).

38. Wang Liren, "Lihun Biaozun Buneng Donyao [the Criteria for Divorce should not be Changed]," http://www.fsou.com/html/text/art/3355758/335575830.html (accessed February 12, 2009).

39. Xu Jialing, "Policy-making Process: Interests Aggregation & Path Choice—Influence of All China Women's Federation on the Revision of the Marriage Law" (in Chinese), *Journal of Beijing University* (Philosophy and Social Science Edition) 41, no. 4 (July 2007): 95-102.

40. Gong Xiantian, "The Proposed Property Law is Unconstitutional," Chinaelections.org, http://www.chinaelections.org/NewsInfo.asp?NewsID=45986 (accessed June 25, 2008).

41. Zhang Fan, "Behind the 52 Oppositional Votes," *Phoenix Weekly*, May 12, 2007.

Chapter 5
Community Governance in Action[*]

In the previous chapter, we discussed formal and informal political consultation systems the national and local levels. Now let us look at deliberative policy-making process, either formally or informally, at the community level. One of the key challenges to China's political development is to find effective mechanisms to channel and accommodate the emerging needs for political participation at the grass-root level. There are two reasons why community governance deserves special attention. On the one hand, the market-oriented economic reform has transformed local communities. Residential neighborhoods are no longer consists primarily factory-build living quarters; increasingly, they are new residential subdivisions built by city governments or property developers. Local governments rely more and more on community support for its decisions related to urban development, policy implementation, and social services. On the other hand, as economic entities gradually transfer their social and welfare functions to the government, individual citizens become more and more dependent on local governments for housing, health care, education, and social services. This dual dependency has consequently uplifted urban residential communities to the center stage of local politics in urban areas.

In recent years, the Chinese government has gradually recognized the importance of community services, development, and governance. The concept of "community services" first appeared in Chinese official lexicon in 1986. In 1991, the MCA added "community building" as one of its main responsibilities.[1] Unlike some other areas of administrative governance, programs designed to promote community work can have a direct impact on the lives of ordinary people who live in the communities. Like politics elsewhere, community governance is all about who make decisions, how decisions are made and implemented, and who will benefit. The traditional approach to community development and governance relies on technocrats and bureaucrats to extend the web of community services, city planning, and political control. The alternative is the "power-to-the-people" approach, which promotes community self-government and grass-root deliberative democracy.

This chapter will examine three cases of citizen reactive participation in urban development projects in the Shenzhen, a modern city created during the reform era. Through these case studies, we want to get a real picture of the

---

[*] The chapter was written with assistant of Dr. Tang Juan of Shenzhen University who provided some data and shared some of her researches with the author. The author wishes to thank her for her contribution.

progress and problems in the emerging system of public policy deliberation at the community level. The reactive participation is a form of civil participation that is a response of community members to the technocratic decision-making process, which is usually dominated by the trained engineers and city planners. We will first examine the development of community as a level of political governance in China. Next, we will analyze three controversial community incidents taking place between 2003 and 2005 in Shenzhen. Finally, we will evaluate these three experiences in community governance. We will make some general observations on the lessons we have learned about implementing deliberative democracy at the community level and the institutional and procedural prerequisites for a meaningful deliberative democracy. The central questions we are about to explore in this chapter include: What should be the role of the government in community building? What are the limits of the technocrats in community development? What are the key characteristics of the new community-based governance reform? What are its theoretical and empirical implications to political reform in China?

Local Communities in Transition

Community governance has been historically significant to political rulers throughout Chinese history. Since the unification of China in Qin Dynasty and the establishment of the unitary system of the administrative structure, the order of the central government could flow directly to the county level. Beyond this level, a semi-military system called the *xiang-li system* was created to serve the needs of the central government. Starting from the Song Dynasty, a *bao-jia* system replaced the *xiang-li system*, and was perfected by different dynasties in the next millennium. The downfall of the Qing Dynasty ended the system briefly. However, the nationalist government restored the system in 1932 in Henan, Hubei and Jiangsu provinces in order to fight communist insurgence. A few years later, the system was promoted nationwide. When the Chinese communists overthrew the nationalist government in 1949, the *bao-jia system* was abolished altogether. The new government established a system of, supposedly, self-governing village committees and urban sub-district offices. Nevertheless, the element of self-government was not fully implemented due to the embracement of a Soviet-style totalitarian political system. During the period of the Cultural Revolution (1966-1976), most of the neighborhood committees ceased to exist. After 1980, the neighborhood committee system was gradually restored. By 1999, there were 115,000 neighborhood committees administered by 5,904 neighborhood offices of 667 city governments.[2] The dissolution of the People's Commons in 1983 also led to the formation of over 300,000 rural village committees.

In the urban areas, each neighborhood committee contained about 100-700 households. Although the committee members were directly elected, the chair and the deputy chair of these committees received monthly salary from the local governments. The neighborhood committees were supposed to be an entity for democratic self-rule, but they quickly became another administrative unit of the neighborhood offices of the local government. They were given over one hundred administrative duties and served many other official functions.[3] The selection of the committee chairs and the finances of these committees were all dependent on the government's neighborhood offices.

The rapid economic development and modernization drive have led to the exponential growth in the number of cities and the number of urban population. China's urban population rose from 18 percent in 1978 to 39 percent in 2002. It is expected that China will reach 55 percent of urbanization rate by 2020.[4] Each year, over 10 million rural populations are absorbed by the urban development, and the total urban population will reach 600 million by 2020. The modern residential housing has mushroomed and new residential communities have transformed the urban landscape. Many old neighborhoods and streets have disappeared almost overnights.

Consequently, the residential neighborhood communities have undergone drastic changes in recent years. By the end of 2007, there are over 80,000 communities recognized by the MCA (see Table 5.1). Currently, there are four types of communities in existence: (1) city block communities; (2) small residential communities; (3) work unit communities; and (4) functional communities.

Table 5.1 Chinese Urban Communities

Category Household	Average Size of Communities	Number of	Percentage
Small	1,000	30,746	38.2
Medium	1,000-3,000	39,825	49.2
Large	Over 3,000	10,213	12.6
Total		80,784	100

Sources: Wei Minli and Li Yajie, "China Build a New Community Governance System," *Xinhua News*, October. 11, 2007, www.chinaelections.org (accessed February 2, 2009).

According to German sociologist Ferdinand Tönnies, in a modern society there will be an increased number of clashes between small-scale neighborhood-based communities and the large-scale competitive market society.[5] A sense of connectedness or common interests will give rise to social capital that may lead to collective social or political actions aimed at promoting community interests.[6] Social capital, thus, can be translated into community power used for political mobilization or control. How to govern the reinvented communities has become one of the major challenges for leaders who are preoccupied with concerns about political and social stability. The escalating number of interest clashes and

Table 5.2 Types of Visits to Government Agencies in Nanshan District, Shenzhen

Year	Group visits		Repeated visits		Higher-level visits		Use of sabotage and violence during visits	
	Cases	Individuals involved	Cases	Individuals involved	Cases	Individuals involved	Cases	Individuals involved
2003	31	852	81	338	14	121	15	225
2004	38	1,801	94	217	11	103	18	1,410
2005 (Jan.-Sept.)	36	921	76	251	10	269	11	136
Total	105	3,574	251	806	35	493	44	1,771

Sources: Nanshan District Government and provided by Tang Juan.

Table 5.3 Letter-Complaints against Property Management Firms in Nanshan District, Shenzhen

Year	Total number of cases handled	Cases dealing with property management firms									
		Total		Include: Related to developers		Related to management firms		Related to home-owners association		Others	
	Sum	Sum	%	Sum	% of cases related to property management	Sum	% of cases related to property management	Sum	% of cases related to property management	Sum	% of cases related to property management
2003	1,188	426	35.86%	136	31.93%	131	30.75%	124	29.11%	35	8.22%
2004	1,516	565	37.27%	233	41.24%	186	32.92%	98	17.35%	48	8.5%
2005 (1-9)	1,440	700	48.61%	310	44.29%	253	36.14%	116	16.57%	21	3.0%
Total	4,144	1,691	40.8%	679	40.15%	570	33.71%	338	6.15%	104	6.15%

Sources: Nanshan District Government and provided by Tang Juan.

mass incidents at the community level has made this task even more urgent. In the Nanshan District of Shenzhen, the number of letter-complaints sent to government agencies and petition-visits to district government offices over property management in the newly built residential communities have increased steadily (see Tables 5.2 and 5.3). Some visitors used tactics of sabotage and violence, while others took street actions to block the construction of the controversial city projects. For political leaders in Beijing, they must find some effective ways to deal with these types of individual and collective actions in order not to compromise China's political and social stability.

Indeed, community building has become a new priority of the Chinese government since the mid-1980s. The MCA has played a major role in promoting community reform. Over twenty-six pilot projects were carried out in different communities in 2,000. Based on these experiments, the nation-wide reform began in 2001. This widely publicized community building effort has drawn some attention. Leaders in Beijing saw this as a positive development in achieving its objective for a "harmonious society." Local leaders viewed this reform as a way to curtail the escalating number of mass incidents and disputes involving laborers, homeowners, property owners, and construction companies. Since then, governments at various levels have been actively promoting community development and extending government services to neighborhood communities.

No matter how promising community services and community building may sound, it does not substitute the community governance. From its very beginning, the neighborhood committees were intended to achieve local self-government. There is a danger that with all of these government interventions, the whole effort may undermine the very idea of democratic self-governance. It is still extremely challenging that self-government can ever be achieved within the state-dominated political structure.

Nevertheless, with the adoption of the incremental approach towards economic and political reforms, and overwhelming concern with political stability, large scale of reform policies are always less risky if they are carried out at the grass-root level in an incremental manner. One of the salient features of China's successful rural reform was the introduction of the rural direct election of the village committees and the village self-rules. Democracy, for the first time in Chinese history, takes a strong hold at the underdeveloped rural villages. However, it is not until the 1990s that the reform of the urban community governance began. The counterpart of the village committees in the urban areas is the traditional neighborhood committees. Direct elections of chairpersons of these neighborhood committees have been carried out in local communities. But democratic decision-making and democratic management remain a distant goal.

The two decades of community reform have produced two very different models of community governance. One is a government-centered governance model with limited community participation. Another one is a community-centered governance model with limited government support and guidance. The government-centered model is represented by Shanghai, and the community-centered model is represented by Shenyang, Jianghan, and Yantian. The Shanghai model of community governance is based on three systems: a decision-making body consisting of the CCP Working Committee, the Neighborhood Office of District Government, and the Urban Management Committee. A community managing and executive body consists of the Urban Affairs Committee, the Community Development Committee, the Social Safety and Comprehensive Management Committee, the Financial and Economic Committee, and a support system consisting of enterprises, social institutions, interests groups, and neighborhood committees. The democratic deliberation is based on three mechanisms: evaluation committees, public hearings, and coordination conferences. The evaluation committee is made up of representatives chosen by the neighborhood committee, and will conduct periodical oversight over the government budget, reports, and neighborhood works. Public hearings are used to allow citizens to testify before a government agency over a planned public project, a price adjustment in public utilities, etc. The coordinating conferences will be held when there are disputes between residents and enterprises over issues such as environmental pollution or excessive street noise. This system strengthens the role of the neighborhood office of district government in an urban area, but leaves little room for community self-governance.

The city of Nanjing, on the other hand, decided to do away with the neighborhood office and replaced it with an administrative affair management center (more like a service center). The business function of the neighborhood office was returned to the district government, while at the same time, the social and service functions were given to community organizations such as the neighborhood committees, social work stations, and community service centers. These civil organizations are independent from the government, but receive government financial support for performing their social functions. They have their own bank accounts, and offer free or fee-based services. The social work stations are responsible for public services as well as welfare services. A large number of civic organizations have been organized, including organizations for the elderly, the disabled, women and children, fine art, and performing art. This model strengthens community's self-governance capability.[7] The similar experiment is also conducted in some communities in Qingdao and Wuhan.[8]

Deliberative and Reactive Participation

According to Talcott Parsons's structure functionalist theory, consensus between members of a society on morals plays an important role in maintaining social order.[9] The consensus, according to Gabriel Almond and Bingham Powell, can only be achieved through the process of interest articulation, interest aggregation, and communication (deliberation) performed by various social institutions.[10] In a stable community, equilibrium will be maintained among various players and institutions. If there is a missing link or malfunction somewhere in the social structure, the equilibrium will be broken, and consequently, social stability may be compromised. Although Chinese society has not developed a fully functional civil society, social dialogs, either peaceful petition or street actions between various social institutions such as government, business entitles, and citizens, are increasingly becoming important forms of political communication since each of the actors is increasingly becoming a more or less independent and self-conscious player. Consequently, consensus-building can become difficult. The lack of a deliberative democracy and inadequate political communication can be a source of conflicts among the players. In the following discussion, we will examine several recent cases involving residential conflicts in Shenzhen between 2003 and 2005.

Rational choice theory suggests that clashes of interests do not necessarily lead to collective actions.[11] Citizens will choose not to get involved in politics and collective actions if the perceived cost of participation is greater than perceived benefits. However, if one's interests are jeopardized, people will have no choice but to participate. In this sense, most participative actions at the community level tend to be a reaction to events or decisions that let the citizens believe their interests are at stake. In Shenzhen, a city that has the highest individual per capita income and highest concentration of the middle class, one would expect citizens' willingness to participate in local politics to be extremely high. However, the reality does not support this. Yes, there were many mass incidents in recent years involving the protection of citizens' rights, but these events were mostly citizens' reaction to unfair business practices and the lack of consultation in government's planning and urban development decision-making process. Clashes, protests, road blockages, and police crackdown characterized some of the reactive participation. In the following discussion, we will take a closer look at three recent incidents: *Dingtai Fenghua* Incident, *Fengzehu Zhuangyun* Incident and the Western Connector Incident.

Case 1: *Dingtai Fenghua* Incident

Dingtai Fenghua is a new residential community located in Nanshan District. Most residents are white-collar professionals in IT and other industries. They are the typical new middle class in the city. The residential development project was approved by the government in 2002, and started its construction in 2003. At the center of the controversy were the demolition of a central garden in the middle of the subdivision and the construction of a 500-meter four-lane public road. According to the original city permit, there was a two-lane city road going through the community. However, the developers built the garden on the planned public roadway without informing the homebuyers about the city plan. In 2004, when the city government began to construct the road, the developers were forced to demolish the garden. Residents of the community, being afraid of the impact of the road on their property value and living environment, waged a three-month long public protest over the road project.

Table 5.4 is the chronology of the incident. This case is a classical example of communication breakdown and reactive participation. The city government officials handled the situation poorly. Their insensitivity, bureaucratic red tape, and the improper use of police force contributed to the escalation of the conflict. Let us look at the problems from all sides. The controversy was initially caused by the illegal building of the garden by the developers on the planned area of a city road. Because of the lack of public disclosure about the planned road, buyers were misled about the construction plan of the subdivision and its residential environment (falsely believing that the subdivision would be a closed community which was what Chinese homebuyers valued the most[12]). So when the road construction began, residents felt cheated by the developers. However, the city government also had its share of blame. Firstly, it did not stop the construction of the garden in the first place, and did give permission at some time to the layout of the first and second phrases of the construction of the subdivision, including the garden. At one time, there was even a lawsuit about the garden, and the court ruled in that case that the garden was a permanent structure, therefore, provided some legitimacy to the residents' claim.

Table 5.4 Chronology of *Dingtai Fenghua* Incident of 2004

April 11-13	The central garden demolished, and the construction company moved in.
April 15	Residents blocked the access road to the construction site, and the construction was stopped.
April 16	City government fined the developers 100,000 *yuan*.
April 16-18	Initial dialogs were conducted among government officials, developers and representatives of the residents.
April 20-28	Residents drafted an open letter to the city government and City People's Congress, and demanded the road project to be suspended.
April 29	Conflicts escalated, city official clashed with residents over protest banners. Residents waged a sit-in in front of the Nanshan District government building.
May 2	Residents published the open letter to the city government to the media.
May 22	Two hundred residents protested before the city government.
May 26-29	More dialog between city officials and residents.
June 9	Police were dispatched to protect the construction site and the road construction began. One thousand residents marched on the street to protest the action.
June 11-12	200 residents met with provincial and city government officials in Guangzhou, and buses carrying additional residents to Gunagzhou were blocked.
June 13	Construction workers clashed with local residents, and police intervened.
June 16	Three residents were detained for fifteen days.
June 19	More residents were detained and were later sentenced to eight months in prison.

Sources: http://house.people.com.cn, July 1, 2004.

for the controversial garden. Secondly, there was no public hearing and notification before the road construction started. That served as a bit of shock to the residents, and led to overreaction by residents because of their lack of information. The road plan was apparently in existence for several years before the construction began. The width of the road changed from 8 meters to 26 meters without any public knowledge and public hearing. Some new buildings already built only were only three meters from the curb of the planned road (therefore violated the city's own building codes). However, city inspection officers issued building permits anyway for these buildings. After the incident became public, the city officials decided to impose a 100,000 *yuan* fine on the developers. However, this did not end the controversy.

The residents were split on what to do with the road construction. If nothing was done, it was perceived that they would suffer financially (lost of property value and vulnerable to crimes) (R_0). Some wanted financial compensation from developers for the lack of public disclosure (R_1). Others wanted the government to hold the construction, and make changes to the blueprint to minimize the impact of the road on the community (R_2). Many would like to persuade the government to abandon the road project altogether and keep the subdivision intact (R_3). Based on the cost-benefit calculation, the preference was clear, $R_3 > R_2 > R_1 > R_0$. The question then become: what was the best means to achieve each of the desired objectives? A functional community would not choose a confrontational or illegal approach, and they should not let emotion and anger to dictate their collective actions. Since there were differences of opinions among the residents, their best strategy should have been to organize a homeowner association, and to speak and act as one voice with measured responses at each of the deliberation steps.

From the government's perspective, officials wanted to build the road quickly and efficiently without any community resistance (G_1). An undesirable scenario with community resistance was that the project would be delayed, and the costs ran over budget (G_2). An even worse scenario would be the cancellation of the whole project under the community pressure, which might be interpreted as letting the government "lose face" and "credibility." It could also jeopardize cooperation of residences from nearby communities on future projects (copycat effect) (G_3). The choice was clear, $G_1 > G_2 > G_3$. The means to achieve the government's most desired objective was to prevent and reduce community resistance. Their choice in this case was to convince the residents that the benefits of the project would surpass the potential costs to them. This could have been done through a lengthy process of education, communication and deliberation. They could even modify their design to minimize the negative impact of the road on the community. The other alternative was to use government coercion to suppress any resistance, and crack down on "lawlessness."

Because of the dysfunction of the deliberation process, both sides ended up with the worst-case scenario. One the one hand, the road was built without any modification, which cut the subdivision into two parts; some leaders of the protests were arrested and sentenced to short jail terms; and community residents felt intimidated and suppressed and were uneasy over the government's heavy-handed approach. The local government, on the other hand, had to postpone its project because of the cost overrun; and the image of the city government was damaged because of the residents' visit to the provincial government, prolonged street protests and sit-ins, and negative publicity by the local news media over the handling of the protests by the city officials. If the leading officials had wished to use this project as a major accomplishment for promotional purpose, this hope certainly vanished. Instead of a win-win outcome, all sides came out bitter and unhappy. Most importantly, social harmony was compromised and social stability was undermined.

It is apparent that the government should have posted public notices before the start of the project, and should have held public hearings on the road construction plan. Once the confrontation began, there were still chances for reconciliation since both sides had the desire to engage in dialog and deliberation. However, because the peaceful petition and violent protests coincided, both sides lost faith with each other. The seizure of protest banners and signs by security personnel and the presence of police forces in the neighborhood antagonized the whole community, and let the emotion of the residents run even higher. The first missed chance for a peaceful solution was the four-day hearing between April 16 and 18. The second one was between May 26 and May 29. From reading the writings of the community organizers of the protests, one found their demands were actually very reasonable initially. The open letter asked the government to reassess the needs for the road construction, and seek majority approval of the residents. The open letter even made a warning to the authority that if the demands were not met, the residents reserved the right for further actions, actions that "authority may not wish to see."[13] This approach clearly backfired since the government side did not want to appear soft and did not like to be threatened.

Another alternative to solve the controversy could be that the government altered its road plan to add a wider overpass on top of the road or an underpass to keep the integrity of the community, and made it easier for the two residential areas to connect with each other. However, the government did not give in. Instead, it considered this a matter of "face" and credibility. The government's effort to put down protest signs and banners by sending anti-riot police destroyed the whole atmosphere of conciliation and cooperation. The community organizers also needed some legitimacy. Without an elected neighborhood homeowners' association, the community was unable to come up with some consistent and reasonable demands, and to prevent disorderly conduct such as breaking up fences setup by the construction company. Deliberative democracy requires informed decision-making and compromise. It should not be based on either ignorance or the sense of pleasure for winning a zero-sum game.

Case 2: *Fengzehu* Subdivision Incident

Fengzehu subdivision is a beautiful lakeside residential development project located in Baoan District of Shenzhen. One year after the first phase was built, the city government decided to build a northern expressway that cut through the planned community. The phase II of the development project would have to be terminated because of the land purchased by the developer was taken aback by the government for the construction project. Like the previous case, the 1,000

families who had move into the new apartment complex recently were shocked
to hear about the road project.

Table 5.5 Chronology of *Fengzehu* Subdivision Incident

Oct. 17, 2003	City Land Management Office approved the developers' Phase II Development plan.
Oct. 18, 2003	City government adopted the plan to build the expressway one day after they just approved the *Fengzehu* development project.
Nov. 9, 2003	*Fengzehu* residents found out the city's plan to build the expressway.
Nov. 10, 2003	Five hundred homeowners went to city office to petition public officials. Unsatisfied by the official response, the residents blocked the Huanggang Road next to the subdivision.
Nov. 11, 2003	Residents organized a preparatory committee of the homeowners' association to coordinate residents' right-protection activities.
Nov. 17, 2003	The committee issued an open apology for the road-block action through the local news media.
Nov. 23, 2003	The subdivision residents organized a community forum on using rational and legal means to protect their rights.
Nov. 28, 2003	Three hundred homeowners went to Guangzhou to petition the provincial government officials to suspend the construction project.
Dec. 10, 2003	The committee canceled its planned 3,000 people march in order to give the government more time to revise its plan.
Dec. 28, 2003	The opening ceremony of the road construction projects was held.
Jan. 17-18, 2004	City officials sought residents comments on the first revised plan, and 90 percent of the respondents rejected the plan.
Mar. 11, 2004	Residents stopped their mortgage payment to banks as a way of protest.
Mar. 16-20, 2004	City Officials sought residents' comments on the second revised plan, And again was rejected by residents.
Mar. 30, 2004	City government officials came to the subdivision to seek residents' opinions on The third revised plan of the road project.
June 29, 2004	City People's Congress held a public hearing on the fourth revised plan.
July 21, 2004	City People's Congress concluded that the fourth revised plan should been accepted based on the hearing.
June 30, 2006	The expressway was completed.

Sources: "Open Letter to People's Daily from Residents of *Fengzehu* Subdivision,"
people.com, July 16, 2004; Xu Wenge, "Protecting Home Rights but not Road-blocking,"
Nanfang Daily, December 23, 2003.

In this case, the residents developed three options in preparation for the ne-
gotiation with the government. One option was to have the road moved to the
north side of the residential areas. This would eliminate all negative impacts the
project had on the community altogether (R_1). The second option was to push
the roadway further south and build a portion of the road underground (R_2). The
third option was to demand compensation for every homeowner in the subdivi-

sion for the depreciation of their property value (R_3). The ranking of the preference was perceived as $R_1>R_2>R_3$. It was apparently more difficult to persuade city officials to achieve the goal of number one and number three. Therefore, residents' best bet was to cooperate with the government and to seek a middle ground.

There are also three options for the government. One option was to build the road as designed since it was the most economic and efficient design (G_1). The second option was to improve the design and increase investment in order to minimize the impact of the road on the local community (G_2). The third option was to move the road to the north side (G_3). For the government planner, the preference is clear that $G_1>G_2>G_3$. Nevertheless, with the strong resistance of the local residents, it was impossible to build the road as planned unless it used some form of coercive methods to pressure residents to give in. The third option would be worse than option one since it would affect more communities. It appeared that option two was also the viable choice for the government planners. The question became: to what extent could the local demands be better accommodated.

The willingness of both sides to make compromise and neither side took drastic actions to antagonize the situation made the deliberation and accommodation possible. Although the community initially took the irrational action of road-blocking, it immediately realized that such an action would upset the public and reduce public sympathy to their demands. It was wise for the community leaders to quickly issue an open apology to the public. They began to organize themselves and to coordinate their collective actions. To educate themselves, the community organized a public forum, and invited lawyers, scholars, and journalists to participate. The government side also demonstrated patient and open-mindedness. They changed the plan four times, and held a first-ever public hearing over this type of controversial road project in China.

Neither sides got their top choices, but both sides came out as winners. The road was completed, though way beyond its original schedule and over its original budget. Because of the revisions, the government added an additional 100 million investment in the project. The section of the road that was close to the *Fengzehu* subdivision was pushed south side 130 meters, and was built underground with green space on the top.

Case 3: The Western Connector Incident

Unlike the two cases we have discussed previously, this controversy involved more than 200,000 residents, multiple residential communities, and lasted for more than two years. Over seventeen public hearings and several hundred democratic consultation meetings were held. The city mobilized literally all resources at its disposal to quiet the massive resistance to the proposed road project. In this incident, there were multiple local interests and demands. The proposed connector did not directly pass through any established community property, therefore, the complaint were mostly about the environmental issues and accuracy of the government's environmental impact study. However, other than demanding government to modify the construction plan to minimize the environmental impact, the locals had little to bargain for since the government had tried its best to accommodate the local residents' demands. The government did reject the demands for monetary compensation for residents living near the outlet of the air duct.

After three years intensive efforts, government officials eventually ran out of patience. They made a decisive move on in April 2005. It issued a legal opinion to answer all legal challenges to the public project. On May 10, it approved the third modification plan, and gave three days for public comments. To reduce popular resistance, the government mobilized all the resources it had.[14] Leaders at every level were asked to persuade their own relatives and friends not to take part in demonstration or group petition activities. Local cadres went from house to house to talk to residents. They tried very hard to communicate with them and answer their questions. The government invited professionals and experts to go to the community and seventeen information meetings were held. The hope was that these face-to-face discussions over the plan's details would help reduce misunderstandings and help residents become better informed about the actual impact of the project. Additionally, city officials also asked property management companies to take down posters and announcements from some unsatisfied residents. They distributed an open letter to parents of school children. The students would bring it home and help persuade their parents to accept the plan. Attorneys hired by the community were also asked to do their share in helping persuade residents not to engage in lawless actions during the deliberation process City officials also put out detailed exhibits of the planned construction projects in the public with an intention to supply residents with real information. According to an official count, over 6,000 local residents visited these exhibits. More than 4,000 educational materials were distributed to visitors of these exhibits. The city also put out programs and information through local newspapers, radio stations, and televisions. Official even set up a telephone hotline to answer residents' questions and inquiries about the projects. The government did try to intimate local activists. City officials organized individual meetings with some of community organizers who had been involved in organizing community resistance to the project. They were warned not to organizing any street demonstrations or marches. For the uncooperative leaders, the government tried to intimidate or isolate them.

With these efforts, the government reportedly convinced two-thirds of residents to change their negative views and made them supportive of the project. However, not all issues were resolved. Residents produced over thirty petition letters and submitted them to various government officials, including a letter sent to Premier Wen Jiabao, and another one sent to the State Environmental Protection Administration (SEPA).

This was indeed a very complicated case. It reflected the reality of community governance at the current time. Government agencies tried their best to educate the public about the project. Extensive deliberative meetings were held to allow citizens to voice their concerns. The city planners also made dramatic

Table 5.6 Chronology of the Western Connector Incident

1997	Western Connector was proposed by the city government.
2000	Initial design was an elevated expressway. Nanshan District government, local people's deputies, and residents called for changes to be made to the plan in order to minimize the impact of the road on local communities.
Aug. 2001	A new design with a semi-underground road was developed.
June 2002	The semi-underground design was approved by the city government.
Jan. 2003	The design was changed again to make it a full underground connector to minimize environmental impact.
Mar. 13, 2003	Feasibility Study of the project was approved by the city government.
Aug. 21, 2003	Environmental Impact Study was approved by an expert group. Residents of *Taohuayuan* subdivision was upset by the proposed waste air outlet next to their community. Worried about the polluting airs, they began a signature drive and fund-raising activities to lobby the city government for a different design.
Sept. 23, 2003	*Taohuayuan* residents submitted an application for a march on the national day holiday.
Sept. 26, 2003	City officials held a dialog with the *Taohuayuan* residents.
Nov. 20, 2003	City agreed to move the outlet of the waste air duct 320 meters west of the *Taohuayuan* community, with a narrowed opening design.
July 2004	*Houhai* Subdivision residents, upset by the decision to move the outlet location to its neighborood, began to petition provincial and national environmental protection agencies.
Aug. 29, 2004	More communities joined *Houhai* to put more demands on the city to revise its designs. More than 50,000 local residents marched to the street in the rain.
April 2005	City government approved the full-underground design plan, and gave additional 1.4 billion *yuan* to fund the project.
April 22, 2005	More dialogs between the city and the residents about the environmental impact studies.
April 28, 2005	City government issued a "Legal Opinion on Certain Issues Relating to the Western Connector Project" to justify the legality of city's decision-making process.
May 10, 2005	City government gave three days for public comments on the project.
June 2, 2005	The project formally began its construction.
July 1, 2007	The project completed and opened for traffics.

Sources: Chen Shanzhe and Jin Sheng, "An Investigation of the Environment Impact Controversy of the Shenzhen Western Connector Project, *21st Century Economic Report*, May 16, 2005.

changes to their original project design to minimize the impact on the community. Nevertheless, the deliberative process could not make everyone happy and solve all disagreements. When this happened, the politics of consensus-building and accommodation became a politics of clashing interests. This was where majority rule had to be invoked. The traditional authoritarian tactics were conveniently applied in the end to close the debate.

What Have We Learned?

Extending the responsibility for public decisions making to citizens at the community level is a growing trend in community governance. The democratic decision-making process turns an otherwise passive citizen into a "stakeholder in a community,"[15] allowing citizens to safeguard their own interests and fostering the manifested explicit consent to and consensus on public decisions. It helps improve the quality of decisions made and enhances the political legitimacy of the local governments.

In each of the three cases we discussed, the citizen demanded participation in the decision-making process, and campaigned for their economic and legal rights. Their participation was not proactive; instead, they were reactive to authoritarian decisions made by the local governments. None of the deliberative processes were perfect, and many problems existed. However, the very fact that these civic participations happened more and more frequently at community level is a positive sign of the emergence of a civil society. It does create challenges to community governance. Although all three incidents took place in Shenzhen between 2003 and 2005, they do represent a growing trend in China's political development, i.e. the incorporation of deliberative democracy at grassroot level.

One of the important lessons we can learn from these events is the need for public forums among the established social institutions to facilitate legitimate interests articulation and peaceful dialogs among multiple players. Rational choice theory tells us that all participants first and foremost concern their self-interests. Everyone wants to maximize individual benefits and minimize individual costs. The conventional cost-benefit analysis and the game theories such as prisons' dilemma also suggest that the government agencies, homeowners, and property management firms involved in the power game have common as well as different interests. Consensus can only be achieved through discovering every player's self-interests, and to seek a middle ground where no one gets maximized benefits while the costs are shared and not concentrated on one set of players. Cooperation with each other and the willingness to accommodate each other's interests and demands may produce the most desired outcome, albeit not the best for the single player. The institutional approach tells us that institutions can create elements of order and predictability. They can constrain political actors, and provide bonds to tie citizens together. Institutions also restrict the possibilities of one-sided pursuits of self-interest, and institutional rules are followed because they provide for legitimacy of decisions made in a community.[16]

There are a number of deliberative forums that have played some positive roles in each of the cases. However, the lack of basic institutional structures and norms did not achieve the full potential of these forums.

Public Hearings

Public hearings are widely practiced in the West. As an instrument for public deliberation, it was first introduced to China in 1996 over administrative penalties cases. Before 2003, public hearings over public projects were unheard of in China's urban planning process. The Shenzhen's experiences were extremely valuable in establishing a project-based public hearing system. Like many other types of public hearings in China, there are three main problems with these hearings. First, the organizers of these hearings are typically the administrative departments which are a party involved in the controversy. The lack of an independent or a third-party organizer has compromised the fairness in the handling of the issues raised in the hearing. Second, there is no third-party assessment of the pros and cons made during the hearing, and the governments does not give a point-to-point response to the arguments made by citizens. Finally, these hearings were one-time events only; no follow-up hearings were held.

Consultation Meetings

Indeed, some of the so-called public hearings looked more like a consultation meeting where government officials made themselves available to listen to public complaints. In each of the cases we discussed, the residents were invited to participate in the initial project planning process. The problem is: can these so-called community members represent local residents? What areas of expertise do they possess in order to assess the impact of the project over the community? Have they communicated with and provided feedback to the communities? They are delegates not trustees after all, therein has no legitimate right to consent or object. The limited number of residents' participation and how they were selected cast doubt on these deliberations. The government officials who were used to the indoctrination of public interests over private interests, quite often had trouble understanding residents' concerns. They treated any citizens' objection to their ambitious plan as a negative thing, and denounced or ignored them easily. Another problem the government officials had was that they did not take these dialogs seriously. Their explanations were often non-convincing. In the Western Connector case, the key controversy was over the pollution data on the proposed waste air emission.

Community Forums

One innovation in Nanshan District's experience with community governance was the use of community forums to facilitate community dialogs. Topics of these forums ranged from community safety to environmental issues. It provided an excellent platform for public discussion. One good example was the *Yueliangwan* Boulevard widening project. The community forum invited the district officials to attend. After reaching consensus over the controversy, the district government decided to invest 1.5 million *yuan* to build a neighborhood road to hold the egress and ingress.

Public Notices and Opinion Surveys

Public notice and community polling are crucial steps in modern community-based projects, and should be done at the beginning of urban planning process. In each of the three cases we studied, the government waited till the last days of groundbreaking to put out public notices and project exhibitions. The purposes of these notices were actually intended to showcase the achievement of the government in urban construction, and educate residents about the benefits of the projects. Public did have opportunity to comments on the project, but these comments are not systematic.

    Another lesson we can learn from these incidents is the importance of social institutions. Shenzhen's model of community governance is based on the Shanghai model with two-levels of governments and four-levels of management. The sub-district offices and community work stations extended the government down to the community level. This may have increased the cost of local governance, but it does have the potential to turn these government dispatches into a channel for public deliberation. In addition, there are several social institutions that may also help the community governance.

Community Work Stations

Community work stations emerged as a new government management unit in 2003 in Beijing Xicheng District. In Nanshan District, there were ninety-six community workstations established in 2004. They replaced the sub-district offices to function as a government management and service center at the community level.   From now on traditional neighborhood committee will become a neighborhood self-governance entity. Each station has five to fifteen staff members.

Homeowners' Associations

There can be no meaningful dialogs if community residents do not have a clear picture of what they want. Because of the diverse interests residents have, it is important to have community members governing themselves in a meaningful way, which includes electing their own homeowners' association, its leaders, and coordinating its positions. In the cases discussed before, case one has no homeowners' association, and the results were chaotic and unfruitful. In case two, the community from the very beginning focused on the institution building, and negotiated with the government patiently through community-elected organizers, and it produced a much better result.

Deputy Work Station

In April 2005, Shenzhen established China's first Deputy Work Station in *Yueliangwan* community. Twelve district people's deputies met periodically with their constituents in their districts to learn about their problems and experiences with local governments. What is interesting is that the some of the leaders of twelve homeowners' associations joined the work station and served as liaison persons between the people's deputies and local residents. They worked together with people's deputies in conducting community forums and opinion surveys. Deputy Work Stations have been proven to be an important social institution that can help build bridge linking the government with the citizens. It makes the day-to-day communication and deliberations a routine. Thanks to the station, over fifty community issues were resolved, and the number of public protests decreased.[17]

As a new innovation, there are many unresolved issues with this organization. The legal status of this type of workstation is still not clear, and there is a lack of public financial support. The Chinese government can look into the experience of the members of the U. S. Congress and strengthen the role of the local people's deputies. In the U.S. each house member typically maintains two to three district offices. Some staff members in these offices are paid by federal funds, and many more are volunteers. They handle casework on behalf of their legislators. The casework staff can help ensure that residents are treated fairly and their cases receive a full and timely review by the appropriate federal agencies. Any individuals can write to their representatives.

Conclusions

Community governance has served as a proving ground for deliberative democracy. One will find both diffused and specific support for the legitimacy of the political regime at the community level. Poor handling of community conflicts and discontent can weaken authority's original and utilitarian appeal for legitimacy, and spark a crisis of governance.

The rising number of disputes over residential communities has become a new source of social disharmony. The lack of channel for social dialog and conflict resolutions led many to "vote by their feet," a term used by the Chinese to describe the mass march incidents. The cases studied in this chapter illustrate different outcomes of government-citizen dialogs. Local governments have consciously begun to engage in more open communication, exchanges, and dialogs with local people. The system is far from perfect. Both sides are learning this new way of democratic decision-making. In 2004, the State Council issued an ambitious plan to streamline the legal system of public administration. It requires all drafts of new administrative rules and regulations, other than those involves in state secrecy, must be published via newspapers and Internet for public comments, and administrative hearings will become a mandatory rather than a discretionary step in finalizing these rules and regulations. The procedures and selections of participants all have to be perfected. The goal is to establish the rule of law in public administration within ten years.[18] This is a promising development. It will make community governance more transparent, and will facilitate deliberative democracy at the community level. The practice of deliberative democracy fosters amongst citizens a sense of empathy for those with different interests, thus enhancing a shared political culture. Conflicts between social groups are resolved openly, rather than secretively by elites.

Notes

1. Ministry of Civil Affairs, "Circular on Strengthening Community Development in Urban Areas," December 22, 2000, http://www.cctv.com/news/china/20001212/366.html (accessed December 19, 2009).

2. MCA, "Circular on Promoting Community Building," December 18, 2000, http://www1.mca.gov.cn/mca/news/news2000121801.html (accessed December 19, 2009).

3. Chen Liping, "China's Grass-root Level Self-government: Past, Present and Future," *China Legal Daily* (in Chinese), November 6, 2007, http://www.legaldaily.com.cn/ (accessed December 19, 2009).

4. Song Yan and Chengri Ding, *Urbanization in China: Critical Issues in an Era of Rapid Growth* (Cambridge, MA: Lincoln Institute of Land Policy, 2007).

5. Ferdinand Tönnies, *Community and Society* (Mineola, NY: Dover Publication, 2002).

6. Robert D. Putnam, *Bowling Alone: The Collapse and Revival of the American Community* (New York: Simon Shutter, 2000), 19.

7. Commission on Reform and Development of Jiangsu Province, "The Experience of the Neighborhood Management System Reform in Huaihai Road," http://www.jsdpc.gov.cn/jsdpc/tzgg/xzgltzgg/200710/t20071017_37274.htm (accessed Decrmber 19, 2009).

8. He Haibin, "China Urban 'Street' Management System Reform and Community Development," *Modern China Studies* 92, no.1 (2006).

9. Talcott Parsons, *The Structure of Social Actions: a Study in Social Theory with Special Reference to a Group of Recent European Writers*, Vol. 2 (Glencoe, IL: Free Press, 1967), 2nd ed.

10. Gabriel Almond and Bingham Powell, Jr., *Comparative Politics: A Developmental Approach* (Boston, Little, Brown. 1966). See also Gabriel Almond ed., *Comparative Politics Today: a World View* (Boston: Little Brown, 1974).

11. Mancur Olson, *Logic of Collective Action: Public Goods and Theory of Groups* (Cambridge, MA: Harvard University Press, 1971).

12. Tang Juan, "Management of Residential Subdivision: Open or Closed?" *Modern Property Management*, in Chinese, September 11, 2008, http://www.xdwy2001.com/ (accessed December 19, 2009).

13. "Open Letter to the City Government and People's Congress," May 2, 2004, http://www.law-bridge.net/bbs/showtopic.aspx?forumid=17andtopicid=4127andgo=prev (accessed December 19, 2009).

14. Data are from Nanshan District government, provided by Dr. Tang Juan.

15. Yang Bo and Huang Weiping, "Deliberative Democracy: The Realistic Choice for Building Harmonious Community", http://www.chinaelections.org/ (accessed on December 19, 2009).

16. James G. March and Johan P. Olson, "Elaborating the 'New Institutionalism,'" in *The Oxford Handbook of Political Institutions*, eds. by R. A. W. Rhodes, Sarah A. Binder, and Bert A. Rockman (New York: Oxford University Press, 2006), 5-7.

17. Tang Juan, "Homeowners' New Invention in Protecting Their Rights in Yu-liangWan Community," *Modern Property Management* (in Chinese), August 12, 2008, http://www.xdwy2001.com/blog/u/%CC%C6%BE%EA/archives/2008/200.html (accessed December 19, 2009).

18. State Council, PRC, "A Comprehensive Implementation Plan for Rule of Law in Public Administration," http://news.xinhuanet.com/zhengfu/2004-04/21/content_1431232.htm (accessed December 2, 2009); see also, Li Li, "Zhongguo Jiang Jian Zhengfu Lifa Xingzheng Zhidu, Baozheng Tingqu Miyin Changtai Hua [China will Establish a Public Hearing System and Take Routine Comments from the Public]" http://www.chinanews.com.cn/gn/news/2009/12-03/1997888.shtml (accessed December 2, 2009).

Chapter 6
The Environmental "New Deal"

In the previous two chapters, we focused our attention on the fairness and openness of the public policy making process. To further test our hypothesis laid out in Chapter 1, we will get into additional public policy areas, including environmental protection policy, labor policy and health care policy. Our goal is to detect if there is any new trend in these areas that substantiates the shift in political orientation in recent years.

As we pointed out earlier, between the 1980s and 1990s, China's economic policy underwent major changes. Improving economic efficiency and promoting economic growth are the key themes in the new policies. To that end, many of the administrative reforms were oriented towards reducing wasteful spending, simplifying administrative procedures and regulations, streamlining civil services, and combating official corruption. The regulatory authorities of the central government went through a process of reduction, decentralization, and elimination.

Not surprisingly, the environmental administration followed the same pattern of development. However, the continued environmental degradation after many years of high-speed economic growth has forced the Chinese government to take a fresh look at its environmental administration. The endorsement of the "scientific development perspective" by the 17th CCP Congress in 2007 is a clear indication that the Chinese government is about to engage a paradigm change, and the environmental governance is ready to embark on a new direction.

The recently concluded Beijing Olympic Games is a good example of this new attitude toward environmental protection. People who travelled to Beijing often witnessed an incredible transformation of Beijing's environment in 2008. Almost overnight, Beijing's sky became blue again. In order to fulfill its promise made to the International Olympic Committee (IOC), China spent nearly 10 billion U.S. dollars on improving Beijing's environmental quality. Many drastic measures were taken in the months prior to the sporting events. Coal-filled power stations in the city were converted to gas-burning stations. More than 1,400 old gas stations and 10 oil depots were closed down for good. Another 200 major polluting factories were ordered to shut down temporarily. Capital Steel and Iron, one of the largest steel makers in China, had to relocate its entire production facilities to a new industrial park 143 miles away from Beijing. To reduce automobile emission, traffic was strictly regulated. The authority also expanded its air quality control measures to cities adjacent to Beijing, and suspended productions of some of the heavy-polluting factories nearby.[1] Thanks to these efforts, Beijing's Sulfur Dioxide emission level decreased nearly 13 percent compare with the same period a year ago.[2] During the month of August when the games were held, almost half of the month's air quality in Beijing was rated as excellent and the remaining days were rated as good.

These massive clean-up efforts are unparallel in the history of Olympic Games. It demonstrates not only the determination of the Chinese government to meet its Olympic obligations, but also the ability of the authority to use its administrative muscles to fight pollution. After years of liberal reform, it is amazing to see that the state still has so much power at its disposal. This administrative capability is almost beyond imagination for a typical politician in a western democracy. One would argue that to close down so many plants and factories without any serious political consequences is nearly impossible in other countries, regardless if the outcome is good or bad.

Now the games are over. The question one will ask is: what will happen next? Will the sky remain blue? Will water continue to be clean? Clearly, the extreme administrative measures put in place during the games cannot be sustained. Beijing's sky may return to its pre-games condition once all economic activities return to normal after the games. In the end, the state simply cannot do it alone. The "command-and-control" strategy must work together with other market and public strategies in order to ensure the regulatory effectiveness.

This chapter examines the dynamics of the politics of the environmental regulation in China. More specifically, it examines how laws and regulations, such as "command and control" regulation, environmental pricing reform, and environmental rating system can be used to reduce the social and environmental costs of economic growth, and how the environmental economy and public involvement can help reduce negative externalities of economic activities. It will first examine the political logic of the regulatory reform in the area of environmental protection. Then a detailed analysis of the regulatory changes taking place in recent years will be presented.

The Political Logics of the New Environmental Politics

China's environmental regulation, which started in the beginning of the reform era in the late 1970s, has gone through different stages. When political leaders in Beijing launched economic reform in 1978, the environmental condition already had some signs of deterioration. In order to strengthen environmental protection, a related provision was added to the 1978 Constitution. In the following year, a provisional Environmental Protection Law was adopted. While relying heavily on the traditional "command and control" approach towards pollution control, the government also introduced the market approach in the 1980s as a way to promote self-control and self-regulation by enterprises and pollution producers. The central government created a system of pollution levy in 1982, but it did not work too well.

As China's economic reform deepened, regulatory powers were gradually decentralized, including the power to regulate the environment. Provincial and local governments were put in charge of enforcing the environmental laws and regulations. Provincial and city governments established environmental protection bureaus (EPBs). They were responsible for collecting pollution levies and other non-compliance fees, monitoring of air and water ambient quality, and doing routine inspections of factories and plants. Table 6.1 lists the number of legislation and regulations made between 1996 and 2006. It shows that before 2002, local governments did most of the work in stipulating environmental regulations. The national government was relatively inactive in this area. Although the system worked in some way, it failed to prevent the deterioration of the environmental qualities that is so typical in a rapidly industrializing nation.

Table 6.1 Environmental Protection Laws and Regulations Enacted (1996-2006)

Year	National Law	National Regulations	Local Laws	Local Regulation
1996	2	1	24	118
1997			26	86
1998			19	98
1999			25	132
2000			27	162
2001		5	25	52
2002		2	32	83
2003		5	25	56
2004		6	22	58
2005		6	30	40
2006		7	38	41

Sources: SEPA/MEP, *China Statistics Yearbook of Environmental Protection*, 1996-2006.

The environmental pollution is typically measured by the levels of chemical oxygen demand (COD) and sulfur dioxide (SO_2). COD is a test that measures the oxygen-depletion effect of a waste contaminant in water, and SO_2 is a chemical compound that is a major factor contributing to acid rain and urban smog. Due to the rapid expansion of economic activities, China quickly became one of the worst polluted countries on earth in just two decades. Air was filled with dirty particles, rivers and lakes became filthy and stinky, and underground water became undrinkable.[3] Industrial pollution contributed greatly to the environmental nightmare. According to an official estimate, industrial pollution accounted for over 70 percent of the national total, including 70 percent for the increase in COD level in water, 72 percent for SO_2 emissions, 75 percent for flue dust (a major component of suspended particulates), and 87 percent for solid wastes. A report by the World Bank depicted the following gloomy picture:

> Unfortunately, serious environmental damage has accompanied this rapid growth. Many of China's waterways are close to biological death from excessive discharge of organic pollutants. In many urban areas, atmospheric concentrations of pollutants such as suspended particulates and sulfur dioxide routinely exceed World Health Organization safety standards by very large margins. As a result, hundreds of thousands of people are dying or becoming seriously ill from pollution-related respiratory disease each year.[4]

After 2002, the Hu-Wen administration intensified its effort in fighting pollution. By 2005, the COD level, though still extremely high, has been stabilized despite the double-digit economic growth in the same period, indicating some success in environmental protection (see Figure 6.1). However, the 2.1 percent reduction still falls short of the targeted 10 percent deduction set by the Tenth Five-Year Plan.

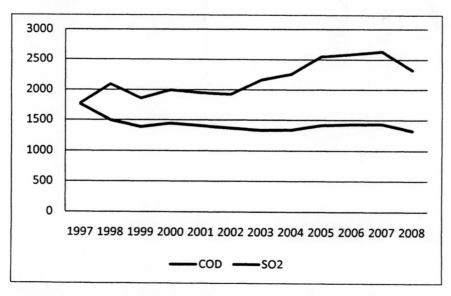

Figure 6.1 COD and SO_2 Pollutant Data   (units: tens of thousands of ton)

Sources, State Environmental Protection Administration (SEPA) *Annual Reports of China' Environment Protection,* 1999-2006, and news from the SEPA.

The targeted goal of SO_2 is 18 million tons, but the actual number increased by 27 percent, to 23 million tons. The main cause was due to the rapid increase in coal-firing power generators and increased consumption of fossil fuel. As a result, areas affected by acid rain increased steadily. A survey of 530 Chinese cities in 2002 showed that 48.9 percent of the cities suffer from acid rain.[5] According to the government's own account, key river basins and regions met only 60 percent of their targets on pollution control and "the emissions of major pollutants far exceed environmental capacity with serious environmental pollution." Furthermore, "the air quality of 46 percent of cities with administrative districts cannot meet Grade II national air quality standards," and "the number of days with haze in some big and medium sized cities has increased and acid rain pollution is not alleviated."[6] To the dismay of the Chinese government, sixteen of Chinese cities were on World Bank's most polluted city list in 2007, and Linfen City in Shanxi Province was ranked as the number one most polluted city in the world.

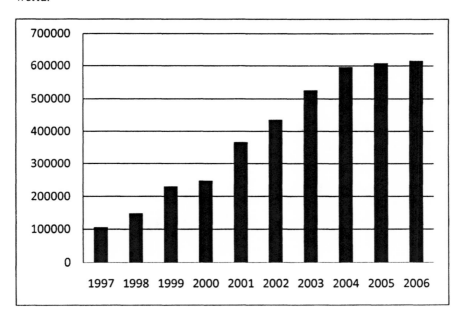

Figure 6.2 Numbers of Environment-Related Complaint Letters Received

Sources: SEPA, *China Statistics Yearbook of Environmental Protection*, 1996-2006.

Pressures for regulatory changes came from both domestic and international communities. Domestically, as China is increasingly becoming a middle-class society, the quality-of-life issue has become a dominant concern. When people's livelihood and health conditions are compromised by a polluter, they are most likely to take collective actions against the polluters. This in turn will have some serious implications for political governance in China. First, the environmental issues can intensify social conflicts and put serious strains on the state-society relationship. In fact, the number of environment-related disputes is on the rise in recent years. The number of complaints in the forms of telephone calls and petition letter-writing increased sharply between 1997-2006 (see Figure 6.1), reflecting in some way the seriousness of public's discontent and the intensity of the conflicts between polluters and local residents. Local protectionism and bureaucratic insensitivity often hampered the handling of these petitions. We do not know how many disputes raised by these petition letters were resolved. It is not unusual for officials to ignore these letters, or simply send them back to the same local officials who have been unable to solve the complaints in the first place.

Another form of protests is group or individual visits of local and national environmental agencies. As shown in Figure 6.2, there was a significant increase in the number of these visits to environmental agencies between 1997 and 2001. The results of these visits are often not promising. There is no formal administrative hearings procedure, and many complaints cannot be solved easily simply because of the lack of recourses and suitable technologies on the part of the environmental agencies. For their own political interests, many local cadres have tried to stop and block people from going to Beijing to register their grievances with the central government. According to a survey report, nearly half of the rural farmers who tried to register their grievances by visiting related offices in Beijing suffered from property confiscation, detention, or revenge by local officials.[7] The "poisonous water" case in Zhejiang province and Baoji amino acids plant case illustrate how local regulatory officials can sit on the wrong side of environmental protection.[8]

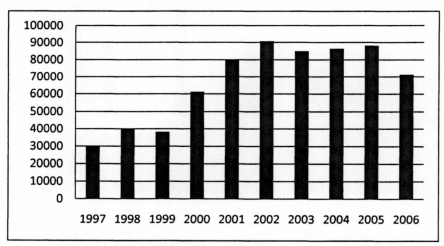

Figure 6.3 Numbers of Group Visits to the State Environmental Agencies

Sources: SEPA, *China Statistics Yearbook of Environmental Protection*, 1996-2006.

Secondly, poor handling of environmental issues can lead to a crisis of legitimacy, and consequently, undermine the regime's stability. Some high-ranking officials have realized that China's environmental pollution is close to a "breakdown," and the developing model China has been pursuing is no longer sustainable.[9] According Pan Yue, a well-know environmentalist in China and the deputy director of the State Environmental Protection Administration (SEPA), "the environmental problem has become one of the main factors that affect national safety and social stability"[10] People already felt frustrated by the inability of the government to improve the environment. According to a recent opinion poll, 75.4 percent of respondents believed that governments did not pay adequate attention to environmental protection. The respondents considered flaws in environmental laws the second cause of environmental problems. Among the same group of respondents, 72.4 percent of them believed that environmental problems were caused by poor enforcement, 70.2 percent thought the penalties were not serious enough.[11] The kind of weak public confidence over the state's governance of environmental protection erodes government's utilitarian legitimacy, and can lead to more social unrests. For instance, in Dongyang, Changxin, and Ningbo, three cities in Zhejiang province, major environment-related protests took place in 2005.[12] In Ningnbo, people surrounded a stainless steel mill for ten days to protest the pollution from the factory. These incidents were small samples of 51,000 reported mass incidents over environmental pollutions that took place in 2005. Additionally, major emergency environmental incidents happened every other day in 2006, and these incidents induced "serious social crises."[13] Stories like the discovery of nearly forty cancer villages in some areas caused much damage to the image of the government and cast shadow on its "specific support" that is vital to its political legitimacy.[14]

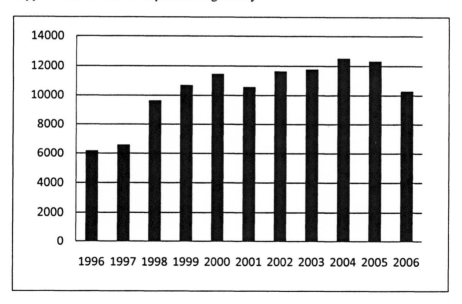

Figure 6.4 Numbers of Recommendations Proposed by CPPCC

Sources: SEPA/MEP, *China Statistics Yearbook of Environmental Protection*, 1996-2006.

Environmental activism has also reached the national level. Many deputies of the CPPCC have been busy in sponsoring legislative recommendations to deal with the mounting pressure on environmental pollution (see Table 6.2). In 2005, the SEPA received 370 pieces of administrative and regulative recommendations from deputies of the NPC, a 61 percent increase from a year ago.[15] As a response, the public investment of environmental protection has increased by double-digits. The overall investment of the whole society in environmental protection doubled that of the Ninth Five-Year Plan period, exceeding one percent of GDP for the first time (see Table 6.3). However, increased spending does not necessarily equal substantive improvement in environmental protection. It is a known fact that Chinese governments at various levels often make wasteful spending decisions on environmental-related projects. During some of the research trips to the remote areas, the author has seen first-handedly some of the useless environmental projects in poor areas that have no environmental impact whatsoever.

Table 6.2 Annual Environmental Investments

Year	Amount (in 100 Million)	Change (%)	GDP (%)
2006	2,567.8	7.5	1.23
2005	2,388.0	25.1	1.31
2004	1,908.6	17.3	1.40
2003	1,627.3	19.4	1.39
2002	1,363.4	23.2	1.33
2001	1,106.6	4.3	1.15

Sources: SEPA/MEP, *China Statistic Year Book of Environment Protection*, 2001-2006.

International pressures on China are also building up quickly. As the largest developing county and the world's fastest growing economy, China has contributed greatly to global warming due to its increased energy consumption and greenhouse gas emissions. Since 1972, environmental protection has emerged as a major issue in world politics. The United Nations Conference on the Human Environment held in Stockholm, Sweden, in June 1972 marked the emergence of international environmental law. The Declaration on the Human Environment also known as the Stockholm Declaration set out the principles for various international environmental issues, including human rights, natural resource management, pollution prevention and the relationship between the environment and development. The conference also led to the creation of the United Nations Environment Program.

Another key event was the Kyoto Conference on Climate Change in 1997. The conference produced the Kyoto Protocol, which required industrialized countries to reduce their emission of greenhouse gases. The conference also produced the United Nation Framework on Climate Change (UNFCC), which China ratified in 2002. In June 2007, China unveiled a climate change plan and promised to put climate change at the heart of its energy policies. During the 2008 G-8 Summit in Japan, the eight industrialized nations agreed to adopt a goal of reducing emissions by 50 percent by 2050. However, China, together with other major developing countries, insisted that developed nations must be treated with lenience. They wanted the developed nations to cut emissions by 25 to 40 percent by 2020, in exchange for developing nations agreeing to cut 80 percent to 95 percent of their emissions by 2050.[16]

The north-south debate continued during the UN Copenhagen Conference on climate control in December 2009. Although China pledged to cut carbon intensity—carbon dioxide emissions per unit of gross domestic product—by 40 to 45 percent by 2020 compared with 2005 levels, the Western countries demanded more from China since China carbon emission continued to increase since 2006. China insisted on the principle of "common but differentiated responsibilities and respective capabilities" and refused to cut the emission at the expenses of its continued economic growth. In a last minute deal, China joined the U.S. to secure the passage of the non-binding Copenhagen Accord that promised to "to reduce global emissions so as to hold the increase in global temperature below 2 degrees Celsius, and take action to meet this objective consistent with science and on the basis of equity."[17]

No one believes that these magic numbers will ever be met. But the domestic and global consensus for drastic reduction of emissions has put a tremendous amount of pressure on China. The Chinese government is in principle in line with these expectations, and it wants China to be a good citizen in the global village. However, in order to keep up with these expectations, China must make some hard choices and look for a new developmental model that is environmental friendly and can provide a balance between the need for economic growth and the need for environmental protection.

The Environmental "New Deal"

Before 2005, China adopted two regulatory strategies: the command-and-control strategy, and the market strategy. The command-and-control strategy involves in the identification of sources of environmental pollution, setting off conditions and emission standards, and inspection for non-compliance. The market-based strategy emphasizes the use of market incentives such as emission quotas and pollution levies to force enterprises to comply with environmental standards.[18] The implementation of these strategies has certainly slowed down China's environmental deterioration. Without these efforts, China's environment could have been even worse than what it is today. However, severe environmental challenges we mentioned in the previous discussion forced China to take more drastic actions. Since 2005, the SEPA has launched four "environmental storms." The newly created Ministry of Environmental Protection (MEP) vows to adopt several new initiatives to strengthen the institutional capabilities in combating pollution and other environment problems. Many observers characterize this new wave of environmental protection efforts as China's "environmental new deal."[19]

Strengthening the Command-and-Control Strategy

The command-and-control strategy focuses on identifying, prioritizing, and achieving strategic and tactical objectives of environmental protection by exercising authority and direction over human and material resources. It relies on detailed regulations followed by routine inspection programs to ensure compliance.

After three decades of legislative work, China has created a basic legal framework of environmental protection. China has enacted and promulgated many laws directly or indirectly dealing with environmental protection. They include the Law on the Prevention and Control of Water Pollution, Law on the Prevention and Control of Air Pollution, Law on the Prevention and Control of Environmental Pollution by Solid Wastes, Marine Environment Protection Law, and Law on Water and Soil Conservation. Between 1986 and 1996, the Chinese government enacted more than thirty administrative decrees regarding environmental protection. Local governments also enacted and promulgated more than 600 local laws on environmental protection.[20] Between 1996 and 2005, the State Council has formulated or revised over fifty administrative regulations and 660 central and local rules and regulations to implement the national laws and administrative regulations on environmental protection.[21]

However, there are still some important pieces of environmental legislation that have yet passed, including laws on handling chemical material, transportation of hazard and radioactive material, farm-raised animal products, and soil erosion prevention. Administrative regulation on emission licensure, environmental monitoring, and drinking water protection are still in the making. Legal liabilities of polluters are not defined clearly by laws. Administrative charges and fines over pollution are too small to deter enterprises from paying serious attention. Additionally, environmental agencies have insufficient power to enforce environmental regulations.[22]

Chinese administrative agencies often used heavy-handed approaches if they saw that problems were out of control regardless of cost to businesses. During the Ninth Five-Year Plan period (1996-2000), the State closed down 84,000 small enterprises known for causing serious pollution. In the period 2001-2004, the State, on three occasions, issued directories listing the outdated production facilities, technologies and products that should be eliminated. More than 30,000 enterprises that had wasted resources and caused serious pollution were weeded out. In 2005, over 2,600 enterprises in the iron and steel, cement, iron alloy, coking, papermaking and textile printing and dyeing industries were shut down for good.[23]

Setting emission reduction is another administrative measure to ensure environmental compliance. In the Tenth Five-Year Plan (2000-2005), the government called for a reduction of the COD and SO_2 by 10 percent. However, none of the goals was met. The 11th National Environmental Protection Five-Year Plan (2006-2010) calls for the strengthening of environmental protection. It sets a national goal of 10 percent reduction in both COD and SO_2 levels. More specifically, the goals require the reduction of COD from 24.14 million tons in 2005 to 12.7 million tons in five years. This requires all cities in China to have sewage treatment facilities treating at least 70 percent of urban sewage water. It also requires an acceleration of the phase-out of heavy polluting enterprises. The plan also targets a reduction in of SO_2 emissions from 25.49 million tons in 2005 to 22.95 million tons by 2010. To achieve this goal, China needs to increase the capacity of existing in-service thermal generation sets with desulphurization facilities to 213 million KW.

One of the major challenges to enforcement is the lack of discretional power and funding for local officials to make environmental protection a priority.[24] As a result, a large number of business owners tend to ignore or violate emission standards. There are a number of other reasons for the poor performance of environmental protection. First, the administrative structure of the agency prevents local EPBs from being tough on polluters simply because the top leaders want to keep business and investment projects in their cities. [25] Second, the lack of power to enforce environment regulation is another major problem. Local EPB officials cannot exercise veto power over the city or county government decisions since the officials are subordinate or the same level of government. EPB officials are afraid of offending their superiors for fear of having budgets cut and losing opportunities for promotion. Finally, the laws are inadequate. Many local officials ignore pollution in order to protect local economies. Quite often, they have a direct financial link or personal relationships with factory owners.

In December 2004, Pan Yue, a deputy director of SEPA, was put in charge of the environmental impact assessment. According to a new regulation he helped draft one year earlier, all new projects must submit reports on the project's environmental impact, and the project could only begin when the report was approved. Facing 2,000 reports for new power plants, he pushed the State Council to re-evaluate all on-going power plant projects. On January 18, 2005, the SEPA launched the first "environment storm" by announcing that 30 major projects, mostly new power plants, were ordered to suspend their operations until submitting the required environmental impact reports. Among the unapproved projects were the 12,600 MW Luoqi Du Hydro-electric Power Station and the underground Hydro-electric Power Station of the Three Gorge Dam.[26] Economic costs for suspending these large projects were tremendous, especially when the country's electric power demand had increased sharply due to rapid economic development. On January 27, the SEPA launched another strike. This time forty-six existing power plants were ordered to install SO_2 reduction devices within a certain period. If the plants refused, the province where the plants were located would be barred from building any new power plant projects. The magnitude of this round of administrative enforcement was unmatched, and surprised many people since the SEPA acted as a rubber stamp to local demands and had no desire to show its teeth towards violators of its own regulations in the past.

Three subsequent "storms" followed. On February 7, 2006, the SEPA announced that it would inspect 127 chemical projects. On January 7, 2007, SEPA used the regional ban on new investment projects against four cities and four enterprises for their violations of some of the regulatory requirements. On July 3, 2007, the SEPA put a ban on new projects for six cities, two counties and five industrial parks to punish their pollution to the Yangtze, Yellow, Hui and Haihe rivers.[27] This new policy gave the state environmental agency and local EPBs a veto power on new construction projects. For example, if a coal-firing power company failed to meet its SO_2 reduction quota, no new generator could be built, and if a region failed to fulfill its emission reduction obligation, there would be no new projects other than environment clean-up projects to be approved.

To build enforcement incentive, the national government began to work on a new system of administrative evaluation and promotion system starting in 2005. This new system would incorporate environmental protection as one of the major performance benchmarks. Guangdong province took a lead in this effort. Guangdong used to be one of the most heavily polluted industrial regions in China due to rapid economic development. In 1991, the provincial government implemented a new assessment criterion for governmental officials that would hold local officials accountable for environmental protections. In 2003, two provincial laws governing the new cadre assessment system were promulgated. Independent survey results of public satisfaction over environmental protection became one of the key measurements. Other measures included the industrial energy consumption rate, green space in urban areas, the percentage of wastewater treatment, and urban air quality.[28] Because of Guangdong government's effort, the province's environmental quality has been stabilized. Based on this successful experiment, the central government has issued a number of directives to ask governments at provincial and local levels to make up their own assessment standards that contains environmental protection components.

The Market Strategy

Administrative measures, though effective, may be very inefficient or very costly sometimes. Naturally, they are the least favored instruments by players in the dynamic games of environmental politics. As China undergoes a market transformation, the market approach has become a preferred choice. Unlike the command-and-control strategy, the market strategy is performance-based and incentive-oriented. Though government still sets quotas and goals, it leaves the decision on how to meet these government mandated reduction quotas and goals to enterprises and consumers.

The foundation of the market strategy is based on the theory of environmental economics. Central to the theory is the concept of market failure. One of the fundamental preconditions of the market is that all costs should be reflected in prices. If the cost of emissions/environmental degradation is not reflected in

prices, it will result in increased pollution, inefficiency, and consequently produce a market failure. Since many polluters simply dump untreated waters and
unfiltered airs from their plants, they are actually waging an unfair competition
by shifting the cost of pollution control to the society as a whole. The way to
correct the problem is to force the producers to internalize the true cost of their
production process. The common instruments of a market approach include
emission quota, environment tax, pollution levy, emission trading, green credit,
green capital markets, ecological compensation, and environmental liability insurance (see Figure 6.4). Unlike classic economics, this approach calls for an
active role of the state in the creation of a system of environmental economy,
but not on the business decision itself; it favors a new political economy which
focuses more on the harmony between men and nature.

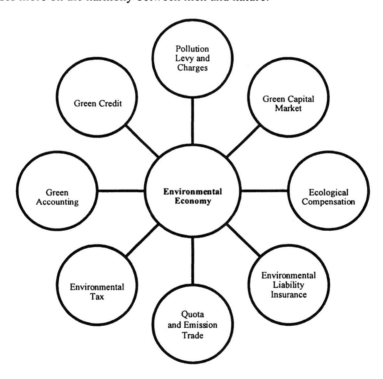

Figure 6.5 The Environmental Economy and the Market Strategy

Prior to 2005, China had already adopted many market-oriented measures,
such as using pollution levies, fees, charges, taxes, and trading of emission quotas to reduce pollution. In 1982, the pollution levy was first introduced and collected. According to the regulation, if the "discharge institutions which has paid
the pollutant discharge fee but have not met the discharge standards for three
years, the charge rate for the pollutant discharge will be raised 5 percent each
year thereafter." On the other hand, if "the discharge institutions which have met

the discharge standards are markedly decreased the quantity and concentration of the discharged pollutants through control and strengthened management may apply to the local environmental protection department for terminating or reducing the discharge fee."[29] However, many factors such as local politics, technical feasibility, or different market priority compromised the strategy's impact. The polluters quite often negotiate with local regulators over the amount of emission fees or charges.[30]

Since then, China has established the most extensive pollution levy system in the world. From the levy's inception in the early 1980s to 1996, Chinese regulators have collected about 30 billion RMB *yuan* ($4 billion) from more than 500,000 of China's major polluters.[31] The impact of government actions taken was mixed. According to a World Bank study of plant-level data from the city of Zhenjiang, government sponsored inspections have a statistically significant impact on firm's environmental performance, but pollution charges do not have a statistically significant effect on firms' performance.[32] A different study done by Huang and Wheeler, however, indicated that plants responded strongly to the levy by either abating air pollution in the production process or providing end-of-pipe treatment for water pollution.[33] Another study done a few years earlier by the two authors suggested that the emissions intensity of Chinese industry was highly responsive to the increases in pollution levy, and from 1987 to 1993 provincial pollution intensities fell at a median rate of 50 percent, and total discharges at a median rate of 22 percent.[34]

However, environmental charges and penalties imposed on enterprises are not severe enough to cause the change of behavior by the polluters. As a part of the central government's new initiative, a new environmental tax is currently under serious consideration. The debates on various forms of environmental taxes are tense since the interests of different players involved. Some people want to abolish the existing levy system entirely and replace it with a general environmental tax, a pollution tax, and a polluting product tax. Another plan is to keep the levy and charge system, but add additional environmental taxes.[35] The third plan opposes a separate environmental tax, and wants to improve or increase existing taxes such as a consumption tax to reach the same objectives. The decision is so controversial that as of today, there are no final words on it. It is expected that the business community will not want the government to use such a tax since this will increase their cost and reduce their profit. Because the potential benefits are widely dispersed, there is no active lobby from the public on this new tax either. This makes a classical case for entrepreneurial politics where policy entrepreneurs such as Pan Yue are crucial to this type of reform.

The development of an environmental economy is another new approach. Since 2008, the government has shifted its focus from punishing polluters to institutional building. As part of the environmental new deal, the SEPA introduced a number of systems to help enterprises and consumers in case of environmental disputes. First, the SEPA recently issued a circular about liability insurance on environmental pollution. The hope is that the insurance system can help enterprises to deal with monetary compensations in case of an environmental disaster without causing too much financial burden on an enterprise. It also helps the interest of the victims and prevents the government from having to pay for the pollution. However, some large corporations have reservations on the insurance requirement, and they believe that it is unnecessary for them to purchase such insurance since they can handle the financial liability by themselves.[36] Nevertheless, several provinces have experimented with a pilot insurance program in several provinces. It is hoped that by 2015, the system will be perfected and promoted nationwide.[37]

Second, the SEPA has initiated a new pilot project on emission trade. The concept of emission trade was introduced to China by Dr. Daniel Dudek, the chief economist of the American-based environmental group called Environmental Defense. In September 1999, Environmental Defense signed an agreement with the SEPA to complete a pilot project on total emissions control (TEC) and emissions trading under the framework of Sino-US cooperation. Benxi and Nantong were selected as the first demonstration cities. In September 2001, the first sulfur dioxide emissions trade was successfully completed in Nantong, Jiangsu Province. In March 2002, the SEPA and Environmental Defense cooperated in launching the "4+3+1" project, an endeavor to initiate an integrated TEC and emissions trading policy in the provinces of Shandong, Shanxi, Jiangsu and Henan, and the cities of Shanghai, Tianjin and Liuzhou, along with the China Hua Neng Group. Each of the jurisdictions completed quota allocations, trading regulations and policy demonstrations.[38] In December 2007, Jiaxing city of Zhejiang province established China's first emission trading center. Beijing and Tianjing are in the process of establishing the nation's first carbon trading centers. Shanghai and Beijing have also established Environmental Energy Exchanges.

All in all, the environmental "new deal" started in 2005 has moved beyond simple command and control phases, and is now concentrated on the institutional innovations and institution-building of an environmental economy. More specifically, seven systems have been gradually introduced, which include green taxation, environmental levies, green capital market, ecological compensation, carbon and emission trade, green international trade, and green insurance.[39]

From State Governance to Cooperative Governance

In the past three decades, the Chinese government has undertaken several major administrative reforms. As China gradually phased out the centrally planned economy and replaced it with a market economy. The reforms undertaken intended to achieve two objectives: decentralization of decision-making power to reduce bureaucratic control at the top, and improve administrative efficiency by incorporating a professional civil service system. However, as we discussed earlier, a number of factors have compromised the reforms, including lack of political support, relatively weak administrative capacity, internal bureaucratic opposition, and mixed support from the general public.[40]

In a joint report issued by the World Bank and Chinese Council for International Cooperation on Environment and Development (CCIED), environmental governance is listed as the number one challenge. The report points out that SEPA does not have enough personnel support and resources needed for the demanding task it is undertaken, and it is poorly equipped to coordinate efforts of multi-government ministries and departments because of the frequent interferences from local government leaders. The report makes a number of recommendations, including upgrading the SEPA to a cabinet level ministry, establishing a close vertical leadership between the SEPA and provincial EPBs, and increasing its budget and staff.[41] The Asian Development Bank also urged China to strengthen its regulatory system to better coordinate the work of many different governmental entities and to enhance its ability to monitor and enforce environmental standards. China was also urged to elevate the SEPA to full ministerial status. It further suggests that China should increase environmental protection investment to 2 percent of its GDP and use these investment funds more creatively.[42]

One of the major weaknesses of the SEPA is the decentralization of law enforcement to local EPBs. These EPBs have significant leeway and independence in interpreting and enforcing the SEPA's mandates.[43] Local protectionism and corruption prevent the EPBs from enforcing environmental laws vigorously. Local governments are able to exercise influence over the EPBs through its budgetary and personnel control. One way to overcome this potential is by making the ministry an independent regulatory agency just like its counterpart in the United States. Another way is to rely on vertical leadership between the SEPA and provincial EPBs. One recent initiative to streamline administration coordination and oversight is the creation of five regional inspection centers. These centers are managed directly by the SEPA. However, only 180 staff members are assigned to these centers.

The new round of administrative reform started in 2007 emphasizes the changing role of government from command and control to a service-oriented government. It continues to make adjustment of governmental powers by cutting the number of administrative approvals and delegating regulatory powers to social organizations. However, environmental protection was one of the few policy areas that were not trimmed. Instead, the NPC approved the proposal to create five new "super ministries." Ministry of Environmental Protection (MEP) is one of them. The MEP's departments and staff have been given some new responsibilities.

The MEP has already taken measures to strengthen its administrative approval process. It vetoed applications of ten companies for public listing in 2007 due to their deficiency in environmental protection. The total applications were valued at 8.4 billion *yuan* ($1.2 billion). Additionally, a total of 1.5 trillion *yuan* ($214 billion) worth of projects were canceled or suspended in 2007 because they were involved in projects of high energy-consumption and high pollution.[44] On August 8, 2008 the NPC Legal Affairs Committee issued its interpretation of the Environmental Protection Law with regards to the punishment for people who are responsible for release of contaminated materials into water streams.

Based on the interpretation, the MEP issued orders to authorize the public security personal to detain enterprise leaders or anyone who has committed such an act. [45]

Even with the creation of a new powerful MEP, the government still cannot do it alone. What China needs is a cooperative governance among the state, the business community, and the public. All three players are stakeholders in the sustainable development of China. One dilemma of the state governance over environmental regulation is that it is either captured by the interests it supposes to regulate, or it can become extremely adversarial and impose excessive burdens on businesses to hurt their competitiveness. Neither result is desirable in light of China's on-going modernization process. Governance based on cooperation and instrumentalism can minimize the impact of both.

One effective way to build cooperative governance is through transparency of the decision-making process. Administrative hearings can be an important instrument to achieve this goal. In 2004, the SPEA issued a circular on administrative hearings over environmental protection issues. The scope of the hearing ranges between small, medium and large projects that have an impact on the environment. The system has had positive results. In 2005, the Beijing government decided to invest 30 million *yuan* ($ 4 million) to install plastics at the bottom of the lakes at Yuanmin Yuan, a remain of a Qing Dynasty imperial garden, in order to prevent water loses and save money. The SEPA responded to the public criticism of the project by calling the first public environmental hearing on April 13, 2006. Seventy-three representatives, many of them well-known professors and experts, were allowed to attend the hearing. Several representatives from Non-governmental Organizations (NGOs) also appeared at the hearing.[46] People.com and xinhuanet.com broadcast the hearing live. Meanwhile, the SEPA also conducted an on-line survey about the project. Over 4,800 people voted on-line. The SEPA eventually decided to order the project to uninstall the finished plastic anti-filtration plastic films. On September 8, 2006 Changsha held the nation's first ever environmental hearing over a new restaurant construction project. Residents close to the restaurant voiced their concerns and recommendations. As a result of the hearing, the owners had to increase their investment to build necessary facilities to ensure a clear environment.[47]

A new approach in the evolution of pollution control policy involving the investment in the provision of information, commonly referred to as the "third wave" of environmental regulation," also draws attention from the state regulatory agency. Beginning in 1998, the World Bank and the SEPA established GreenWatch, a public disclosure program for polluters. It uses the Environmental Performance Rating and Disclosure System to rate firms' environmental performance from best to worst in five colors: green, blue, yellow, red and black. The ratings are disseminated to the public through the media. The pilot program was initially tried in Zhenjiang, Jiangsu Province, and Hohhot, Inner Mongolia, with funds from the Bank's Information for Development Program. After Green Watch pilot projects proved successful in twenty-two Chinese municipalities in seven provinces, the Chinese national government decided in November 2006 to extend GreenWatch to every city in the country by 2010. In an assessment study done by the World Bank, it found that the "informal regulation" was very effective in changing polluter's behaviors, and the program had substantial impact on environmental protection efforts.[48]

Environmental NGO and activists have played some roles in this area as well. In May of 2007, students and professors at Xiamen University sent out one million text messages urging citizens to protest the planned construction of a $1.4 billion petrochemical plant nearby. On June 1, 2007, between 7,000 and 20,000 people marched through the city, despite threats of expulsion from the school or from the CCP.[49] On December 28, 2007 China's environmental regulator promised that public hearings will become part of the approval process for major projects. The decision was reached after residents' protests forced the suspension of the controversial Xiamen city P-Xylene plant project. The right to know is recognized by the state regulators as a fundamental right of Chinese citizens. The SEPA has taken a number of initiatives in this regard. A new regulation on the release of environmental information takes effect in May 2008. The rules mandate a reply from the government within fifteen days after a public inquiry is submitted.[50] A regulation on citizen participation in environmental protection is being drafted. In February 2006, the SEPA issued a set of guidelines on public participation in their environmental impact assessment, which require that the public must be given ten days to make comments on the environmental impact report of a project before it is submitted to the government for approval.

Currently, there are about 2,768 registered environmental groups in China, employing over 220,000 employees. Many more are probably unregistered volunteer groups, student organizations, web-based groups, or registered as business entities.[51] In 2005, these environmental NGOs raised nearly 3 billion *yuan* (US$425 million).[52] Officially established in 1994, the *Friends of Nature* is the oldest environmental NGO in China. Their activities include public awareness education, biodiversity protection, energy conservation, dam protests, and filing lawsuits against polluting factories. Most of their activities are non-confrontational and are welcome by the authority with some exception. However, a corporatist style of control over NGOs is evident, for example, there is a requirement that a NGO must be sponsored and supervised by a government agency or state sanctioned institutions. Overall, "the Chinese government has generally adopted a positive attitude toward environmental NGOs, recognizing that they fill a critical gap in the state's capacity to protect the environment effectively." [53]

A good example of cooperative governance between government, NGOs entrepreneurs and citizens is Alxa's treatment of the sandstorm project. Alxa is located to the west of Inner Mongolia, which is the main source of China's sandstorms in northern China. The ecological deterioration in the area has threaten the livelihood of 196,300 local herdsmen and created many ecological refugees. On June 5, 2004, 100 entrepreneurs pledged to donate 100 million *yuan* (US$14 million) to the Environmental Protection Public Welfare Fund to Control Sandstorms. The Alxa SEE Ecological Association was established based on this initiative. The SEE Ecological Association has engaged in several pilot projects, including "Alternative Energy and Natural Haloxylon Woods Zone Protection," project and "Improving the Sustainability of ALEXA Ecological Migrants" project. Its investment models are centered on multilateral cooperation among the association, government agencies, local herdsmen, entrepreneurs, and international organizations.[54] The government of Alxa Meng (Meng is an administrative unit, usually seen in Inner Mongolia) launched a "migration and transfer, centralized development" project to relocate herdsmen in Helan Mountain and Tengger to the Barunbielli town of Alxa, and built 100 greenhouses for them. The SEE Ecological Association was invited to be a partner of this project and provided technology training to herdsmen and support for the migration transfer. An important difference between SEE invested projects and government-run projects is that the association does not impose its own initiatives on local people; instead, it emphasizes its role as a facilitator and will only sponsor and finance a project if local people choose to participate and co-invest in it. This community governance model is fully documented by a study by Xiao Jin over the established cooperative dairy farm in Helan Mountain area, and this model has proven to be a very effective way in relieving poverty.[55] Alax Meng were so interested in SEE's pilot project, it has joined the effort by injecting additional funds to help SEE-coordinated projects.

International Non-governmental Organizations (INGOs) have also cooperating closely with the Chinese government in recent years in the area of environmental protection. Since the mid-1990s, the number of international NGOs and philanthropic foundations conducting or funding environmental conservation campaigns has grown at an extraordinarily rapid pace. While the number of INGOs with offices in China has grown gradually, the size and resources of these offices has grown dramatically since 2000.[56] World Wildlife Fund (WWF), for example, has worked very constructively with government officials at various levels to protect pandas and other endangered spices, to preserve ecologic sustainable development, and to promote environmental education. It currently has over forty projects in many provinces. In 2007, WWF held its world annual conference in China for the first time. It also launched campaigns like "20 Ways to 20 percent" and "Go for Gold" to help China achieve its goal of reducing energy consumption by 20 percent by 2020, and it staged a green Olympics in 2008.[57] Another well-known INGO is the Nature Conservancy (NC). In recent years, it has been invited to help guide a nationwide assessment of China's conservation priorities and help manage over fifty of China's 2,400 Natural Reserves because of its successful partnership with the Chinese Government. To reduce the demand for wood and address the serious threats to health and biodiversity, the Conservancy and local governmental agencies are providing joint subsidies and technical assistance to local communities to install energy alternatives in rural homes and schools. In addition, it is also working with local communities, government agencies, and tourism enterprises to develop strategies for "green" tourism that will limit the footprint of mass tourism while generating income for local people.

Another attempt to increase public pressure on environmental protection made by the state is the compilation of various environmental indexes. In January, 2007, under the instruction of the SEPA, the China Environmental Culture Promotion Association (CECPA) compiled and released its first Environmental Protection Index. The Index showed that people worried about pollution and the misuse of chemical fertilizers.[58] On January 9, 2008, the CECPA released the Chinese Public's Environment and Inhabitant Livelihood Index 2007, which shows that Chinese people are dissatisfied with air pollution. The report shows that the general score for environmental awareness is 42.1 points, for environmental behavior is 36.6 points and for environmental satisfaction is 44.7 points. According to the Index, none of these ratings is considered good. Nearly 25.8 percent of responded say they are angry about the air quality.[59] China's first corporate responsibility index on the environment, the Taida Environmental Index, was also released on January 3, 2008. Forty listed companies from ten environment-related industries compiled the Index. As the first social responsibility index for China's capital market, the Index is mainly aimed at evaluating listed companies' social responsibilities. Companies with strong social responsibility focuses will be heralded by government and consumers and are likely to gain more opportunities for sustainable development.[60] This new system is part of the new market strategy that focuses on building a system of green capital market. It prevents enterprises with environmental problems from raising capital indirectly through loans from banks, or issue stocks from the stock market. To that purpose, the MEP has released over 30,000 pieces of information about companies' environmental violations in 2008 to commercial banks so that these banks will use them when they make load decisions. In the meantime, the MEP accepted thirty-eight applications for environmental clearance being listed on the stock markets in order to raise more capital. The MEP rejected more than half of the applications for their investment in the pollution-prone projects.[61]

Cooperative governance is impossible without good corporate citizenship and keen partnership between the government, business and community. Environmental protection should not be the goal of only the state and the public; it should be a goal for business as well. Research shows that a positive report on corporate citizenship makes consumers more prone to purchase their products.[62] According to the a report on corporate social responsibility conducted by the Institute on Private Enterprises of Beijing University, Chinese companies, especially private companies, have not given enough attention to this area. Only fifteen large state-run corporations began to publish annual reports of its corporate responsibilities in 2006, Including China Petroleum and Natural Gas, State Grid, and China Mobile. Many local governments have required all state-run enterprises to periodically issue Corporate Social Responsibility (CSR) Reports since 2007. By July 2008, 144 companies have issued similar reports.

There are many successes in some of the corporate efforts to develop strong social responsibility. Elion Resource Group of Inner Mongolia, for example, combines environmental protection with ecological conservation, and adheres to the principle of "lower input, lower consumption, higher benefits, being recyclable, and being sustainable" in the development of the corporation. To grow licorice, the company's main herb plants used for medicine, it has treated 2,000 square km desert, and constructed five desert highways. These efforts not only helped the local economy, but also helped reduce soil erosion to the Yellow River.[63] With a strong government push and public demands, more and more companies will take the CSR more seriously and invest more in projects and technology to ensure a recyclable and sustainable development model.

Enterprises will ultimately become the key players in environmental protection. Large companies and state-run companies are more likely to embrace the idea of corporate social responsibilities. However, major challenges remain ahead. As of September 2008 only 181 businesses and business groups have joined the United Nation Global Pact, a global network founded in 2001 aimed at promoting global corporate responsibility, including environmental responsibility.[64] The majority of Chinese companies is small and medium size, and is privately owned. There needs to be more state action and public efforts to have these companies shoulder their social responsibilities.

Conclusions

From command-and-control strategy, to market-based environmental economics, and from state governance to cooperative governance, the new regulatory politics in China represents a new direction in China's environmental protection. It mirrors a fundamental shift in China's developmental strategy. The combined efforts should help produce some significant improvements in China's environment in the years to come. The success of these efforts may have some lasting impact on China's political development. The state is no longer the monolithic actor in the decision-making process, but rather it has become more open and democratic. Civil participation will help foster a participatory culture in China and educate people how to be a partner in the governing process.

There is no doubt that many uncertainties still lie ahead. Whether or not the new deal will succeed remains to be seen. China has laid out its ambitious goal of quadrupling its GDP in the first two decades of the twenty-first century. At least people in China have realized that the growth cannot be achieved at the expense of their environment. It is very likely that a trade-off between economic efficiency and environmental protection has to be made in order to sustain the continued economic development in the years to come.

Notes

1. Paul Meidment, "Striving for Blue Skies for Beijing's Olympics," *Forbes*, July 29, 2008.

2. MEP, News Release, http://www.mep.gov.cn (accessed September 24, 2008).

3. Elizabeth C. Economy, *The River Runs Black: the Environmental Challenge to China's Future* (Ithaca, NY: Cornell University Press, 2004).

4. Susmita Dasgupta, Hua Wang, and David Wheeler, *Surviving Success: Policy Reform and Future of Industrial Pollution in China*, World Bank Policy Research Working Paper No. 1856, World Bank, February 1997, 2.

5. Jinnan Wang, Jintian Yang, Chazhong Ge, Dong Cao, and Jeremy Schreifels, "Sulfure Dioxide Emission Trading in China: Piloting Programs and Its Perspective," Chinese Academy for Environmental Planning, http://www.caep.org.cn/english (accessed December 19, 2008).

6. The State Council, PRC, China National Environmental Protection Plan in the Eleventh Five-Years （ 2006-2010 ） , http://www.caep.org.cn/english/paper/China-National-Environmental-Protection-Plan-in-11th-Five-Years.pdf (accessed December 19, 2008).

7. Yu Jianrong, "Protecting the rights of the people to visit higher government officials is a Constitutional principles," *Xuxi Shibao*, http://news.sohu.com/ (accessed December 19, 2008).

8. The *Zaoshu* case deals with polluted water in a local mine. Several villagers were detained repeatedly for registering their grievance over the water pollution problem caused by a local molybdenum mine. The local environmental bureaus stood guard for the interests of the mine owner, and blamed the villagers as troublemakers. See Chen Zhiqing, "Investigation of "Poisonous Water Incident" in *Zaoshu* Village in Zhejiang," from China http://env.people.com.cn/GB/6898637.html(accessed December 19, 2008). The Baoji case involves complaints made by local residents over an amino acids plant. When people staged a sit-in protest, the local government used police to disperse the crowd, http://www.ep.net.cn/cgi-bin/jbts/doc.cgi?id=901(accessed December 19, 2008).

9. "China's Environment Close to 'Breakdown'," *China Daily*, July 4, 2007.

10. Lin Fangchao, "Environmental Issues Addressed More Urgently," *China Daily*, May 4, 2006.

11. China Environmental Awareness Program, *2007 China General Public Environmental Survey*, http://www.chinaceap.org/download/9.pdf (accessed December 19, 2008).The poll was conducted jointly by the Chinese Academy of Social Sciences (CASS) and the China Environment Awareness Program (CEPA), a program sponsored by the United Nation Development Program (UNDP) and SEPA.

12. The Dongyang Incident involved the pollution in a Chemical Industrial Park. Several thousand people clashed in the park, and led to one hundred people injured, and park was subsequently deserted and abandoned. The Changxin Incident was caused by pollution from a battery manicuring plant. Due the incident, 75 percent of companies moved out of the industrial park. The Ninbo Incident took place in the Beilun Port area, where a local people protested over pollution caused by a steel mill. "A revisit of the Mass Protest over Environmental Pollution in Zhejiang Province: Life or Death," *Jingji Cankaobao*, November. 9, 2007 http://www.ce.cn/cysc/hb/gdxw/200711/09 (accessed December 19, 2008).

13. Yang Dongping ed., *China Environment Green book: Environmental Transition and the Games* (2006) (Beijing: Zhongguo Wenxian Chuban She, 2007).

14. For example, Lao Guanzui is a village located in Jun County of Henan Province. Due to river pollution caused by factories built along the Wei River, the underground water was seriously contaminated. Between 2002 and 2003, seventeen people died of cancer each year. "The Fearful Northern Henan: the Cancer Village," Xinhuanet.com, April 29, 2003, http://news.xinhuanet.com/focus/2003-04/29/content_852405.htm (accessed on Dec 19, 2008). More details see "A Map of Cancer Villages," *China Digital Times*, http://chinadigitaltimes.net/2009/05/a-map-of-chinas-cancer-villages/ (accessed May 9, 2009).

15. SEPA, News Release, March 2, 2006, http://www.zhb.gov.cn/ (accessed May 9, 2009).

16. Carin Zissis and Jayshree Bajoria, "China's Environmental Crisis," Council on Foreign Relations, August 4, 2008, http://www.cfr.org/ (accessed May 9, 2009).

17. United Nations Climate Change Conference, December 9-December 18, 2009, http://en.cop15.dk/ (accessed May 9, 2009).

18 Tom Tietenberg, "Design Lessons from Existing Air Pollution Control System: the United States," in Susan Hanna and Mohan Munasinhe ed, *Property in a Social and Ecological Context* (Beijer International Institute of Ecological Economics and World Bank, 1995).

19. Pan Hongqi, "Huanbao Xinzheng Xu 'San Guan Qixia'" (Environmental New Deal Needs to Involve Three Parties)," *Beijing Youth Daily*, September 11, 2007, http://bjyouth.ynet.com/article.jsp?oid=23684074 (accessed May 9, 2009).

20. Information Office of the State Council, *Environmental Protection in China 1986-1996*, http://english.mep.gov.cn/environmental_education/ (accessed May 9, 2009).

21. Information Office of the State Council, *Environmental Protection in China 1986-2005*, http://english.mep.gov.cn/environmental_education (accessed May 9, 2009).

22. Zhou Wei, "The SEPA: There Are Five Weakness in the Environmental Legislation," Xinhuanet.com. May 17, 2005, http://news.xinhuanet.com/zhengfu/2005-05/17/content_2966173.htm (accessed May 9, 2009).

23. Information Office of the State Council, *Environmental Protection in China 1986-2005, op cit.*

24. Hon S. Chan, Koon-kwai Wong, K. C. Cheung and Jack Man-keung Lo, "The Implementation Gap in Environmental Management in China: The Case of Guangzhou, Zhengzhou, and Nanjing," *Public Administration Review* 55, no 4 (July/August 1995): 333-340.

25. Stephanie Beyer, "Environmental Law and Policy in the People's Republic of China," *Chinese Journal of International Law* 5 no. 1 (2006):185-211.

26. Han Lin, "The SEPA Suspended 30 Project for Violating Environmental Regulation," China.com.cn, January 18, 2005. http://big5.china.com.cn/chinese/huanjing/763371.htm (accessed May 9, 2009).

27. *Beijing Morning News*, February 2, 2007.

28. *South China Daily (news addition)*, August 8. 2008. http://theory.southcn.com/ (accessed May 9, 2009).

29. Ministry of Environmental Protection, "Interim Measures on the Collection of Pollution Discharge Fee," August. 2, 1982.

30. Chinese Academy for Environmental Planning, *International Experience: Incorporating Environmental Costs in Prices*, http://english.mep.gov.cn/environmental_education/publications/200710/P020071016296190725212.pdf (accessed May 9, 2009).

31. Hua Wei and David Wheeler, *Endogenous Enforcement and Effectiveness of China's Pollution Levy System*, World Bank Policy Research Working Paper No. 2336. World Bank, June 2000.

32. Susmita Dasgupta, Benoit Laplante, Nlandu Mamingi, and Hua Wang, *Industrial Environmental Performance in China: the Impact of Inspections*, World Bank Policy Research Working Paper No. 2285. World Bank, February 2000.

33. Hua and Wheeler, *op cit.*.

34. Hua Wei and David Wheeler, *Pricing Industrial Pollution in China: An Econometric Analysis of the Levy System*, World Bank Policy Research Working Paper No.1644. World Bank, September 1996.

35. Wen Jing, et al., "Green Tax: outline of the three proposals," Xinhuanet.com, December 1, 2005.

36. SEPA and Insurance Supervision Administration, *Research Report on Liability Insurance for Environment Pollution*, June 5, 2007, http://news.163.com/07/0823/03/3MI4POB70001124J_2.html (accessed May 9, 2009).

37. Qi Jianrong, "Can Green Insurance Be a Good Solution?" *Legal Daily*, February 19. 2008.

38. Environmental Defense in China, China Emission Trading, www.cet.net.cn

39. Pan Yue, "Tantan Huanjing Jingji de Xin Zhengce (On the New Policies of Environmental Economy)," lecture made at the Central CCP Central Party School, September 27, 2007, http://swdx.nc.gov.cn/web/showStudyDetail.aspx?StudyId=15 (accessed May 9, 2009).

40. John Burns, "China's Administrative Reform for a Market Economy," *Public Administration and Development* 13, no. 4 (October 1993): 345-360; Susan Shirk, "The Chinese Political System and the Political strategy of Economic Reform," in Kenneth Liberthal and David M. Lampton, eds., *Bureaucracy, Politics, and Decision-making in Post-Mao China* (Berkeley, CA: University of California Press, 1992).

41. Chinese Council for International Cooperation on Environment and Development, *Research Report on China's Environmental Governance*, http://www.china.com.cn/tech/zhuanti/wyh/2008-01/11/content_9518780.htm (accessed May 9, 2009).

42. C. Lawrence Greenwood, Jr., "Environmental Protection in China: Challenges and Solutions," speech at China Development Forum 2007, Asian Development Bank.

43. Srini Sitaraman, "Regulating the Belching Dragon: Rule of Law, Politics of Enforcement, and Pollution Prevention in Post-Mao Industrial China," *Colorado Journal of International Environmental Law and Policy* 18 (2007), 267, 291-292.

44. *Beijing Review*, June 2008.

45. *Xinhua News*, August 8, 2008, http://www.news.cn (accessed May 9, 2009).

46. People.com.cn, April 13, 2005.

47. Shenzhou Shangmaowang, December 28, 2006, http://www.chinaicp.net/ (accessed May 9, 2009).

48. Hua Wang, et al., "Environmental Performance Rating and Disclosure: China's Green Watch Program," World Bank Policy Research Working Paper No.2889. World Bank, June 2002.

49. Joey Liu, "Xiamen Residents Say No to Toxic Plant; Hostility Toward Works in Rare Public Meetings," *South China Morning Post*, December 15, 2007; Christine Xu, "China: Locals Turn to Environmental Activism," Climate Institute, http://www.climate.org/topics/international-action/chinese-environmental-action.html (accessed on May 9, 2009).

50. *China Chemical Reporter*, January 16, 2008

51. Yang Guobin, "Environmtnal NGOs and Institutional Dynamics in China," *The China Quarterly*, no. 181 (2005), 50.

52. Data quoted from Chen Gang, *Politics of China's Environmental Protection* (New Jersey: World Scientific Press, 2009), 42.

53. Elizabeth Economy, "Environmental NGOs in China: Encouraging Action and Addressing Grievances," Statement made before Congressional-Executive Commission on China, February 7, 2005, http://www.cecc.gov/pages/roundtables/020705/ (accessed May 9, 2009).

54. Society Entrepreneur Ecology (SEE), *ALXA SEE Ecological Association: Duty and Dream*.

55. Xiao Jin, "Research Report to Lee Hysan Foundation" (unpublished manuscripts)

56. C. Chad Futrell, "Evolution of International NGOs in China: broadening environmental collaboration and shifting priorities "in Yang Dongping ed., *China Environ-*

ment Yearbook: Changes and struggles, Vol. 2 (Brill Academic Publishers, 2008), 225-257.

57. WWF, *2007 WWF China Program Annual Report*, http://www.wwfchina.org (accessed May 9, 2009).

58. ChinaCSR.com January 19, 2007.

59. China CSR.com, January 9, 2008.

60. ChinaCSR.com, January 3, 2008.

61. CECPA, "The 14th Green China Forum held in Shenzhen on September. 12, 2008," http://www.tt65.net/zonghe/cecpa/02/14luntan.htm (accessed May 9, 2009).

62. *Corporate Responsibility Survey*, http://www.yfzs.gov.cn/gb/info/dywz/2005-10/04/1238368993.html (accessed May 9, 2009).

63. Golden Bee Center for Corporate Social Responsibility, "Case studies of Corporate Social Responsibilities," http://www.csr-china.org/Html/yugao/ (accessed May 9, 2009).

64. UNGC, "Global Compact 'Progress and Value' Workshop Held in China," http://www.unglobalcompact.org/newsandevents/news_archives/2008_04_21.html (accessed May 9, 2009).

Chapter 7
Changing the Balance of Power in Labor Relations[*]

The fate of Chinese workers serves as a barometer of changes taking place in recent decades. For many years, the ruling party in China has maintained that workers were "masters of the society." However, since the introduction of market-oriented economic reforms, the "masters" were once again demoted to wage laborers. The glorious crown used to hang over their heads has become nothing but a part of a fading memory of the "good old days." The decline of workers' social status and their frequent protests have raised some tough issues for the ruling party since the proletarian social class, in Marxist terms, is always deemed as the social basis of a communist party's political support.

Many scholars have done extensive studies on the emerging labor issues in China. According to a recent study by Ching Kwan Lee, Chinese workers suffered two types of deprivations during the prolonged period of economic transition. One was the loss of their equity in the state, which resulted in the loss of social status, and guaranteed fringe benefits in areas such as employment, health care, retirement, housing, and education. Another was the loss of their equity in their workplaces. Inhuman treatment, long working hours, unsafe working conditions, and substandard pay were common complaints among workers. This "decremental deprivation," a term used by Ted Curr,[1] has resulted in two types of protests: "protests of desperation" and "protests against discrimination." The "protests of desperation" were seen in many parts of the country, especially in those old industrial bases where business restructuring, mergers and bankruptcies have eliminated much of the state-run enterprises established in the 1950s and 1960s. The "protests against discrimination" took place mostly in the southeast part of China where private and foreign-invested companies were booming. Most of the protests involved changes in labor practices and standards, the mistreatment of rural migrant workers.[2]

The changing fate of Chinese laborers presents a good example of the cyclical pattern of political development in China. In this chapter we will first examine the labor policy in the early days of the PRC. Our focus will be on how

[*] A portion of this paper was published by *American Reviews of China Studies* under the title of "From Master to Wage Labor: Chinese Workers at the Turn of the New Millennium," (1, no. 1 (2000): 111-128). The author wishes to thank the journal editor for giving me permission to include part of the article into this chapter.

the ruling party patronized workers of the state-owned enterprises and institutions by changing their social and economic status and extending their safety net. Next, we will study the transformation of labor policy that took place between the 1980s and the 1990s and illustrate how workers were forced to be subjected to the terms and conditions of the market economy. Finally, we will examine recent developments in labor legislation under the new equity-oriented reform regime. More specifically, we will analyze the efforts made by the state to improve China's labor standards through labor-friendly social legislation, and the role the official trade unions have played in protecting labor rights in recent years.

From Wage Laborers to "Masters of the Workplaces"

Urban workers have an important place in socialist theory and practice. The ideology of Marxism is based on the assumption that after the "conquest of power by the proletariat," labor will no longer be a commodity, and the accumulated labor, the capital, "is but a means to widen, to enrich, to promote the existence of the laborer." Marx and Engels declared that by overthrowing capitalism, "[t]he proletarians have nothing to lose but their chains."[3] Guided by this ostentatious vision, the Chinese Communists fought for nearly three decades in armed struggles and eventually seized political power. The founding of the PRC in 1949 marked the beginning of the first transformation of state-labor relations.

The size of China's modern industry was relatively small before 1949. Industrial work forces were mostly first-generation rural migrant laborers. Many studies have documented the working conditions of Chinese workers before 1949.[4] In general, low wages, long hours under meager working conditions, and poor treatment were common in workplaces. There was no job security, and the fringe benefits were literally non-existent. In order to ensure profits and improve efficiency, employers adopted western "scientific" management systems such as the "Taylor system" used in the United States. Various unfair employment systems such as the contract-labor system (*baogong zhi*), apprentice-labor system (*xuetu zhi*), probation-labor system (*yangchenggong zhi*), slave-labor contract system (*baoshengong zhi*), and child-labor system were widely used. The contract labor system or "blood-sweating wage system" allowed the subcontractors (*baogong tou*) to control and exploit workers using piecework wages.[5] The wages of employees in commerce, schools, transportations, postal services, and banks were mostly paid by the hour. The feudalist tradition also made the sacrifice of workers' personal freedom a part of their employment conditions, particularly in the use of apprentice contract, probation contract and the slave contract systems.

The Establishment of a Socialist Labor Regime

The CCP's victory over the Nationalist government on the mainland was due partly to the strong support of the industrial workers in the urban areas. What made the CCP attractive to those workers at the time were its popular appeals to have eight-hour working days, and to "liberate" workers from exploitation by domestic and international capitalists. Russia's "October Revolution" of 1917 inspired many Chinese revolutionary pioneers to follow the Bolshevik's footsteps and establish a workers' state. The Stalinist theory of socialist transformation, which shaped much of the CCP leaders' mental picture of socialism, demanded a transfer of the ownership of the means of production to the state and the public, the elimination of the wage labor system, and a fair distribution of economic wealth. Based on this theory, Mao and his comrades nationalized or collectivized privately-owned enterprises, lands, commerce, transportation and craft-making industries. The equal employment system replaced various old employment systems. The size of the industrial work force increased steadily due to the accelerated industrialization and urbanization. Millions of farmers joined industrial labor forces (see Table 7.1). In 1949, there were only eight million workers in the state-own enterprises. By 1981, this number had jumped to 83.7 million. It is ironic to point out the fact that the very social class that is supposed to make the communist revolution is, in fact, largely a creation of the communist revolution.

Table 7.1 Numbers of Workers in the Public Sector   (units: millions)

Type of enterprises	1949	1952	1965	1975	1981
State-owned	8	15.8	37*	64*	83.7
Collectively owned	–	0.2	12*	22	25.7

Sources: CCP Secretariat and ACFL, *The Condition of the Working Class in China* (Beijing, Central Party School Publishing House, 1983), trans. *by International Journal of Political Economy* 25, no. 1 (Spring 1995). *Estimated numbers.

Labor reforms in the areas of wage, management, and social security were carried out nationwide. The wage reform standardized wages and salaries. State-owned enterprises and institutions had to follow guidelines and wage standards set up by the State Council. Eight-hours of work were required in most workplaces. Although the state managed to keep the real wage significantly lower than what workers deserved, workers obtained many generous fringe benefits in return, including free or nearly free medical care, childcare, kindergartens, education, pensions and public housing. For instance, in 1950, there were only 1,800 kindergartens enrolling 140,000 children in the Chinese mainland. By 1958, there were 700,000 kindergartens, enrolling over 29 million children. Each work unit built its own employment housing, and the number of housing units built increased steadily (see Figure 7.1).

Working conditions and workplace safety were improved. In 1951, a new labor insurance regulation issued by the State Council set up a generous welfare system for workers. According to the regulation, enterprises were obligated to pay for laborers' life, health and retirement insurances to cover injury, sickness and retirement. Workers paid no premiums to the insurance schemes. Disability insurance was also established. If a worker was disabled due to work-related

injuries he or she could get health care costs covered in full, plus 75 percent of their regular wages paid until their death. The state guaranteed individuals' pension payment. Normally retirees received 30-60 percent of their regular wages or salaries. Special attention was given to the protection of female workers. Female workers could get up to two-months paid maternity leave.[6] Unions and enterprises established rehabilitation and leisure facilities, such as worker sanatoriums, disability homes, orphanages, etc.[7] State-paid health insurance coverage expanded gradually (see Figure 7.2). In 1952, only four million workers enrolled. By 1958, nearly seven million workers were covered. Most workers were included in the unit-based welfare system in the next two decades. A cradle-to-grave welfare system was gradually coming into sight.

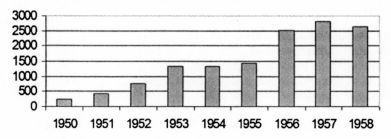

Figure 7.1 State-Built Workers' New Housing Units   (units: square meters)

Sources: National Bureau of Statistics: *Weida de Shinian* [*The Great Ten Years*] (Beijing: People's Publishing House, 1959), 192.

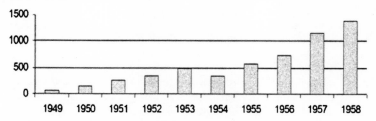

Figure 7.2 Beneficiaries of the Labor Insurance System   (units: tens   of thousands)

Sources: National Bureau of Statistics: *Weida de Shinian* [*The Great Ten Years*] (Beijing: People's Publishing House, 1959), 193.

Workers' political and social rights were improved considerably. Women joined the work force in large numbers, and gender discrimination was made illegal. Physical abuse of workers was prohibited. Workers were asked to concern themselves with national and enterprise affairs. Political meetings and study sessions were common in workplaces. A model worker system was established to reward workers who excelled in their work performance. Emulation, rather than competition was encouraged to promote work efficiency and raise productivity. Employees who were employed by the state sectors were paid with a fixed wage, and their employments were considered fixed or lifetime. The piecework wage system and contract labor system were largely gone by 1958. Even though temporary workers and rural labors were used, the household registration system prevented a large scale of rural laborers from migrating into cities.

The most important change was workers' social status. Since the wage labor system was replaced by the equal employment system, labor was no longer a commodity to be sold in the market place, and workplaces were no longer meant to be "sweatshops." A sense of equality and ownership was established. At the center of the improvement were the manager-labor relations. The system of "two participations" required managers to participate in manual labor, and workers to participate in managerial tasks. Managers were mostly chosen from workers, and were supposed to be "civil servants" of workers. The distinction and function of laborers and management was un-clarified and non-differentiated. Managers functioned in many ways as social service providers who were concerned not only about production issues but also overwhelmed with workers' welfare issues. They acted as bargain-hunters to negotiate with the paternal state to maximize the tangible and non-tangible benefits for their own employees.[8] Some managers resented the policy of workplace equality and resisted substantive workers' participation in a factory's decision-making process. This discrepancy might have contributed to workers' rage during the "cultural revolution" and led to the breakdown of the industrial orders.[9]

The Role of the Official Unions

To be sure, there were many sectional and regional variances in workers' political status, social prestige and economic welfare. Small-scale labor disputes or work slowdowns did happen from time to time. Overall, the relationship between the state and workers was collaborative rather than adversarial. This cooperative relationship was also due to the CCP's control over labor unions. In June 1950 the government proclaimed the Trade Union Law. The government organized workers' congresses and labor unions at workplaces and then grouped them together under the umbrella of the ACFTU. Workers could join the union on a voluntary basis. Nevertheless, each work unit could establish only one union. The government never allowed any independent union to exist. There was no collective bargaining either.

The ACFTU was treated as a peripheral organization of the ruling party. The CCP claimed absolute leadership over it. According to Lenin's labor union theory, labor unions were "schools of communism" or "transmission belts," and their primary duty was to protect state interests and to promote production and worker discipline. Representing workers and channeling their concerns and voices were only secondary, thus making it differ in an important way from the role of trade unions in the West.

However, for most workers, the union was merely another "*yamen*" and a welfare organization. Although there were five attempts by the union leaders at various times to acquire some autonomy from the party, each time, it ended up with a complete failure.[10] From very early on, the ruling party controlled the selection of union leaders. Many key union leaders were communist leaders at the same time. Financially, most of the half million union leaders were on the government's payroll. Union cadres at and above the county level were considered to be state cadres who could receive a salary equivalent to a deputy administrator in the government, and enjoy all other admired material benefits such as pensions, travel and health care. Union members paid 2 percent of their wages or salary as union dues. Enterprises and institutions contributed another 2 percent of their total wages and salary payments to unions. Government also subsidized unions in many ways. In addition to direct financing tied to the government, enterprises and institutions also provided union offices and meeting places.

Many recent studies have pointed out the corporatist nature of China's labor policy.[11] Like many European countries in their initial stage of industrialization, the Chinese new state actively promoted cooperation and collaboration between the state and labor. The state wanted workers to believe that the antagonistic relationship between the state and capitalists on the one hand and the working class on the other was no longer in existence. Consequently, cooperation and collaboration should characterize the new relationship between the state and labor.

From Masters to Wage Laborers Again

Since 1978, China has moved away quickly from the command economy. Labor reform is an important part of the economic reform. Although the reform experienced many ups and downs, it became clear by the early 1990s that the reform was geared towards the dismantlement of the "moral arrangements" between the state and labor.[12] Under the new condition of market socialism, labor's social and economic rights came under siege.

Urban Enterprise Reform

China launched the urban enterprise reform in the 1980s. The first new initiative introduced was the Factory Director Responsibility system. The long-discredited Taylor management system returned to workplaces in the name of improving efficiency and productivity. Personnel system reform and wage reform soon followed. The "Regulation on Transforming the Management Mechanism of State-Owned Enterprises" issued in 1992 further strengthened the power of factory managers. They were now free to hire workers under their conditions and free to set their employees' wages. The government also decided in 1986 to restore the contract labor system.[13] Under the new system, workers' "iron rice bowl" was broken, and so was their privileged social status as well as their guaranteed economic, health, housing, and education securities.

To be sure, reforms did have many positive impacts on workers' lives. Although workers lost their lifetime employment privileges, they gained their economic freedom and social mobility. Their income also increased steadily. Various schemes of wage reform have been experimented with at the enterprise level. Floating pay, piecework pay, and obscure wages (*mohu gongzi*) replaced the fixed wage system. Both foreign-owned enterprises and state-owned enterprises are beginning to adopt the Concealed Income Distribution System in which managers decide the workers' actual wage, bonus and allowance. Employees were supposed to keep their wages or salary confidential and not to share that information with their coworkers.

During the 1990s, the reform of state-owned enterprises was accelerated. The separation of government and enterprises (*zhengqi fenkai*) left economic decision-making power in the hands of enterprises. State-owned or state-invested businesses became self-sufficient and were responsible for their own profits and losses. To improve efficiency, state enterprises began to let go millions of surplus labor forces. Throughout the 1990s, the annual reduction of worker forces in state-owned enterprises exceeded 15 million.

When Zhu Rongji became Premier of the State Council in 1998, he pushed for the completion of three more labor market reforms in three years: social insurance reform, health care insurance reform and housing reform.[14] The goal was to end the role of enterprises as distributors of state-sponsored welfare, and to improve enterprise vitality and efficiency. The social insurance reform included an unemployment insurance program–to be paid for by a one percent payroll tax on all types of enterprises. The insurance would provide unemployment relief to an unemployed worker for up to two years. A new pension system–paid for by mandatory individual contributions from both employees and employers–was also established during this time. The health care reform, which will be discussed in detail in Chapter 8 was also carried out nationwide.[15] The housing reform started in July 1998. All free housing allocation by the enterprises and the government in the urban areas was to cease. Existing housing units were sold to workers at a subsidized price.[16] New employees had to purchase their own apartments from that time on.

The Plight of Chinese Workers

The labor reform certainly benefited many laborers and improved their standard of living. However, the income gap between managers and workers, technicians and non-technicians, workers in state-owned enterprises and workers in foreign owned enterprises widened appreciably. The key value served to maintain the cooperative relationship among all players in the traditional labor relations, namely, the sense of equality and ownership, was lost. The phenomenon of relative poverty, a term Marx used to describe labor conditions in late nineteenth century, now turned out to be a new reality despite the increase in workers' real wages. The percentage of labor incomes in GDP actually decreased from 15.7 percent in 1978 to 11.7 percent in 2006.[17] The lack of labor pressure on wages was a major cause of the decline. Income inequality between laborers and managers increased. By early 2009, the ratio of the highest average industrial income and the lowest one had expanded to 11 to 1.[18] Income disparity between the blue-collar and white-collar workers also reached an intolerable level.

The effort to reform the public sectors through closure, shutdown, merger, transfer and bankruptcy hit industrial workers hardest, resulting in a sharp increase in the number of out-post workers. Compared with 1997, the number of workers in state-owned and collective-owned enterprises in 1998 was reduced by 15 million people (see Table 7.2). The total number of unemployed workers reached 12.54 million.[19]

Table 7.2 Numbers of Workers in the Public Sector   (units: millions)

	1981	1993	1997	1998
State-owned	83.7	109.2	98	88
Collectively-owned	25.7	33.9	23	18.9

Sources: *China Labor Union Statistical yearbook (1993).*

Although the registered unemployment rate stood at 3.1 percent, the real unemployment rate was believed to be 7-9 percent in the 1990s.[20] For those who could not find a new job, their only chance to survive was to depend on the newly-created unemployment insurance system and poverty relief programs. Many of them became the new urban poor. According to a survey in Henan province, some of the troubled workers also faced absolute poverty (see Table 7.3). In 1994, there were seven million workers nationwide living under the poverty level, or 20 million individuals, when workers' family members were also taken into consideration. The per capita income of these families was only 62 *yuan*, or 42 percent of the national average.[21] In Liaoning province, 70 percent of the unemployed were women. Only 50 percent of them had a chance to find new jobs. Many who did find jobs saw their income significantly lower than what they had before (see Table 7.4).

Table 7.3 Unemployment and Retirement Population in Henan (units: tens of thousands)

	Total	Lost insurance or pension payment	Ratio
Unemployed †	97	39	40%
Retired ‡	95	14	19%

Sources: He Lisheng and Lin Shixuan, "Tizhi Zhuanhuan Shiqi Henansheng Chengshi Pingkunceng Yanjiu (A Study of Urban Poverty in Henan in the Period of System Changes" *Henan Sheke Jie*, December 30, 1998.
†1996; ‡ July 1997

The reform's biggest impact was the marginalization of workers in the workplace. The Factory Director Responsibility System gave managers tremendous amounts of powers to terminate employees, to decrease and increase employees' pay or bonus, and to promote employees to managerial positions. Many newly established township factories and foreign-owned factories became modern day sweatshops.[22] The concept of workplace equality was replaced by hierarchical structures and a differential wage system. In private-owned and foreign-owned companies, the sense of mastership is totally lost. Workers in most situations dared not to challenge managers and had no guts to even complain about their unfair treatment for fear of losing their jobs or revenges against them.[23] Cruel treatment, physical abuse, compulsory overtime, high task quotas, military style of rules and regulations, arbitrary fines and punishment let workers taste the bitterness of a capitalist-style management system. Suffering from personal insult and physical abuse, many workers were forced to take extreme actions.[24]

Table 7.4 Reemployment Situation for Suspended Employees from State-Run Enterprises in Ten Cities and Provinces   (units: percentage)

	Returned to work after training	Absorbed internally	Transferred other department	Found own work in tertiary sector	Remained without work
Jiangxi	6.4	10.4	5.1	28.1	50.0
Gansu	1.7	71.3	7.2	5.3	4.5
Hebei	9.3	21.4	1.3	21.4	31.6
Shanxi	10.0	21.0	4.0	5.6	53.4
Shanghai	–	32.2	13.9	14.2	39.7
Shandon	13.1	23.9	19.9	9.0	34.1
Wuhan	–	28.6	6.6	5.0	59.8
Xi'an	8.0	–	31.6	47.0	14.0
Wenzhou	–	2.3	–	44.3	53.4
Harbin	–	5.0	16.0	23.0	48.0

Sources: Chang Kai, "A Survey and Investigation of Unemployment and Reemployment of Female Employees in State-Owned Enterprises," *Chinese Sociology and Anthropology* 30, no. 2 (Winter 1997-98), 38, Table 7. The data refers to 1994.

Political Responses to the Emerging Labor Issues

As a sign of labor discontent, the number of labor disputes increased steadily every year. The Complaint Receiving Bureau (*Xinfangju*), under the joint control of the Central Party Committee and the State Council, documented that it handled 87 percent more cases of workers' collective complaints and 164 percent more individual complaints in 1993 than in 1990. During the same period, among twenty-seven provinces surveyed, eighteen provinces had a marked increase in collective complaints and twenty-one provinces had a sharp increase in workers' individual complaints.[25] Most of them were related to unpaid wages or pensions. There are no accurate yearly statistics about the number of labor disputes. In 1993, official figures registered 233 labor strikes, even though strikes are outlawed in China's Constitution. In 1996, there were 48,121 labor disputes, an increase of 50 percent over the previous year. More than 1,700 enterprises had experienced workers strikes or slow-downs. In 1998, workers in Zigong, Mianyang and Wuhan reportedly went on strike. Some labor activists went even further by calling for the creation of an autonomous labor union or labor party to compete with the official unions.[26]

Although the labor movement in China during this time remained largely reactive and passive, it could have jeopardized the economic reforms in China. The labor reforms in the 1990s brought back the chronic problems faced by laborers prior to the 1950s, namely, alienation, poverty and resentment. When workers became commodities in the marketplace, their production activities inevitably became passive, involuntary and coercive. They lost their sense of pride on what they did and why they did it.[27] These kinds of economic alienation generated political frustration and resentment over the official image of workers that the government had propagated over the years.

An underground labor movement emerged in China during this time. There were many attempts on the part of workers to set up independent trade unions. Some even tried to establish a Chinese Labor Party. The stability-minded government was determined to put down any demand for labor autonomy. Many labor activists were jailed or forced into exile overseas.

To mitigate the suffering of the out-post workers and reduce potential labor resistance to reform, the government proposed in 1998 a policy of "dual guarantees," namely, to guarantee the minimum standard of living payment for the laid-off workers and pension payments for retirees. In September 1999, the government raised the monthly pension and unemployment payment by 15-30 percent. Unpaid pension money would be paid in a lump-sum payment by the central government. Employment centers were established by all enterprises that had downsized their labor forces. Over six million workers registered with these centers and sought government relief.

During this period, legislators also enacted a number of important labor laws to reflect the rapid changing labor relations. The Labor Law of 1994 was the first comprehensive labor standards law. The law covered minimum wage, child labor, working hours, protection of women, forced labor, collective bargaining and group contracts, overtime pay, vacations, holidays, labor protection, labor inspection system, and many other areas. The labor standards set in this law raised the bar of labor employment. It codified many labor practices adopted since the reform started. It stipulated that labor contracts had to be offered to all workers in all types of enterprises. Labor disputes arbitration and inspection divisions were to be established at all levels. The law allowed collective bargaining for all types of enterprises, but it also permitted enterprises to lay off workers for economic reasons without prior consultation with local governments.[28] The law codified the new industrial relations that emerged during the reform era. Workers became once again free agents in the market places, and were free to sell themselves as commodities in the market place. All the rights and protections they had under the equal employment system were gradually chipped away.

The Trade Union Act of 1992 codified a unitary form of trade union system and gave labor unions a broader role in collective bargaining, the settlement of labor disputes, and enterprise management. With the enactment of this law, China established the largest network of trades unions with memberships currently exceeding 130 million. Although the membership in a union was non-mandatory, employees in state sectors were thoroughly unionized with an over 90 percent labor participation rate. Private sectors in urban areas were only partially unionized. According to the law, only one union was allowed in each company and institution. All of them must belong to the official ACFTU.

Overall, the labor reforms of the 1990s reversed labor regimes established during the labor reforms of the 1950s. The labor reform in the 1950s was indeed a revolutionary one. It drastically improved labor's social status in society and established a whole new system of labor relations in the workplace. However, rationalization, reorganization and retreat characterized the second reform. While the first one focused on breakthroughs, coercion, and control, the second one focused on improving efficiency, management coherence and coordination.[29] The number of state-owned enterprises was dropped significantly, but the number of employees they hired remained quite large. Workers' job security and safety net were overhauled, but a new market-based income security system model was slow in taking shape. Social services provided by the work units were phased out, but the government struggled to establish a new state-sponsored system of social services to fill the vacuum. Trade unions had more responsibility in protecting labor's interests, but party maintained its strong control over the labor organization. Overall, the new reform was neither a complete rejection of the first one nor a simple return to the pre-1949 wage labor system.

Changing Nature of Labor Relations

The nature of labor relations after the 1950s labor reforms was cooperative rather than antagonistic. Ideological principles and the "shared" interests of the state, management and labor were the main themes. The mechanism of coordinating labor relations was based on tight administrative control over employment conditions, wages, labor administration, labor protection, health care and pensions, and union activities. The state was not only a manager but also a party in labor relations. This type of labor relationship was essentially bipartite. The sweet relations were based on the ideology of egalitarianism in which income gaps between managers and workers were relatively small.[30] Workers were in general complacent. The first labor reforms featured an enlargement of the size of the working class, added economic benefits, and created a more cooperative relationship between the management and labor. Laborers depended on the state for welfare, for job security and for health care security; they relied on the state for justice and fair treatment. The state tied workers together through its patronage. The most commonly accepted notions of labor rights, such as the right to organize unions and the right to collective bargaining were denied to workers at the time.

The labor reforms in the 1980s and 1990s turned the traditional cooperative relationship between the state and the laborers into an antagonistic one. The state withdrew from enterprise-level management. Market, instead of state command, dictated for the most part business operations. Under the new labor contract system, workers sold their labor, and employers bought it in the labor market. All products and profits were employers' property. The relationship between workers and enterprise management was based primarily on an exchange of economic interests rather than on cooperative camaraderie or social equality.[31] The decentralization of labor management power to the enterprise level caused deterioration of labor-management relations, and created many theoretical challenges to the socialist state. Were workers still masters anymore? Was economic exploitation justified? For the disgruntled workers the continued use of "mastership" was simply a "big joke," or a "fancy rhetoric." Were managers still "servants of workers" anymore? For many high-paying managers, they insisted that they should not be blamed for the income gaps. After all, according to many of them, they were the ones who had to make their companies profitable, and deserved the big perks they got from their jobs.[32]

All signs have indicated the formation of a new tripartite labor relationship: the state, the employers and the employees. Each player in this new relationship possesses relative autonomy. The labor reforms of the 1990s separated the state from the bipartite labor relations, restored the state's role as a third-party manager of labor relations instead of being a direct participant in that relations.[33] The state functioned as a rule-maker and rule-keeper. Its primary mission was trying to maintain a balanced approach to both employees and employers. Now, the state is still preoccupied with enterprise reform. It gives an impression that the state is abandoning workers, and makes an alliance with employers. However, in the end, the state will have to maintain an intricate balance the two conflicting parties, or else it will lose legitimacy in the eyes of both parties.

Table 7.5 CCP's Influence over Labor Unions   (units: people)

	Union full-time chair and deputy chair	Receiving benefits of deputy party chair	Members of CCP Committees	Members of CCP local standing committees
Local Unions	195,648	105,443	82,320	9,212
National Total	234,833	118,828	93,631	10,952

Sources: ACFTU, *The Statistical Yearbook of Chinese Trade Unions*, 1993.

There exists an unbalanced political equilibrium in labor relations. While businesses are given all the necessary powers and freedom to improve efficiency and increase economic output, the laborers are still subject to tight state control. Labor activists argue that if the state is willing to let enterprise managers become independent to run their businesses, it doesn't make sense for the state to continue to maintain a tight grip on laborers. At present, the CCP does not allow any union organization outside the ACFTU's network of official unions. The official unions have maintained their bureaucratic and administrative nature, and do not act as true agents of workers. Union officials are guaranteed state benefits and incorporated into various party and governmental institutions (see Table 7.5). In order to avoid the image of being another bureaucratic agency of the government and the party, unions have to strengthen their role as representative of the interest of the working people.

New Directions in Labor Policy

The neglect of workers' rights throughout the 1980s and 1990s has already created a negative image of labor administration. Many workers, especially the old workers, felt that they were abandoned by the state, and that the state had now formed a close alliance with businesses in the name of attracting business investment and promoting economic development. Labor laws were not enforced aggressively. Business owners who ignored labor standards went unpunished. Many Chinese workers wanted to defend their interests, but only found themselves powerless in front of the powerful developmental state whose primary concern was to protect the interests of investors, maintain economic growth, and improve economic efficiency. Business owners were also very powerful in local politics. Investors or business owners often pulled their business out of certain areas if they saw labor activism. Once again, we see the presence of the trade-off between efficiency and equity here.

Taken as a whole, China's labor policy prior to the 1980s can be characterized as one of state corporatism. The state managed labor relations in its favor, and patronized the working class by serving in a redistributive role. After the 1980s, this traditional model of labor relations underwent a major transformation. A new, tripartite industrial relation emerged. Today, the state owes only a small number of businesses and, in most cases, no longer runs factories or firms directly. According to the second national economic survey of 2008, among the five million business entities, the state owns only 3 percent of that total, which is a 20 percent decrease over a decade ago. Although there were still over 76 million workers worked for state-owned industrial entities, most workers were no longer state employees.[34] Furthermore, the government rarely interferes with the decisions in the state enterprises. This enables the state to act more like a third-party regulator and broker.

Since 2002, there have been some positive signs in remaking labor policy. To change the balance of power in labor relations, the administration has paid more attention to the protection of labor rights. Its goal is to enhance its political legitimacy among its traditional support base. The wave of labor legislation opens the door for strengthening labor protection. China's entrance into the WTO also creates opportunities for China to improve its labor standards to meet international obligations.

Strengthening Labor Protection Through Labor Legislation

The year 2007 was the year of labor. Three important labor laws were adopted by the NPC. They are: Labor Dispute Mediation and Arbitration Law, Employment Promotion Law, and Labor Contract Law. The passage of these laws marked the establishment of a basic legal framework to regulate labor relations under the market economy and the beginning of an era of active labor protection through legal means.

Labor Dispute Mediation and Arbitration Law

The law on labor disputes was an important milestone to the legal protection of labor rights. The main purposes of this law are to settle labor disputes fairly and in a timely manner, to lower the burden on employees when safeguarding their legal rights, and to simplify the settlement process for labor disputes.[35] In the new law, there are many provisions favorable to labor. In order to discourage enterprises from manipulating their legal muscles to increase the legal costs to labors, the law treats the arbitration decision made by local labor arbitration boards as the final decision should an employer's appeal to the court be rejected.

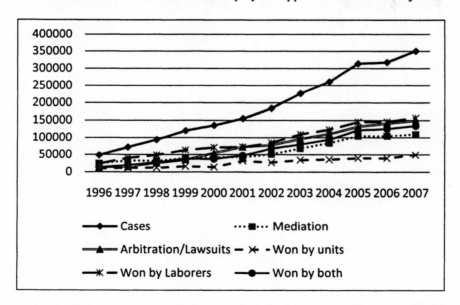

Figure 7.3 Numbers of Labor Disputes and Their Ways of Settlement (1996-2007)

Sources: NBS, *China Statistical Yearbook* (1997-2008), http://www.stats.gov.cn.

The law also extends the legal time limits for labor arbitration to sixty days from the date of the labor dispute, and reduces the time within which an arbitration decision must be made. In order to reduce the burden of evidence gathering, especially on document proofs of employment relations that are controlled by employers, the law shifts the burden to employers. A worker who files a case for arbitration is no longer required to pay an arbitration fee. If an employer refuses to make the required payment to a worker, the law also allows a worker to file an injunction to force the payment to be made.[36]

Figure 7.3 indicates that while the number of labor disputes nationwide continues to rise, the number of cases that went to mediation and court increased signficantly after 2006 due to the passages of the new laws governing labor disputes and labor contract. Local data also support this finding. In Beijing, the city's arbitration committee received 26,000 labor dispute cases in 2007, 49,000 in 2008, and 70,000 by November 2009. Beijing's Second Intermediate People's Court alone accepted and heard 4,506 cases involving labor disputes by November 10, 2009, a 180 percent increase over a year ago.[37] In Guangdong province, six months after the new law took effect, the number of labor disputes increased 300 percent, and the number of court cases also increased by 158 percent in the same period.[38] One factor contributing to the increase is that workers no longer have to pay 300 *yuan* to apply for arbitration. Another factor is the passage of the new labor contract law which raised the labor standards to a higher level.

Another notable developmental trend suggested by Figure 7.3 is that 2001 is a turning point in the settlement of labor disputes. The number of settlement won by laborers rosed sharply while the number cases won by employers remained relatively stable. The number of settlements won by both sides, meaning some kind of compromises, also increased at a greater rate. These are all positive signs suggesting that laborers have learned how to use the legal means to defend their rights. The number of cases won by laborers also indicates the balance of power is moving in a direction that is more favorable to laborers. The labor administration has moved away from its pro-business practices in the 1980s and the 1990s.

Employment Promotion Law

The law on employment promotion is an important piece of labor-empowering legislation. The government now for the first time takes job creation and employment service as its top priority. It wants to ensure equal opportunity and nondiscrimination in the job market. It obligates the government to provide employment assistance and job training and education for the unemployed. The law prohibits job discrimination based on ethnicity, race, gender, religious belief, age, health, or any physical disabilities. For example, discrimination against workers who are carriers of infectious diseases such as Hepatitis B or HIV was once widespread. Now it is against the law. An employer may not give priority to foreigners if their qualifications are the same as Chinese and may not increase the threshold for the employment of females because of their gender. The most important change in the law is that employees who suffer discrimination have a specific right to lodge a lawsuit in a people's court. It is also the first law that prohibits the discrimination against migrant rural laborers.[39]

Many business owners have strong reservation about the new law. They believe the law violates their autonomy and hiring control and may hurt their company. Hidden prejudices remain a major barrier for many job seekers, which a job seeker may find hard to prove. Because of the surplus laborers, employees are most likely to choose keeping silent over discriminative practices.[40] China has over 120 million people known for being carriers of the Hepatitis B virus. Because of the physical examination requirement for job seekers, these carriers suffer frequent discrimination. Since the passage of the Employment Promotion Law, many people have taken their cases to court and won many court battles.[41]

Labor Contract Law

The Labor Contract Law codified the new contract labor system. Since 1996, China had attempted to draft a labor contract law but without much progress. In 2005, according to a Sino-U.S. legal cooperation agreement, the U.S. Labor Department provided 5 million U.S. dollars in aid to help China draft a labor contract law. The legislative process finally started again. Between 2005 and 2007, business groups and labor groups engaged in fierce debates and battles over the new legislation. Never before have so many people participated in the debate, and never before has any law received so much attention in China's legislative history. The revision of the proposed bill was dragged in different directions as the domestic companies, foreign business firms, and laborers lobbied intensively. Businesses worried about the negative impact the bill may have on their business costs and profits. The workers wanted to improve fair labor standards and job protections. The final bill passed by the NPC in July 2007 represented a major victory for the laborers.

The legislative deliberation went through three stages. In the first stage, the Ministry of Labor and Social Security (MOLSS) revised an earlier version of the draft made in 2001 and submitted it to the State Council's Legal Affairs Office for revision in 2005. This office made four major changes before it submitted it to the Standing Committee of the NPC. During this time, the Legal Affairs Office joined the MOLSS, the ACFTU, and the China Enterprise Confederation (CEC) went to different part of the country to hold discussion meetings and sought feedback from businesses and trade unions about their suggestions. However, participants did not get a chance to see the legislative draft. In December the NPC made the first reading of the draft. The legislators struggled to balance the needs for a strong protection of labor and the concerns over its impact on business costs. The October draft contained the language to protect the interests of both sides. However, when the MOLSS submitted its final draft to the NPC in October 2005, the tune changed to give more the protection to workers' rights. This change was apparently in response to the mounting pressure from society about the flights of labor conditions that was reported by many mass domestic and international media at the time.

The business community was unhappy with the new legislation, especially on the issue of offering long-term contracts. Both business and labor organizations waged intensive campaigns to influence the legislative process, though not in a direct confrontational way. The second stage began in January 2006 when the NPC sent the draft bill to governments at all level for further consultation and deliberation. The NPC also held three deliberation sessions inviting representatives from the All China Federation of Industry and Commerce (ACFIC), the CEC, and the American Chamber of Commerce-PRC (AMCHAM). The opinions and comments were overwhelmingly from business and enterprises, and their reaction to the first draft was overwhelmingly negative. The AMCHAM even wrote a sixty-four-page document with detailed comments on the proposed legislation to the NPC. Many of these business objections were sent to various national leaders, thus making their opinions irresistible. Consequently, the NPC adopted many of their suggestions, including the AMCHAM's in its second draft.

In March 2006, the NPC published the drafted bill for public comments, and invited citizens to submit their comments on line. This was the final stage of the legislative battle. In order to counterattack the business lobby, the ACFTU launched its own grassroots campaign to defend labor's interests. It asked local trade unions to solicit workers and comments. Eventually the NPC received 191,000 online comments. Among them, 65 percent were from ordinary workers. However, the second draft responded to the business concerns more than those of labor. It returned to the language that the law must protect labor's interests as well as the interests of employers. Among the eleven major revisions made to the first draft, eight were based on employers' concerns. Trade Union denounced the second draft as a major step back. However, things took another turn when international pressure began to build up after the controversy was made known to the INGOs and governments for the weakened protection of labor rights. In the subsequent revisions, the law writers strengthened the protection of labor's rights again. When the final draft was put to a vote by the Standing Committee of the NPC, it received unanimous support.

Throughout the process, the ACFTU demonstrated that it could become a strong advocate for workers if it chose to do so. In fact, because of its activism, about 70-80 percent of its suggestions were adopted by the NPC.[42] The business community did not have the same capability to mobilize public support as the unions did.[43] According to a survey conducted by *Chinese Entrepreneur Magazine*, 70 percent of enterprises wished to revise some part of the new law, and most of them strongly objected to the no-fixed term labor contract. Over 70 percent of enterprises believed that the new law would increased their labor costs significantly, and half of them worried about the subsequent rise of costly litigations since the new laws gave labor more rights to sue.[44] Most of them believed the labor standards set by the new law were too high and would hurt their competitiveness in the market place. However, the ACFTU insisted that the business community exaggerated the negative impact of the new labor contract law, and since China's labor costs were so low, there was still some room for wage increases without compromising China's competitiveness. It condemned the tactics used by some companies to stall the legislative process.[45]

From labor's standpoint, the new law had clearly put more teeth in labor protection. First, it strengthened the protection of new employees hired on probation. Enterprises often hired workers by imposing a probation period. Workers on probation received very little pay, and could be easily terminated. The duration of probation was arbitrary. Many were too long. The new law limited probation time to a maximum of six months and set the minimum wage of probationers to 80 percent of wages of the job hired. The probationers could only be terminated if they proved to be unqualified for the job. Workers, on the other hand, could terminate their contacts with an employer without penalty if the employer did not provide social security insurance, or if the working conditions were not safe.

Secondly, the new contract law encouraged long-term labor contracts. The most controversial provision of the law was the addition of the non-fixed term contract. This applied in the following situation: have signed fixed term contracts for more than ten years, and have signed two consecutive fixed-term contracts. If an employer failed to renew a yearly contract, it would also imply an automatic extension of the non-fixed-term contract.

Finally, the law gave workers some say in major enterprise decisions. The law stipulated that an enterprise must consult equally with employee meetings or trade unions. Though it did not require employees' approval, it did encourage some level of industrial democracy and workplace participation. The law also stated that if a company wanted to terminate more than twenty employees, the company must consult with its union first.

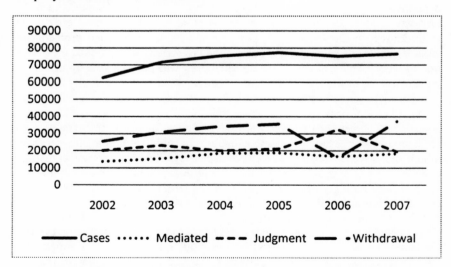

Figure 7.4 First Trial Cases of Labor Contract Disputes (2002-2008)

Sources: NBS, *China Statistical Yearbook* (2003-2008).

Figure 7.4 suggests that while labor contract disputes increased risen over time, there was no particular pattern as to how the cases were handled. The number of cases mediated and decided by the courts fluctuated in 2006 and 2007. The long-term impact of the new labor contract is still not entirely clear at the moment.

The new contract legislation highlights the new interest group politics today. Both business and labor are engaging in a zero-sum game. The state, in order to promote social harmony, is willing to side with labor and create the toughest labor protection since the enactment of the Labor Law in 1994.

WTO and the Improvement of Chinese Labor Standards

At the turn of the twenty-first century, the Chinese labor regime faced not only domestic challenges to its labor standards, but also pressures from the international community. Internationally, foreign trade unions and human rights groups have campaigned for years to press China to improve its human rights protection, including labor rights. Certainly, these gestures are not altruistic in nature; they are motivated mainly by their own self-interests; namely, to protect their own job markets from Chinese competition. When China applied for membership in the World Trade Organization (WTO), their lobby intensified. The most important demand from the unions was to add a social clause into the bilateral and multilateral trade agreements. They repeatedly made accusations about China's use of unfair labor practices and the abuse of labor rights in order to gain comparative advantages.[46]

As a response and concession, China adopted many International Labor Organization (ILO) conventions and amended some of its domestic laws and regulations. In 1990, the NPC ratified the International Labor Organization's Convention 144 on tripartite consultation to implement international labor standards. The Trade Union Law of 2001 and the Labor Contract Law of 2007 all contains clauses about the mandatory tripartite consultation system. At the national level, the representatives from the Ministry of Human Resources and Social Security (MOHRSS, formally the MOLSS, representing the state), the ACFTU (the workers) and the China Enterprise Directors' Association (CEDA, the employers) have met many times since 2003 to discuss issues related to employment, wages, social insurance, job training, labor disputes, working conditions and labor contracts. The system played a positive role in the drafting of the Labor Contract Law of 2007 and the Labor Dispute Mediation and Arbitration Law of 2007.[47] The system now has a permanent liaison office and a joint committee on laws and policies on labor relations.[48] By the end of 2007, there were 10,702 provincial and local tripartite consultation organizations. Various labor arbitration boards handled over half a million cases, involving over 650,000 workers.[49]

Additionally, China has ratified eighteen Conventions of the International Labor Organizations but has not ratified several key conventions, including No. 87 (freedom of association), No. 98 (the right to organize and collective bargaining) and No. 105 (abolition of forced labor).[50] The International Labor Organization (ILO) is the world's recognized body for formulating international labor standards. Over the years, ILO has adopted over 170 international conventions. Through these conventions, ILO has developed a set of core labor standards that include freedom of association and collective bargaining, freedom from forced labor, equality of employment opportunity, gender equality, safe and healthy working conditions, etc. [China has joined twenty-three of these conventions but only twenty are in force]. All others were ratified during the era of the Republic of China (ROC) prior to 1949, but were later honored by the PRC. In comparison, the United States has not been very active in adopting these international treaties either. The United States has joined only fourteen of these conventions and ratified only twelve of them by the Senate so far.

The WTO also had major impact on China's domestic laws. According to an official estimate, in order to comply with WTO requirements, China has clarified 2,300 laws, abolished 830, and modified 325 at the national level so far. At the local level, a total 190,000 laws and regulations were clarified, abolished or modified. It is not clear how many of these revisions are related to labor laws and regulations.

The practice of collective bargaining in China remains in its infancy. Many more changes need to be made in order for the system to work. Unions' role in settling labor disputes will also need to be strengthened. The sign of the unions' expanded role was the new rules set up in the "Regulation on Handling Enterprise Labor Disputes in the PRC" of 1993. The regulation mandated the establishment of Labor Dispute Committees at the enterprise level. It stipulated that (1) such a committee must be presided by the chair of the enterprise trade union and (2) enterprises' decisions to reduce surplus workers must be made with participation of trade union representatives.

Due to recent efforts to upgrade its labor standards, China also has set some of the highest labor standards. The new labor contract law pushes for long-term labor contracts. New wage regulations have imposed some toughest provisions over unpaid wages and overtime. While the national wage regulations were still under discussion, the government in Guangdong issued a tough regulation in April 2005. It required enterprises to pay 50-100 percent penalty payments on the amount of unpaid wages. It empowered the labor inspectors to go to court to force payment if the enterprise does not pay a worker for two months or more. It stipulated sickness pay and disability pay. For legal holidays, a worker could get paid for up to four times of their regular wages.[51]

In order to ensure social stability, the Chinese government continues to put some restrictions on labor's political rights. Article 35 of the Chinese Constitution of 1982 removed labors' right to wage strikes. Chinese workers must seek mandatory arbitration of labor disputes they are involved in before they can file a lawsuit. Chinese authority also prohibits independent and multiple unions to be organized in workplaces, thus limiting workers' freedom of association, a key component in ILO conventions. There have been some reports on the arrests of labor leaders who organize such underground unions or strikes.

Some scholars in China believe that the criticism of China's labor standards is a scheme of the West to impose Western values on China in an effort to change China peacefully.[52] There are some weaknesses in this claim. Most of the internationally accepted core labor standards have very little to do with a country's economic status. There are four core labor standards recognized by the ILO to which China is also a member nation: freedom of association and the right to engage in collective bargaining, abolishment of forced labor, ban on child labor, and elimination of discrimination in employment. China's existing laws have already addressed many of these core standards. China does not compare unfavorably in all areas with other countries.

The key weaknesses in China's labor legislation are lacks in enforcement. Not only do Chinese companies ignore frequently the nation's labor laws and regulations, so do many foreign companies. Labor standards practiced in foreign enterprises are uneven. Some are very careful about their image in China and back home, while others routinely violate China's official labor standards, especially companies from Taiwan, South Korea and Hong Kong. Although China's labor standards are higher or comparable to their American counterparts in many areas, yet these standards have been seriously compromised for several reasons. The lack of willingness of local labor administrations to enforce the laws certainly contributes to the problem. However, overseas investors and managers also take advantage of China's weak administration to exploit Chinese workers to maximize their profits. They are chief violators of Chinese labors laws. Because the areas of violation fell mostly in the categories of non-core standards such as minimum of wages and working hours, there has been some attention paid from domestic and international authorities to deal with these abuses.[53]

The common problems reported on the abuse of labor rights include sweatshops, wages and pension arrears, poor treatment of farm laborers, illegal use of child labor, unfair labor contract practices, and discrimination against women. Workplace safety was also a big problem. Most reported cases about violation of labor rights took place in companies owned and managed by overseas Chinese, Taiwanese, Koreans, and business people from Hong Kong. Western companies have a much lower number of incidents involving labor abuse. According to Chan's own investigation, workers outside of China's state-owned industrial sector are the primary victims of labor rights violations. Many of them are migrant farm laborers. Some factory owners used forced and bonded labor practices by charging workers "safety deposit" or withholding their resident permits. Others required workers to work prolonged hours with only subsistence or below subsistence wages. In the worst cases, intimidation, physical violence, corporal punishment and control of bodily functions were used.[54]

The case about organizing unions in Walmart stores in China was an interesting case since Walmart never allows unions in any of its stores, including the United States, since its creation in 1976. Walmart entered into Chinese mainland in 1996. For over ten years, the ACFTU has pushed Walmart to follow Chinese labor law and allow its workers to organize unions. Walmart resisted. Local governments also did not want to push Walmart too hard since their priority is to attract foreign investment. The government began to launch the unionization drive after an AFCTU study revealing that that only 25 percent of foreign companies had established unions. The government and the official union believe that once workers are unionized they will be able to better protect

Table 7.6 Comparing PRC and U.S. Labor Standards in Several Key Areas

Items	China	United States
Health insurance	• Urban-based public insurance scheme to cover all employees	• No public insurance program for employees
Overtime pay	• 1 ½ for over 40 hours per week • 2 times for weekends • 3 times for national holidays	• 1 ½ for beyond 40 hours for non-exempt employees • none • none
Maternity leave	• Paid leave for at least three months • A half-hour breast-feeding time, up to twice during working hours	• Unpaid leave for up to twelve months • None
Holidays and vacations	• At least sixteen days • Paid vacation not implemented	• Five -six days • Paid vacation two-four weeks (based on years of service, not required by federal laws)
Employment involvement	• Worker's Congress labor participation in democratic management	• None
Labor disputes	• No right to strike • Mandatory arbitration before taking legal actions	• Right to strike after a cooling period • Voluntary arbitration before taking legal actions
Wages	• Minimum wage law • Increased sixteen times in the last two decades	• Minimum wage law • Increased very slowly

themselves. With this change of attitude in mind, the ACFTU and its local branches began aggressively to push for unionization in private and foreign-owned companies. Jinjiang is a small city in Fujian province. By 2006, 90 percent of foreign-owned companies had already established unions. Walmart established its first store in Jinjiang in 2005. Local government and trade union representatives approached the store managers a number of times about establishing a labor union among store employees, but the requests were repeatedly denied. Subsequently, the local union leaders contacted store employees directly, and 30 of the 500 employees were convinced and decided to establish their own union.[55] In the past, Walmart would rather close its stores if it could not stop a union from forming among its employees. However, the attraction of the Chinese market and the determination of the Chinese government to push for unionization left the Walmart with little choice but to yield. After communicating with the ACFTU, Walmart finally agreed to allow all stores in China to establish unions. The only justification from the company's side for breaking this so-called "Walmart philosophy" is that they believe Chinese unions are not inherently antagonistic; instead, Chinese unions tend to help business owners in promoting productivity and facilitate the formation of a cooperative enterprise culture.[56] According to the ACFTU,

> By making active coordination, seeking co-operation, relying on workers, mobilizing workers, concentrating manpower and tackling difficult problems, the All China Federation of Trade Unions and the trade unions at various levels have finally made the Walmart headquarters and its branches in China set up trade unions, which is a big event in the history of Chinese trade unions and has produced huge influence in international trade union movement.[57]

By November 2006, all sixty-three Walmart stores had established unions. This helped convinced other foreign companies to follow the trend. By 2008, over 83 percent of subsidiaries of Fortune 500 companies in China were unionized.[58] The ACFTU has increasingly become more aggressive in its effort to unionize workplaces. Between 2002 and 2008, it added 86 million workers to unions, including 66 million migrant laborers from rural areas. All together, the ACFTU has 209 million union members.[59] This makes it the largest union in the world.

Overall, China's labor standards have improved greatly in recent years. In comparison with that of the United States, China does not fall behind in every area (see Table 7.5). In the core standards area, such as the right to collective bargaining, and the right to be free from forced labor, the existing laws need to be strengthened. The problem of forced and bonded labor is clearly a violation of China's existing labor laws. However, existing laws can only protect workers if they can claim injuries from such treatment; and very few workers are willing to take a more assert effort to openly challenge their mistreatment. Some scholars suggested the government must strengthen this area by allowing public prosecutors to sue violators. In the area of collective bargaining, private business owners quite often are unwilling to engage in negotiations with trade unions since such bargaining is not mandatory in the existing laws. Since Chinese law did not clearly authorize workers to use means of strikes to force employers to come to negotiating tables, trade unions simply cannot do anything if employers chose not to enter collective agreements with their employees.

Conclusions

Labor relations in China have gone a full circle since 1949. From rejecting market to embracing market, workers have witnessed a rough ride all the way. Each time the state shifts its course in its developmental objectives, workers see their fate change as well.

Workers remain in a much weaker position to negotiate since China's employment situation is so severe. It is also unrealistic to expect that labor unions will be transformed into a pivotal voice of workers overnight. Due to the lack of freedom of association, especially the freedom to organize independent unions, China will, for the foreseeable future, remains a corporatist state. Under the existing political conditions, the state is still the most effective means to improve labor protection. Yet this does not prevent the incorporation of some elements of societal corporatism into play and does not stop the existing labor unions from playing a more assertive role in protecting their interests. Indeed, we already see some positive developments in the process.

Notes

1. Ted R. Curr, *Why Men Rebel* (Princeton, NJ: Princeton University Press, 1971).
2. Ching Kwan Lee, *Against the Law: Labor Protests in China's Rustbelt and Sunbelt* (Berkeley, Los Angeles and London: University of California Press, 2007).
3. Karl Marx and Frederick Engels, *The Communist Manifesto* (New York: International Publishers, 1948), 24-25, 44.
4. See Elizabeth J. Perry, *Shanghai on Strike: the Politics of Chinese Labor* (Palo Alto, CA: Stanford University Press, 1993) and Lynda Shatter, *Mao and the Workers: the Hunan Labor Movement 1920-1923* (Armonk, NY: M.E. Sharpe, 1982).
5. Merton Don Fletcher, *Trade Unions in Communist China*, Ph.D. dissertation, 1968, UC Berkeley, University Microfilms, Ann Arber, MI, 1969.
6. The revised "Provisional Measure Regarding Worker's Retirement and Resignation of the State Council" in 1978 further increased retirement pensions to 70 percent of retiree's regular wages if workers had worked over twenty years. Workers with a disability could receive 80 percent of their regular pay as nursing fees. Female workers' maternity leave later changed to three months.
7. Peng Qingzhao, *Gongren Zhengzhi Keben* [Workers' Political Textbook] (Beijing: Workers' Publishing House, 1952).
8. See Andrew Walder, "Wage Reform and the Web of Factory Interests," *The China Quarterly* 109 (March 1987): 22-41; Yimin Lin, "Between Government and Labor: Managerial Decision-making in Chinese Industry," *Studies in Comparative Communism* 25, no. 4 (December 1992): 381-404.

9. Jackie Sheehan, *Chinese Workers: a New History* (Florence, KY: Routledge, 1999), 97.

10. Peihua Chen, "Geming Hu? Zuhezhuyi Hu?: Hou Mao Zedong Shiqi de Gonghui He Gongren Yundong [Revolutionary? Or Corporatism--Trade Union and Labor Movement in the Post-Mao Era]," *Modern China Studies*, no 4, (1994), 5.

11. See Howard Wiarda, *Corporatism and Comparative Politics: the Other Great "ism,"* (Amonk, NJ: M. E, Sharp, 1997); Daniel Chirot, "The Corporatist Model and Socialism," *Theory and Society*, no. 9 (1980); Anita Chen, "Revolution or Corporatism– Trade Union and Labor Movement in Post-Mao Era," *Modern China Studies*, no. 4 (1994).

12. Cai Yongshun, *State and Laid-off Workers in Reform China: the Silent and Collective Action of the Retrenched* (Florence, KY: Routledge, Taylor and Francis Group, 2005), 2; Xin Gu, "Unemployment in Transition and the Reform of Chinese Socialist Welfare System," *Modern China Studies*, no. 3 (1998).

13. CCTV News, May 5, 1999, http://www.cctv.com/news/dailynews/199905/05/ (accessed December 29, 2009).

14. See a discussion of these reforms by Wei Yu, "Financing Unemployment and Pension System: What's Wrong with China's Policy," *Modern China Studies*, no. 3 (1998).

15. *Zhongguo Ribao*, January 8, 1999, Sinanet http://dailynews.sinanet.com/ (accessed December 29. 2009).

16. According to the latest official statistics, more than 60 percent of public housing has been sold to private owners.

17. National Bureau of Statistics, PRC, *China Statistics Yearbook*, 2006.

18. Zhang Haiyan and Yang Mu, "Chinese Income Disparity by Industry Reaches a Rate of 11:1," CPPCC News Portal, http://cppcc.people.com.cn/ (accessed December 26, 2009).

19. *People's Daily*, October 10, 1998.

20. Hu Angang, "Xunqiu Xinde Ruzuolu (Seeking New Soft Landing)," *Liaowang (Beijing)*, 31 (1997).

21. Feng Tongqing, "Workers and Trade Unions under the Market Economy: Perspectives from Grassroots Union Cadres," *Chinese Sociology and Anthropology* 28, no. 4 (Spring 1996), 23.

22. Anita Chan and Robert A. Senser, "China's Troubled Workers," *Foreign Affairs*, (March/April 1997): 106-107.

23. See Zhao, Minghua and Theo Nichols, "Management Control of Labor in State-Owned Enterprises," in Greg O'Leary ed., *Adjusting to Capitalism* (Armonk, NY: M.E. Sharper, 1998).

24. Detailed accounts of some of the labor strikes can be found in "Zhongguo Gonghui Minaling Xintiaozan: Laozi Jiufen, [Chinese Trade Unions Facing New Challenges: Labor Disputes]," *China Press (Qiao Pao)*, October 26, 1998; *China and the World*, no. 1, (1999), http://www.china bulletin.com (accessed December 26, 2009).

25. Feng, *op cit.*, 12.

26. Han Dongfang, "A Long Hard Journey: the Rise of a Free Labor Movement," *China Rights Forum*, Winter 1995, http://www.igc.apc.org/ (accessed November 25, 2008).

27. C. H. Chang, "The Nature of Labor Problems," *Labor Research Quarterly* (Taiwan) 95 (April 1989), 102.

28. U. S. Department of Labor, *Foreign Labor Trend: China* (1996), 6.

29. Lawrence D. Brown, *New Policies, New Politics: Government's Response to Government's Growth* (Washington D.C.: The Brookings Institution, 1983).

30. Feng, *op cit.*, 7-8.

31. *Ibid.*, 7.

32. *Ibid.*, 40-41.

33. Luigi Tomba, *Paradoxes of Labor Reform: Chinese Labor Theory and Practice from Socialism to Market* (Honolulu, HI: University Hawai'i Press, 2002), 103-107.

34. National Bureau of Statistics, "The Statistics Release of the Second National Economic Survey," Xinhua News Agency, December 26, 2009, http://news.xinhuanet.com/politics/2009-12/26/content_12705184.htm (accessed December 29, 2009).

35. Jim H. Young, Lin Zhu, "Overview of China's New Labor Dispute Mediation and Arbitration Law," Davis Wright Tremaine, LLP, http://www.dwt.com/LearningCenter/Advisories?find=2230 (accessed December 28, 2009).

36. "China Will Deal with Labor Disputes with Speedy and Satisfactory Settlement," http://www.molss.gov.cn/gb/news/2008-01/02/content_218238.htm (accessed December 29, 2009).

37. Wang Wen, "Labor Disputes Skyrocket in Beijing," *China Daily*, December 10, 2009, http://www.chinadaily.com.cn/metro/2009-12/10/content_9154121.htm (accessed December 28, 2009).

38. "Why There is an Eruption in the Number of Labor Disputes" (in Chinese) http://e-magazine.beijingreview.com.cn/VOL_001/05_CN_a.html, (accessed December 28, 2009).

39. Nicolas Groffman and John Shi, "China's New Employment Promotion Law," http://www.mallesons.com/publications/2007/Sep/9123337w.htm (accessed December 28, 2009).

40. ACWF, "Fight against Employment Discrimination," *Woman of China Magaing*, http://www.womenofchina.cn/Issues/Employment/14032.jsp (accessed December 28, 2009).

41. Beijing Renyiping Center, *Jiuye Weiquan Falu Shouce (Legal Handbook Against Job Discrimination)*, http://www.hbvhbv.name/files/Guide2009v6.doc (accessed December 28, 2009).

42 "Zhuanjia Jiedu Hetongfa (Experts Discussed the Contract Law)," Labor Contract Law Web, http://finance.sina.com.cn/g/20080201/15154483679.shtml (accessed July 30, 2008).

43. Liu Tao and Wang Qi, "The Labor Contract Law: the Debate and the Shock Wave," *Chinese Entrepreneur Magazine*, http://finance.sina.com.cn/g/20080201/ (accessed December 29, 2009).

44. Zeng Lan, "An Opinion Survey on the New Labor Contact Law," *China Enterprise Magazine*, carried by sina.com.cn, February 1, 2008, http://finance.sina.com.cn/g/20080201/15214483699.shtml (accessed December 29, 2009).

45. Leiyang Xiu Yucun, "Some Companies Exaggerated the Negative Impact of the Labor Contract Law," *People's Daily*, December 29, 2007, http://npc.people.com.cn/GB/6718517.html (accessed December 29, 2009).

46. AFL-CIO, John J. Sweeney, President, AFL-CIO, testimony before the Senate Finance Committee, "U.S. Trade with China and China's Accession to the WTO," http://www.afl-cio.org (accessed on March 12, 2003); International Confederation of Free Trade Unions (ICFTU), ICFTU China Policy, November 2002, http://www.icftu.org/ (accessed April 3, 2002).

47. Feng, *op cit.*, 11-12

48. MOHRSS, "Memorandum of the 10th Tripartite Consultation Meeting," http://w1.mohrss.gov.cn/gb/ywzn/2006-12/11/content_152776.htm (accessed December 29, 2009).

49. MHRSS, *2007 Annual Statistics Reports of Labor and Social Security*, http://w1.mohrss.gov.cn/gb/zwxx/2008-06/05/content_240415.htm (accessed December 29, 2009).

50. U. S. Department of Labor: *Foreign Labor Trend: China* (1994), 21.

51. Wang Daobin, "New Wage Regulation Will Take Effect in Guangdong," http://www.pconline.com.cn/pcjob/rs/wkch/0504/592290.html (accessed December 29, 2009).

52. Chang Kai, "WTO, Laogong Biaozhun Yu Laogong Quanyi Baozhang [WTO, Labor Standards and the Protection of Labor Rights]," *China Social Sciences*, 1 (2002), 126-134.

53 . Anita Chan, "Labor Standards and Human Rights: The Case of Chinese Workers under Market Socialism," *Human Rights Quarterly* 20, no. 4 (1998), 903.

54. *Ibid.*

55. "The Breakthrough at Walmart after Ten Years of Resistance: Six Unions Established," Aug. 15, 2006. http://info.finance.hc360.com/2006/08/15093652383.shtml (accessed December 29, 2009).

56. Ye Yongbi, "The Case of Walmart Unions: Whose Interests Are Protected?" August 10, 2006. http://info.finance.hc360.com/2006/08/10141052136-2.shtml (accessed December 29, 2009).

57. ACFTU, *Blue Paper on the Role of the Chinese Trade Unions in Safeguarding the Legitimate Rights and Interests of the Workers*, http://www.acftu.org.cn/template/10002/file.jsp?cid=67&aid=399 (accessed December 29, 2009).

58. ACFTU, "The Steady Growth of Chinese Labor Unions in Thirty Years," http://www.acftu.net/template/10004/file.jsp?cid=222&aid=80797 (accessed December 29, 2009).

59. Chen Jinsong, "China's Labor Union Become the Largest One in the World," *People's Daily* (overseas edition), http://acftu.people.com.cn/GB/67560/8202431.html (accessed December 29, 2009).

Chapter 8
The New Equity-Oriented
Health Care Reform

Cost, access and quality are three important values in health care. The issue of cost is a matter of providing health care efficiently at an affordable rate. The issue of access is a matter of distributing scarce health care resources equitably and fairly. Quality of medical care is a function of the cost and access. When health care becomes unaffordable and when the distribution of health resources is inefficient and unequal, the overall status of citizens' health suffers. Experiences in various countries have indicated that efforts to improve access tend to increase the overall costs of health care and efforts to reduce costs often result in compromises in access to health care or quality of health services provided. The efficiency-equity trade-off is present in the politics of health care as well.

Since 1979, China has attempted to use market mechanisms to restructure its outdated health care system and improve its coverage and delivery systems. In the urban areas, the government introduced many new market-based reforms in an attempt to streamline the health care industry and slow down the escalating costs of providing health care. Health insurance reforms introduced built-in incentives for consumers to reduce unnecessary utilization of health services. The hospital reform reduced government subsidies and put the burden of institutional finance on hospitals. To increase their own income, doctors have to improve their skills and compete with other doctors for patients. To control costs, the government also set up a prospective payment system, a public bidding system, and reclassifying hospitals as non-profit or for-profit entities.

These market-oriented reforms have resulted in a major overhaul of both health care finance and delivery systems. While the welfare functions of health services are phased out gradually and public expenditures on health care dropped substantially in relationship to the overall government expenditure, the efficiency of health care services and resource allocation have improved somewhat. However, the market reforms also resulted in the erosion of the political legitimacy of the government since the equity of health care took a big step back. Health care became more and more unaffordable and disparity in health finance and services got worse. Many Chinese have begun to develop a negative view about these reforms since they have started to feel the pinch on their wallets.

Beginning in 2002, the health care reform began to move away from the direction of marketization. The equity issue was once occupied the central stage of the policy debate. This chapter will examine various new programs launched in recent decades and assess their successes and failures. Part one provides some background information on the health-related reforms. Part two examines some key components of the health-care system launched between 2000 and 2009. Part three looks at the new comprehensive proposal for health care reform and the future direction of health reform in China.

Growing Disparities in Health Care

Prior to 1979, the Chinese government managed to set up a comprehensive health insurance system for the majority of its citizens through a three-tiered health care system, which include a public health insurance scheme, a labor insurance scheme, and a rural cooperative health care system. The public insurance scheme covered all employees in government, academic and social institutions, college staff and students, military personnel, and disabled veterans. The labor insurance scheme provided coverage for workers in all state-run enterprises, as well as some large collective-owned enterprises. By 1979, these two urban schemes enrolled over 137 million people. Heavily subsidized by the government, these two health insurance schemes served an important welfare function to urban workforces since no employee contributions were required. In rural areas, People's Communes established various cooperative health care schemes, covering about 93 percent of the rural population, with rural collective entities contributing an average 50 percent of costs of the medical funds.[1] Over 1.8 million bare-foot' doctors were active in providing essential health services at affordable rates to poor farmers.[2]

When China began its ambitious economic reforms in 1978, the health-care system crumbled as governments at various levels no longer guaranteed the health care insurance coverage. The reduction in public expenditures resulted in diminishing public health services and prevention. Emphasis in investment in high technology and facilities reduced the available resources for services and treatments. With the dismantlement of People's Communes, rural cooperative health care insurance coverage dropped from 90 percent in the pre-reform era to just about 10 percent in 2005. Almost all village clinics were contracted out to individual doctors or sold to private practitioners. In urban areas, employees no longer received health care for free. Urban economic reforms created many new groups of labor forces who were outside the traditional urban health insurance schemes, such as the laid-off workers, the employees of privately owned businesses, and the migrant farm laborers. In just a decade, the near universal health coverage disappeared.

Meanwhile, health-care costs increased at an alarming rate. Total health-care spending rose by 28 times between 1978 and 1997, much faster than the inflation rates during the same period. Health care wastes and overutilization were widespread among insured public employees. While their numbers were declining steadily, the resources the state provided for their coverage continued to rise uncontrollably, despite the overall decline of government spending in total health expenditure during the same time. According to a report of the

World Health Organization (WHO) published in 2000, based on the statistics of 1997, China ranked 144th in the overall health system performance, and 188th in fairness in financial contribution (among the 191 member states).[3] China's own data suggested that the ratio between urban and rural public health resource allocation was 7.4:1.[4]

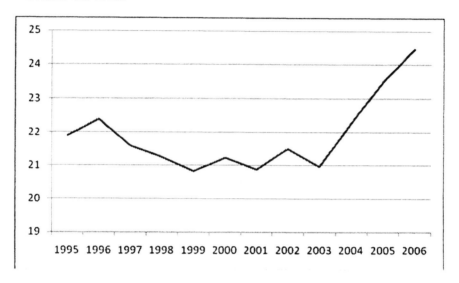

Figure 8.1 China's National Health Care Spending (1995-2006) (units: hundreds of millions)

Sources: Ministry of Health (MOH), *Health Care Statistical Annual Report* (1995-2006) http://www.moh.gov.cn.

China's own official national health survey conducted in 2003 confirmed the worsening inequality in health care. Due to the high cost and diminishing insurance coverage, more than one-third of people who were sick did not go to doctors for treatment, and 13 percent of these sick people were not treated at all. More than 80 percent of government health spending went to urban areas, and 80 percent of public spending went to major health care institutions. All together, only 20 percent of the population benefited from public health insurance programs. Even in the cities, health care inequality was also evident. By 2003, more than 76 percent of urban low-income families had no health insurance coverage at all. Uneven distribution of healthcare resources resulted in some disturbing statistics. While 90 percent of pregnant women of low-income families in urban area still received some level of prenatal care, and 85 percent of them delivered their babies in a hospital, only 75 percent of pregnant women of low-income rural families got some prenatal check-up and only 45 percent of them gave birth to their children in a hospital.[5] As a result, the infant mortality rate between rural and city was 2:1 before 2001.[6] In some of the poorest counties, the infant mortality rate increased from 50 per thousand in 1970 to 72 per thousand at the end of 1980.[7] Between 1998 and 2003, while average personal income in urban areas increased by 8.9 percent, urban health care expenditures increased 13.5 percent.[8] Ironically, as China's population continued to grow, the number of patients' visits to health care institutions kept a downward trend between 1996 and 2003, and then rose up again since that time (see Figure 8.1). By 2008, the total patient visits to health facilities reached 3.5 billion times, due to the establishment of various new health care schemes, which we will examine in the second part of this chapter.

Additionally, with the diversification of the employment system, the labor forces became more and more mobile than ever, and most of the 140 million migrant rural laborers, and millions of self-employed small business owners and their employees in the new economy went uninsured. By 2001, only 30.2 percent of urban employees were enrolled in the urban employee medical insurance. The increase in the number of retirees presented another challenge. As more and more workers reached retirement age or got into some early retirement arrangement, state-owned companies found it increasingly difficult to provide them with adequate pensions and health-care benefits.

Figure 8.2 reflects the changes in public health spending between 1952 and 2007. Between 1952 and 1982, public spending on health care rose significantly, but declined for the next twelve years. The trends began to move up again after 1996, but at a much slower rate. The public complaints about the rising costs of health care were largely a result of the decrease in public spending on health care. The profits of health institutions went up, but at the expense of equity and accessibility.

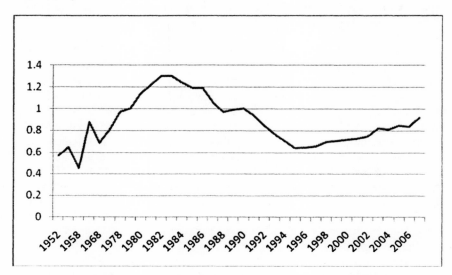

Figure 8.2 Government Health Expenditure as Percentage of GDP

Sources: Du Le-xun, Zhao Yu-xin, and Liu Guo-xiang, "Reflection on 60 Years of Development of Government Health Investment and Total Health Expenditure Accounting in China: Respect and Prospect," *Chinese Journal of Health Policy* 2, no. 10 (October 2009), 19, Table 2.

One of the causes for the initial decrease was the introduction of the second round of health care reform in the urban areas. A study of the new health-care system in Zhenjiang, one of the earliest pilot cities to begin the reform, indicates that in 1999, the city's overall health-care expenditures decreased 8 percent for the general population and 18 percent for the system's users. There was a 17 percent drop in the length of hospital stays, and 14 percent and 11 percent drops in the utilization of health services for outpatients and inpatients respectively.[9] According to a survey conducted in the 1990s, China's national sickness rate increased by 7.3 percent over the past year. However, the health-care utilization rate declined. Compared with 1993, the health-service utilization rate declined by 19 percent, and the hospitalization rate declined by 4.3 percent. Over 50 percent of urban residents chose not to receive any treatment when they got sick, and 30 percent of people needing to be hospitalized chose to stay home or opted for traditional treatment methods, fearing that health-service options would be too expensive.[10] This survey was not related to the new medical insurance plan. However, since out-of-pocket health-care expenses in the future will be at least 10 percent of a worker's wage, we will see more and more of this kind of reticence.

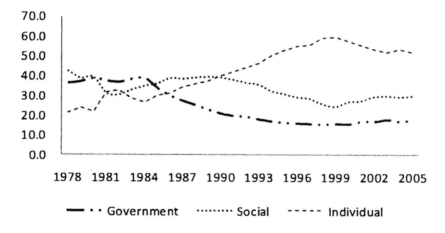

Figure 8.3 Percentage Share of Health Care Expenditures (units: percentage)

Sources: MOH, *2007 Health Care Statistics Yearbook.*

The drop in hospital utilization rates could be a correction for the old problem of overutilization of health services, which was a byproduct of the previous system for financing health care. The drop could also be a sign that the financial burden on medical care has become excessive, at least psychologically. If people postpone treatment and do not receive early diagnoses, minor illnesses may develop into ones that are more serious. Such a trend is worrisome because it may actually add to the overall health-care costs in the end. This impact will require future research.

The effect of the cost-shifting of the new reform was also evident (see Figure 8.3). In Hunan province, only 25 percent of all drugs were listed as Class A drugs, which will be reimbursed at 70 percent. The other 75 percent were all Class B medicines, and can only be reimbursed at 63 percent of the costs. On average, the individual cost of health care has increased 25 percent compared with previously.[11] In the city of Zhengzhou, the average individual health care cost between 1984 and 2005 increased 244 times, but during the same period, the average individual disposable income only increased 14 times.[12] Any major illness or chronic conditions can lead to a financial drain on any family.

Figure 8.3 also shows that the percentage of government contributions to health care declined steadily in the 1980s. Individual contributions now make up more than half of all health care expenditures. The unwillingness of the government to share the costs of health care is in sharp contrast with many of its neighbors. In Japan, the percentage of public financed health care is 81.5 percent.[13] The direct impact of the shrinking public health spending is the increased financial burden on health care consumers, and makes health care one of the new "three mountains" on top of every family.[14]

Expanding Medical Care Coverage

Losing their health benefits and coverage, state employees became increasingly irritated. According to a state document, health care has created hardship for many workers, and "[t]heir motivation for productivity and trust toward the reforms as well as the government are in serious doubt" and this in turn "has intensified social contradictions, and become a potential threat to social stability."[15] To achieve Pareto efficiency or Kaldor-Hicks efficiency, which we discussed in Chapter 2, would require the state to provide remedies to compensate workers for what they have lost. To establish a new market-driven health care system has become an urgent task for the reformers. As one commentary published by the official newspaper *People's Daily* stated that health-care reforms, as well as other social security reforms, are strategically important to not only the overall success of the entire economic reforms, but also to the "survival of the Chinese Communist Party (CCP) itself."[16]

In response to the crumbling national health insurance system, the central government started to work on developing a nation-wide new employee medical care system in the 1990s, although incremental and small-scale health-care reforms began as early as the 1980s. These reform experiments were designed to incorporate various market mechanisms into the health care system. The main concern was to cut down health care costs and to make the industry more efficient and more profitable.

The Urban Employee Medical Care Insurance Scheme

The nationwide drive for health care reform was initiated in 1993. According to a decision made by the CCP Central Committee on market reform, the new urban basic medical care insurance system for staff and workers (UBMCI-SW) would be based on the concept of social risk-pooling in which work units would no longer be providers of free health care, and employees must bear some of the costs.[17] Under the new system, a participant's medical costs will be cover by two separate medical accounts. An individual employee contributes 2 percent of his/her wages or salary to his or her individual medical account. The participant can use this balance to pay for outpatient services and medications. Employers contribute 6 percent of the sum of their employees' total wages or salaries to the general medical trust fund, but 30 percent of the employers' contributions will be allocated to employees' individual accounts.[18] The general medical trust funds are currently pooled at the city and county levels, primarily to pay for employees' in-patient and major health services.[19] City or county governments will provide operating budgets and personnel to collect, manage, and run the general trust accounts as well as the individual medical accounts. The government agencies will negotiate with health-care providers on the terms, coverage, and reimbursement of health-care services. This new system was initially experimental in many cities, starting in 1994.[20]

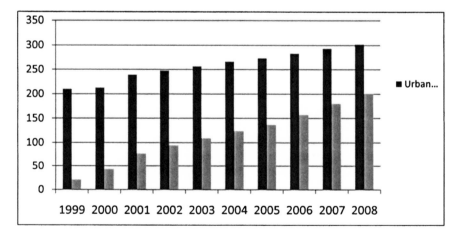

Figure 8.4 The Growth of Urban Basic Medical Care Insurance Coverage for Staff and Workers (1999-2008) (units: millions)

Sources: National Bureau of Statistics of China, *China Statistical Yearbook* (1999-2008), http://www.stats.gov.cn/.

The government launched a nation-wide campaign in 1999 to promote the new system.[21] The initial goal was to enroll within one year all urban employees and all who were self-employed. However, inexperience and bureaucratic red tape hampered the implementation process. By 2008, about two-thirds of the urban labor forces are covered by the UBMCI-SW (see Figure 8.4). With the current expansion rate, 90 percent of urban employees will be covered by 2012. At the same time, to reduce the burden of enterprises, over 7,000 enterprise-owned and -operated hospitals and health-care facilities have been turned over to local governments. [22] The separation of health insurance and service functions from enterprises paved the way for building a modern enterprise system.

The new health insurance program consolidated the old public insurance and labor insurance schemes into a single employee medical insurance program, covering employees in all types of enterprises, governmental institutions, and semi-official social groups in urban areas. Employees of private-owned and foreign-owned companies, which now consisted of the majority of urban labor forces, became eligible to enroll in the system. The coverage also included laid-off workers (6 million) and retirees (37 million).

Compared with the number of beneficiaries in 1980 (137 million), this meant the new plan would increase health-care coverage from 75 percent to 85–90 percent of urban workers. This is not in itself a significant extension of coverage demographically. There are millions of family members, non-working people, and farmers who will not directly benefit from the current insurance schemes. There are 32 million small business owners who are not required to join the plan. Therefore, the new insurance scheme is not a comprehensive health plan for all urban residents.

The success of the entire new financing system depends upon the soundness of its fiscal management. Currently, the ratio of health insurance premiums to medical funds is based on individual wages or total employee wages, not on the previous year's cost of running insurance programs. Therefore, the system could run into potential solvency problems since there certainly will be incidents with discrepancies between funds available and actual program expenditures. At the current time, the overall balance sheet is still in the black. However, the program may have to increase both employee and employer contributions if this should become an issue. For instance, in Shanghai, the employer contribution is already double the national average. In the long-run the city or county-based risk-pooling will not solve the unequal distribution of health resources since the poor regions may not have sufficient fund to provide adequate coverage to all enrollees. The only solution may lie in a gradual change towards national level risk-pooling to enhance horizontal equity.

One potential cause for budget deficits is the way retirees are being incorporated into the same insurance plan. Under the current plan, existing retirees will not pay any premiums to the system. Portions of funds from employers' contributions will be allocated to establish retirees' individual medical accounts. Considering the following three factors: the sheer number of retirees exiting jobs, the projected growing increase in the retirement population in the near future, persons who have paid very little into the program, and much higher medical system utilization rates among the elderly. We can anticipate that the cost to cover these retirees can be a tremendous financial drain on the entire system. Therefore, additional government funding is needed to make up the gap.

The New Rural Cooperative Medical Care Scheme

The rural-urban divide created the most unfair allocation of health resources. The lack of adequate access to quality health care systems has resulted in higher infant mortality, higher death rates of pregnant women, and lower life expectancy. With the collapse of the rural cooperative health care system, farmers became very vulnerable to sickness. Many fell into poverty because of chronic or major illnesses.

To address this issue, the government decided in October 2002 to reestablish the rural cooperative health system.[23] However, since the rural collective is gone, there is no public financial support to sustain the system. The government eventually decided to use public funds to fill the vacuum. The sheer size of the rural population demands a substantial amount of resources to be allocated to cover the 900 million plus rural population.

The effort to restore the cooperative health care system actually began in 1993. In 1994, the Ministry of Health (MOH), Ministry of Agriculture (MOA) and the World Health Organization (WHO) launched an experimental project on a new cooperative health care scheme. The experiment was carried out in fourteen counties and cities. It was not until 1997 that the MOH decided to promote the new system nationwide.[24] However, the new system asked local people to organize the system and relied mainly on individual contributions to support the system financially. By 2002, less than 10 percent villagers had signed up for the system. Most farmers were unable to shoulder even the modest cost of the program.

In the new program promoted after 2003, the government organized, guided, and supported the system. However, the program would only cover major illness and some of the out-patient services. The central government, local governments and participants (each party contributes 10 *yuan* initially) would contribute to the program's finance. Participation in the new program is voluntary. Their contribution would be put in their individual account, and would be used to pay for outpatient visits. The state and collective contributions would be put into a pooled account to help pay for the cost of the treatment of major illnesses. In 2006, the central government decided to increase public financial support in order to increase the program's coverage. The central government and local governments would each double their contributions to 20 *yuan* for each participant. In another words, the government now will pay 60 percent of the total cost of insuring each rural participant. In 2008, these contributions were doubled again, with the state and county governments each contributing 40 *yuan* to each insured and the each participant would pay 20 *yuan* annually. It was hoped that with the increased public subsidies, the coverage would be extended to most rural residents by 2010.

The 2003 plan proved to be a workable one. Enrollment in the program has increased rapidly. By the end of 2007, nearly 90 percent of rural residents already enrolled, and 260 million peasants benefited from the program (see Table 8.1). Compared to the urban health insurance plan, the benefits of the rural pro-

gram are still very limited. It only pays for 50 percent of the cost of hospitalization initially (now it is about 60 percent). For doctor's visits, a patient can only
be reimbursed for 7-8 *yuan* per visit. The annual maximum of patient reimbursement for doctor's visits varies greatly from county to county. Some limit
annual individual reimbursements to 140 *yuan*, while other set it at 400 *yuan*.[25]
One direct result of the new insurance system is the increase of the rate of health
services utilization. Farmers are more likely to visit a doctor in case of an illness. For in-patient services, the system encourages patients to seek services at
the township level. A regressive payment system is in place to provide financial
incentives for patients to seek services locally instead of going to the more expensive health centers and hospitals. For instance, the patient will only receive
20 percent of reimbursements if services are provided at a hospital beyond the
county level, but will cover 50 percent if treated at the township level. Patients
still have to pay a deductible of 300-600 *yuan* per illness.[26] As a result, village-
level health clinics provide most basic services. By the end of 2008, every village now has at least one village clinic. More than one million village doctors
and nurses worked in these village clinics. They are mostly privately owned.
Over 60 percent of farmers go to these clinics first when they become ill. In
Qinghai province, some of the clinics are equipped with X-ray machines, Type-
B Ultrasonic Imaging Systems and ECGs. However, in other provinces, these
clinics are prohibited from providing imaging and laboratory services. The training of medical stuff remains a main issue. It is hard to find good doctors who
want to work in these village-level health clinics.

According to the 2008 National Health Survey, only one-third of rural patients received reimbursements for out-patient services; 85 percent of farmers
who received in-patient services were reimbursed, and reimbursement was only
34 percent of their total expenses for their hospital bills.[27]

Table 8.1 Development of the New Rural Cooperative Medical System

Year	Counties that have the program	Peasants enrolled (In millions)	Percentage of the population
2005	678	179	75.7
2006	1,451	410	80.7
2007	2,451	730	86.2
2008	2,729	814	91.5
2009	--	833	94.0

Sources: MOH, *Statistic Almanac of Health Care Development in China* (2005-2009),
http://www.moh.gov.cn.

The new rural health care system is based on a three-tiered model that is
promoted in the urban area. Each county will have a government-owned hospital
that is responsible for treatment for more serious illnesses. At the *xiang* and
township level, there will be only one government-owned health service center.

At the village level, there will be at least one health clinic in every village. Its main responsibilities include public health, basic service for routine care, and health education. The existing health service centers at town and county levels will be consolidated. For that purpose, the governments will maintain one public clinic in each town. Some of them will be designated as the central clinics. All facilities will receive government funds to improve their infrastructures and build necessary facilities before 2010. This has been the largest government investment in rural health care facilities since the collapse of the old rural cooperative health care system in the 1980s. Additional government-owned clinics will be privatized and turned into joint-holding entities. Market mechanisms will be used to ensure their operational efficiency. All employees will be put on labor contracts. The management of the clinics will be separated by ownerships. Individuals can contract with the government for the management of these facilities. In the city of Ninbo, since 2004, the city government has invested over 490 million *yuan* to build 121 standardized township health clinics, has established 1,250 community health service stations, and has extended its coverage to 93 percent of its rural population.[28]

The Urban Resident Insurance Scheme

With the rapid expansion of the employee insurance scheme and the rural cooperative health insurance scheme, most of the working-age populations are now covered. However, some groups of the populations are still left out. One is the elderly who are not part of the retirees of state-owned enterprises. The second group is the children, and the third group is the family-operated small business owners and their employees. The final group is the 140 million migrant farmer laborers. State-owned enterprises generally allowed coverage to the family members of an employee, but usually at half the cost.

To provide health insurance coverage for these groups, starting in 2007, various forms of medical care insurance schemes were established. The goal was to create a mandatory urban resident insurance by 2010. Like the rural cooperative health care scheme, the government would provide sizeable subsidies to individual participants. Under the new program, an adult would pay a monthly premium of 100 *yuan* with a state subsidy of 50 *yuan*. Children's cost was 30 *yuan* a month with 50 *yuan* state subsidy. For the disabled, the premium was only 40 *yuan* with 110 *yuan* state subsidy. The insurance would only cover major illnesses and urgent care on an outpatient basis or inpatient hospitalization. The annual deductible was quite high, ranging from 540 to 980 *yuan* per illness. The co-payment ranged between 20 percent and 50 percent. Most of the services were limited to community health centers. Referrals were needed to go to a regional hospital for further treatment. Maximum insurance benefits ranged between 16,000 to 20,000 *yuan* annually.[29] The main beneficiaries of the new resident-based health programs were children under age of eighteen, including students in technical schools.

By 2008, there were 116.5 million people enrolled in the new health insurance system. The new system was also extended to migrant laborers. About 42.5

million or one-third of migrant labor forces had enrolled in the program by 2008.[30] Table 8.3 is the summary of the enrollment status of employees and residents in various medical insurance schemes.

After some intensive efforts since 1999, China has reestablished a basic national health insurance system. The new system has several features: First, it is no longer a free public welfare system and individuals must contribute to their health insurance premiums. Second, the health benefits remain very different from plan to plan, with the employee health plan as the best plan. Third, the central and local governments had to provide heavy subsidies to ensure the affordability of these plans. Finally, the level of risk-pooling remains very low, and may take a while to develop into a comprehensive national plan. Nonetheless, thanks to these efforts, the inequality of health care has been reduced, and the health care utilization rate has gone up again, a positive sign indeed. More and more people are no longer postponing their treatment because of financial restraint.

Table 8.2 Social Insurance Composition of Residents   (units: percentage)

Item	Total		Urban		Rural	
	2008	2003	2008	2003	2008	2003
Basic Medical Insurance of Employees	12.7	8.9	44.2	30.4	1.5	1.5
Government Insurance Program	1.0	1.2	3.0	4.0	0.3	0.2
Basic Medical Insurance of Resident	3.8	--	12.5	--	0.7	--
New Rural Cooperative Medical Scheme	68.7	--	9.5	--	89.7	--
Other Social Insurance	1.0	12.0	2.8	15.2	0.4	10.9
No Social Medical Insurance	12.9	77.9	28.1	50.4	7.5	87.3

Sources: National Survey on Health Service in 2003 and 2008; *Statistical Summary of China's Health Care from MOR (2009)*, Ministry of Health, http://www.moh.gov.cn/.

Medial Relief Systems

To help people who live under the poverty line to pay for their medical expenses, China expanded its medical relief program after 2003. On February 26, 2005, the Ministry of Civil Affairs (MCA), the MOH, the Ministry of Labor and

Social Security (MOLSS), and the Ministry of Treasury (MOT) issued a joint directive on establishing a rural medical relief system for the rural poor. The directive called for the establishment of the new system within four to five years. Local governments were asked to establish special medical relief funds with money allocated by general revenue, lottery proceeds, and social donations.

On the same day, the four ministries also issued another directive calling for the establishment of an urban-based medical relief system. However, the medical assistance was restricted to major illnesses and procedures with high out-of-pocket deductible payments. In Xinzheng city of Henan province, for example, a family living in poverty had to pay the first 1,000 *yuan*, and the assistance could only be applied to twenty-six serious medical conditions. The maximum assistance a beneficiary could receive was 5,000 *yuan*.[31] The process of applying the assistance was burdensome. In the rural medical relief program, a patient or his or her family had to pay all the costs upfront. After being treated, he needed to apply to village committee with a number of supporting documents and the application for assistance. A villager representative meeting would then meet and approve his application. After that, the application went to the county or township government for approval. Once this was done, the application went to the civil affairs department for final approval.[32] The process could take more than a month. Despite the limits and complications, the number of people who applied for medical assistance grew rapidly from 2003 to 2008.

Table 8.3 Medical Relief Beneficiaries and Expenditures

Indicator	2004	2005	2006	2007	2008
Number of Recipients (10,000)	641	970	1,746	3,338	4,247
Urban	--	115	187	442	513
Rural	641	855	1,559	2,896	3,734
Medical Relief Expenditure (100 million)	4.4	11.0	21.2	42.5	59.3
Urban	--	3.2	8.1	14.4	23.5
Rural	4.4	7.8	13.1	28.1	35.8

Sources: Source: National Survey on Health Service in 2003 and 2008; *Statistical Summary of China's Health Care from MOR (2009)*, http://www.moh.gov.cn/.

In June 2009, the four ministries issued a new directive to further expand the pool of potential beneficiaries and simplified the procedure for receiving the medical relief. Today, a patient no longer has to pay everything upfront. The relief fund can kick in while the patient is still being treated. The amount of government contributions and the maximum amount of reimbursements also increase considerably. In Tianjin, the maximum annual reimbursement for a patient covered by the relief program has been raised from 10,000 to 100, 000 *yuan*. The outpatient services are now covered with a maximum allowable reimbursement between 60 to 200 *yuan*.[33] To assist the enrollment of the new urban resident health insurance program, the medical relief fund can also be used to help some families pay for their premiums.

Apparently, the medical relief program remains to be very restrictive even with the latest expansion. According to official figures of 2009, China's urban population living under poverty line can was 23.4 million, and the rural population living under poverty line was about 47 million. Another 6 million urban employees suffered from economic hardship due to personal or family difficulties.[34] With only 5 million of them receiving some medial relief, the government certainly can do more in helping this underprivileged social group.

The reluctance to set up a more generous welfare program in health care may have something to do with the concern over its abuse and the possible negative impact on the work ethic. It is here we see the classical dilemma of the trade-off between equity and productivity. The government may want to think twice if it wants to create a similar welfare program such as the Medicaid program in the U.S., which has caused so much of the financial burdens to the state and federal governments and is known for rampant fraud and abuse.

The Elimination of Public Health Insurance System

The public insurance system established in the early 1950s continued to exist after 1979. The public insurance provided free coverage for all government employees, military personals, college students and graduate students, and employees of state affiliated social institutions such as full-time employees of trade unions and the so-called "democratic" parties. By 2009, most local and provincial governments have eliminated the public health insurance, and replaced it with the new employee-based medical care insurance schemes. By 2012, college students, employees of central governments, and staff of social institutions will all complete the merger with the new urban medical care insurance schemes.

With the establishment of the urban medical insurance of employees, the new rural cooperative medical system, the urban resident medical insurance program, and the medical relief system, China has overhauled its entire medical insurance systems. These systems have expanded rapidly since 2005. Despite the notable achievement, medical coverage remains very limited, and the financial burdens of the people are still considerably higher than what it was before the economic reforms. China still needs some time to consolidate and perfect these new systems before they can be expanded into a unified national health insurance system that is equitable and fair.

The Future Direction of Health Care Reform

During the last two decades, there was a series of heated debates on the direction of health care reform. Generally speaking, there were two groups in the debates.

The pro-market advocates were in favor of marketization of health care industry. The opponents of this approach insisted on the welfare and social functions of health care, and demanded an active role for the government to ensure adequate access to health care and services.

The effort to turn hospitals care institutions into self-sufficient economic entities in the 1980s forced hospitals to increase their charges and fees, causing the loss of accessibility to health care. Health ethics was compromised due to rampant corruptions, such as doctors taking bribes from patients and drug companies, prescribing unnecessary medication and technology usage, and making false advertisements. As a result, the relationship between doctors and patients was at all time low. In 1993, the vice minister of the MOH, Yin Dakui, openly opposed to the marketization of health care. He argued that health care was a public product serving the public interest and it should have an important role in ensuring social justice and fairness.

One of the major problems with China's existing health care system is that health care resources are not distributed equitably. The high out-of-pocket expenses have limited access to health care. City residents consume a majority of the limited health dollars while the majority people who live in the rural area have little or no access to adequate health care. In 1998, government invested 58.7 billion *yuan* in health care. Only 9.25 billion went to the rural areas.[35] The percentage of public spending in the total spending declined sharply. So the latest health care reform is concentrated in two areas. One is to rebuild the rural health care system, and the other is to reemphasize the public service functions of health care institutions.

On July 29, 2005, the Development Research Center (DRC) of the State Council shocked the nation by releasing its final report on China's health care policy reform. It claimed that, taken as a whole, the market-oriented reform in health care was unsuccessful, and the reform had contributed to the escalating costs of and difficulties in access to health care.[36] This negative assessment triggered a new round of debate on health care reform in China and paved the way for the second round of health care reform that was unveiled at the end of 2008.

The year 2005 was a turning point in China's health care reform. Once again, attention was shifted away from pushing for further marketization and focused more on fairness issues. In September 2006, the State Council put together a new health care reform coordination committee, which consisted of eleven ministries and agencies of the State Council. The committee engaged in extensive debates on ten different reform plans submitted by various agencies.

On October 14, 2008, a new comprehensive health care reform proposal was published for public comments. It targeted 2020 as the date for the establishment of a comprehensive system of basic health care, which included public health, health services, health insurance, and pharmaceutical supply subsystems. It emphasized the public service functions of health care system, and the dominant role of the government in providing health care financing and services. It promised to increase the share of health care spending in the government's total expenditures and to provide budgetary support for all public health care institutions so that they do not have to rely on incomes generated through charges on in-house pharmacies and prescribing unnecessary procedures and medical tests. It moved away from the total free market approach and brought pricing control back, especially for non-profit public hospitals. It called for increased governmental subsidies to participants of urban resident medical insurance and rural cooperative medical systems.

No significant new changes were made to the health insurance schemes that were put into place since 2002. Under the plan, the urban employee medical insurance system will be expanded to provide coverage for the uninsured, employees in the private sectors, retirees, and companies in economic hardship. The urban resident insurance program will extend its coverage for the elderly and the poor. The rural cooperative health system will be promoted nationwide. It is hoped that eventually the three separated public systems will be unified. The government determined to strengthen areas that are the weakest in the current system, namely, public health, community health services, and rural health services.

In the wake of the global financial crisis of 2009, the State Council took a swift action by announcing a four trillion *yuan* economic stimulus plan. As a part of the stimulus package, the state issued its much debated ambitious health reform plan with a total projected 850 billion *yuan* investment to support these reforms. The following is some of the highlights of this plan:[37]

(1) Expand basic health insurance coverage to 90 percent of the population in three years and reduce out-of-pocket costs of the covered population on health care and increase the amount of state subsidizes to participants of urban resident and rural cooperative medical insurances to 120 *yuan*. This sounds very ambitious, but since a majority of the urban and rural population have already enrolled in some type of social insurance programs, so that the goal can be easily met in probably one or two years ahead of the schedule. At the end of 2007, over 86 percent of the rural population already enrolled in the rural cooperative medical care insurance. Over 180 millions workers in urban areas also enrolled in the employee medical insurance program.[38] In Henan province, 92 percent of farmers already enrolled in the rural medical insurance scheme by 2008, and in some areas, the government subsidies had already been increased to 160 *yuan* per enrollee. The maximum plan benefits were also increased from 10,000 to 30,000 *yuan* in some places.[39] The MOH wanted to increase the reimbursement for in-patient services from 60 percent to 65 percent. In 2009, the government subsidizes for the rural health program amounted to 62.7 billion *yuan*, and paid for 490 million people's medical expenses.[40] By 2010, the subsidized amount could go up to 100 billion *yuan* due to the proposed increase in state's contributions to individual enrollees.

(2) Establish a national medicine index. The idea behind this is to control the costs of medicines and stop abuses in prescribing expensive drugs. In order to be reimbursed, patients and doctors must choose medicines listed in the national index.

(3) Strengthen the health service delivery system. Under the plan, the state will invest significant amounts of money to modernize 2,000 county hospitals, 290,000 township health hospitals, 5,000 township health centers, 3,700 urban

community health service centers, and 11,000 neighborhood health service stations. To improve the quality of rural health services, the government promised to offer trainings to nearly two millions doctors and nurses who worked in the rural health care system.

(4) Promote equality in basic public health services. The government will provide free annual checkups for the elderly, wellness care for children under age three, prenatal and post-natal care and follow-ups for pregnant women, prevention and treatment consultation for people who have high blood pressure, diabetes, mental illness, and TB. The government will also provide free immunization and treatment for TB and AIDs, assistance to rural pregnant women to have hospital delivery,

(5) Increase government-provided subsidies to public hospitals and eliminates surcharges on drugs imposed by hospitals. While the number of public hospitals will be reduced, some of the existing public hospitals will be privatized.

Under the plan, the government continues to promote basic health care coverage and services and fair distribution of health care resources. However, these new policies will not reduce the financial burdens of health consumers in any significant way. One interesting development in 2009 is the universal health insurance program established in Shenmu County, Shaanxi province. Shenmu is a main producer of coal. Between 1998 and 2008, the county's revenue increased 100 times due to the development of Shenhua Coal Mine Company. In 2008, its per capita GDP surpassed US$10,000, three times more than the national average. The 1.7 billion *yuan* local tax revenue also made the county one of the richest ones in the country. With this financial strength, the county decided to establish a universal health insurance program that enabled all county residents to receive health services literally "free." Although it still separated the urban resident medical insurance from rural cooperative medical insurance schemes, the county government allocated on average 400 *yuan* per resident to subsidize their health care, far exceeding the 120 *yuan* goal set by the national government by 2012. As a result, a patient, after paying 400 *yuan* annual deductible, will have his or her medical bills covered by the insurance up to a maximum of 300,000 *yuan* per year. The county spent about 170 million *yuan* to support this new program. All residents, regardless their employment and household-registration status, were covered by the program with the same benefits. Since the system started in March 1, 2009, for a while, all hospitals were filled with patients and hospital beds were in short supply. The direct beneficiaries were those poor families who had been unable to pay for their services, and now received the treatments or operations they needed.[41] While some worried about the potential abuses by consumers and its long-term financial consequences on the county government's budget,[42] some celebrated this model as a return to socialism.[43]

The experiments of Shenmu County may point to the future direction of China's health care reform. The current health care insurance schemes can only be considered a transitional one since it still embraces different treatment of citizens based on their occupation, residence, and economic status. This is probably the direction China should strive to achieve in the long run. However, the current government is not in such a position to offer this kind of universal coverage to all of its citizens. If the State Council is willing to increase the public contribution to 400 *yuan* per person, like Shenmu did, it will solve most of the problems with inequality of health care service. But the total cost will be 520 billion *yuan*. This is certainly unbearable financially at the moment.

The State Council's decision to deepen health care reform has clearly redefined health care as a public utility and should be treated as a public product, managed and provided by the government. This decision represents a departure from the decades-long pursuit of market-driven health care reform, and a refocus on the issue of equity in health care. The goal is to achieve basic universal health coverage for all.

Conclusions

China's health reform is struggling with different models. In the early days of the republic, socialized health care provided a universal health care system for the public employees in urban areas. During the reform era, the efficiency-oriented guiding principles pushed China toward a market-driven system similar to the United States. The reform since the 1990s has embraced a social insurance model similar to that of Germany and Japan. The recent reform initiative strengthened the role of the government in the new health care system and reestablished the public nature of the health care services. The Shenmu model, however, challenged this model and shed some lights on the future direction of China's health insurance systems. So in the foreseeable future, we will continue to see more debates about the pros and cons of the two very different approaches. Some have already warned the government not to get too involved in health care.[44]

Notes

1. Ministry of Health, PRC, *1998 Health Statistics Index*, http://www.moh.gov.cn (accessed May 30, 2002).

2. Chen Meixia, "Danizhuan: Zhonghua Renmin Gonghe Guo de Yiliao Weisheng Gaige [The Big Transformation: the Reform of the Health Care Reform in the People's Republic of China]," Wuyou Zhixiang [Utopia], http://www.wyzxsx.com/ (accessed January 10, 2010).

3. WHO, *The World Health Report 2000*, 152.

4. Wang Yonghun, "Zhonguo de Caizheng Jundenghua yu Zhuanyi Zhifu Tizhi Gaige [China's Fiscal Equity and Reform of Fiscal Transfer System]," *Zhongyang Caijing Daxue Xuebao [Journal of Central China Finance and Economics University]* 9 (2006): 1-15.

5. MOH, "Statistical Release of the 3rd National Health Survey," December 12, 2003, http://www.moh.gov.cn (accessed January 2, 2010).

6 MOH, *Statistical Summary Report of China's Health Care (1997-2001)*, http://www.moh.gov.cn/ (accessed January 10, 2010).

7. Chen Meixia, *op cit.*

8. *Ibid.*

9. Gordon G. Liu, et al., "Urban Health-care Reform Initiative in China: Findings in Its Pilot Experiments in Zhenjiang City (I), *International Journal of Economic Development* 1, no. 4 (1999): 504-525.

10. MOH, "The First National Heath Survey," http://moh.gov.cn (accessed January 10, 2008).

11. Hunan Urban Study Team, "An Analysis of Problems with the Current Health Insurance System," National Bureau of Statistics (NBS), http://www.stats.gov.cn (accessed May 17, 2001).

12. Xing Jin and Zhang Zhiying, "A Survey of Health Spending in Zhengzhou Found a 244 Times Increase," *Zhengzhou Wanbao*, August 10, 2005.

13. Chris L. Peterson and Rachel Burton, *U.S. Health Care Spending: Comparison with Other OECD Countries*, Congress Research Service Report, September 2007.

14. The other two are education and housing.

15. MOLSS, *op cit.*, no. 13 "Why the Health-care Insurance Reform Is Essential to the Long Stability of the Country."

16. *People's Daily*, July 26, 2000.

17. CCP Central Committee, "Decisions on Market Reform."

18. It varies among different age groups. Younger workers will get much less from employers' contribution, while older workers will get more.

19. Although it is currently pooled together by cities and counties, it may go up to a higher level, such as provinces, in the future, according to an official document.

20. Commission on System Reform, State Council, "Decision on the Experiments of Employee Health-care System," Commission on System Reform Document No. 51 (1994); Office of State Council, "Decision on Expanding Employee Health-care Reform Trials," State Council, Document, No. 16 (1996).

21. The CCP Central Committee and the State Council, "Decision on Health-care Reform and Development," CCP Document, No. 3 (1997), January 15, 1997.

22. Zhou Beichuan, "Investigation and Discussion on the Separation of Hospitals from Enterprises," *People's Daily*, November 24, 2000.

23. The CCP and the State Council, "Decisions on Strengthening the Works of Rural Health Care," October 20, 2003, http://www.people.com.cn/ (accessed January 10, 2010).

24. MOH, "Circular on Developing and Perfecting Rural Cooperative Health System," May 28, 1997. http://www.people.com.cn/ (accessed January 10, 2010).

25. Hao Xiao and Yuan Zhou–kang, "Analysis of the Implementation of Out-patient Pooling Funds of the New Rural Cooperative Medical System in the Central and Western Areas of China," *Chinese Journal of Health Policy* 2, no. 5 (May 2009): 45-49.

26. Wang De-hua and Lu Yao, "An Analysis of Issues of the New Rural Cooperative Medical System in Heilongjiang Province," *Chinese Journal of Health Policy* 2, no. 5 (May 2009): 50-53.

27. Chinese Center for Disease Control and Prevention, "Main Statistical Result of the 4th National Health Survey," http://www.chinacdc.net.cn/ (accessed January 10, 2010).

28. "Recommendations to Speed up the Construction of Township Health Clinic and Community Service Station in Xiang and Township" from website of Ninbo Committee of Chinese People's Political Consultative Conference, http://www.nbzx.gov.cn/ (accessed January 10, 2010).

29. The State Council, "Opinions on the Pilot Project of Urban Resident Health Insurance System," http://www.gov.cn/zwgk/2007-07/24/ (accessed December 29, 2009).

30. NBS, *Annual Statistical Report* (2008), http://www.stats.gov.cn/ (accessed January 10, 2010).

31. Xinzheng City Government, "Implementation Plan on Urban Medical Relief," http://xinzheng.gov.cn/html/20080703/248269.html (accessed January 10, 2010).

32. The Department Civil Affairs, Jilin provincial government, "Application Procedure of Rural Medical Relief for People under Poverty" http://www.jl.gov.cn/ (accessed January 10, 2010).

33. http://news.xywy.com/ (accessed January 10, 2010).

34. Pan Hui, "Qianjia Wanhu Wen Nuan Liu [Poverty Relief Went to Many Poor household]," People.com.cn., http://politics.people.com.cn/ (accessed Jan. 10, 2010). Rural poverty lines are determined by the State Council. In 2007, a farmer earning an annual income of less than 1,067 *yuan* (US$156) was considered poor. If his income was less than 785 *yuan*, he was in the absolute poverty category. http://www.syfpb.gov.cn/ (accessed on January 10, 2010).

35. http://www.ce.cn/finance/insurance/zbdjt (accessed January 10, 2010).

36. The Development Research Center (DRC) of the State Council, *Assessment and Recommendations of China's Health Care Reform (Executive Summary)*, http://www.china.com.cn/chinese/health/927874.htm (accessed on January 10, 2010).

37. The State Council, "The Implementation Plan of the Near-term Priorities of Pharmaceutical and Medical Care Reform," the State Council, Document No. 12, 2009, http://www.gov.cn/zwgk/2009-04/07/ (accessed January 16, 2010).

38. MOH, *Statistical Almanac of Health Care Development in China* (2005-2007), http://www.mor.gov.cn (accessed January 10, 2010).

39. *Shangdu.com*, January 31, 2009, http://news.shangdu.com/ (accessed January10, 2010).

40. http://moh.gov.cn (accessed January 10, 2010).

41. Zhu Wenyi, "An Investigative Report of the Shenmu Health Reform," Chinaelections.org, http://www.chinaelections.org/Newsinfo.asp?NewsID=150074 (accessed January 10, 2010).

42. http://money.163.com/09/0518/ (accessed January 10, 2010).

43. Wang Mei, "The Debate over Shenmu Health Reform," Chinaelections.org, http://www.chinaelections.org/NewsInfo.asp?NewsID=149345 (accessed January 15, 2010).

44. Jiang Yunyun, "New Health Reform Should Avoid Excessive Government Involvement," Chinaelections.org, http://www.chinaelections.org/ (accessed January 10, 2010).

Chapter 9
Conclusions:
Toward a New Chinese Polity

Since 2002, the Chinese political leaders have invested a lot of energy to steer the high-speed running train of development in a new direction before its crash. In the name of "scientific development," a new politics of equity is replacing the politics of efficiency. The issue of sustainable growth is not only an economic issue but also a political one as well. The achievement-based utilitarian legitimacy has helped the ruling party to maintain its utilitarian-based legitimacy despite the significant weakening of its original legitimacy in the wake of the June 4 crackdown. Now the decades of efficiency-driven development have created new social problems and new political forces that the old system of political legitimization can no longer accommodate. To make the state sustainable, there is a urgent need to strengthen its original and procedural justification.

This book is a study about the rising politics of equity-enhancement and its impact on the political legitimacy of the Chinese state, and most importantly, on the future of China's social and political reforms. The new politics has produced a set of new governing philosophies, a new group of political elites, and a new round of social and political reforms aimed at promoting equity and equality. In the following discussion, we will summarize major findings of this book.

The New Mandate of Heaven

At the current time, the overwhelming consensus is that there is a great need for social and political equity as well as economic equality. At beginning of 2010, People's Daily ran a special edition on income distribution on its website people.com.cn. The title of the edition is "Do We Want Equity or Efficiency?" The opinion survey carried by the same site collected 4,028 responses in just a few days. An overwhelming majority of them believed that equity should be given priority (Figure 9.1). It is no doubt that equity-enhancement has become the new mandate of heaven. Leaders in Beijing have to take these calls for actions more seriously in order to stay in power.

Since 2002, Beijing's focus has shifted toward overcoming various economic disparities such as income, regional development, and the urban-rural divides. The power transition from the so-called third generation to the fourth one has created the momentum for this major reorientation. At present, it appears that the new leaders in Beijing are busy formulating new reform schemes designed to address their innate deficiency in political legitimacy. As we found in Chapters 2 and 3, a set of new governing philosophies, based on "scientific development" and "harmonious society," has replaced Deng Xiaoping's pragmatism. A new group of non-engineer elite is ascending to power steadily.

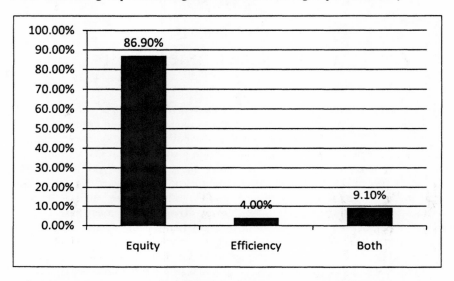

Figure 9.1 Responses on the Question "Which One Should Be Given Priority: Equity, Efficiency, or Both?"

Sources: people.com.cn,   http://voting.people.com.cn/vote_show/index.php?qid=9783 (accessed January 18, 2010).

If Deng's reform was a major breakthrough in contemporary Chinese politics, then the new politics of equity is a process of rationalization of that breakthrough.[1] It is the new problems produced by the economic breakthrough that have triggered the latest political efforts to find new policy solutions and formulate a new developmental model. These new policies will necessitate many changes in the existing political institutions (such as Big Ministry Reform, the endorsement of deliberative democracy, the change of the election law to embrace equal representation of rural and urban population) and leadership styles (such as the new slogan of "governing for the people"). These new institutions, styles and behaviors constitute what we termed the new politics of equity.

The revival of the politics of equity is part of the political cycle that has characterized Chinese politics in modern history. On the one hand, efforts to maximize efficiency will compromise equity, and consequently, invite efforts to correct the equity deficiency. On the other hand, excessive efforts to enhance equity will likely have a negative impact on efficiency. This balancing act between the achievements of these two objectives constitutes a dynamic force for political development in China.

The politics of equity differs significantly from the politics of efficiency. Equity is a function of political power. An unbalanced distribution of political power will lead to political as well as economic inequality. If the institutions that produce the inequality in power and wealth are not reformed, the goal of equity will be unattainable. If the developmental model is unsustainable, then the regime's legitimacy will be in question. That's what is behind all the rush to the policy innovations. The renewed call for political reform and a gradual opening up of political participation may offer a promising solution to the problem of legitimacy deficiency, which will be discussed later; they have reignited the hope for getting the stalled democratization process going again.

Classic liberalists such as Adam Smith believed that market is the best mechanism to achieve economic efficiency. However, Smith also pointed out that no society can be flourishing and happy "if the greater part of the members is poor and miserable."[2] Unfortunately, as many critics of market have pointed out, market does fail from time to time and will produce various forms of injustice such as unequal and unfair allocation, economic polarization, monopolization, alienation and exploitation. These problems cannot be resolved by continued economic growth. Only a major overhaul of the "superstructure," using a Marxist term, can bring about changes needed to broaden the social support for the party-state. The new politics of equity-enhancement has gradually taken shape since the beginning of the new millennium. The new governing philosophy, the rise of new political elite, and formulation of new public policies have institutionalized this "new politics."

China's move to rationalize its reform is indeed long overdue. It is true that China's success in economic reform has greatly improved China's economic performance since 1979. However, the widening income gaps between rural and urban populations, the emergence of the new urban poor, the worsening regional disparity between the more developed coastal regions and the western part of China, and the widespread public criticisms of market-oriented reforms in health and education in recent years have put the reformers on defensive. The mounting pressure for social justice has resulted in escalating the number of disputes, complaints, protests, and unrests. Will China encounter a similar public interest movement that troubled the United States in the 1970s? Can technocratic managers survive the onslaught of the moralists who demand the government provide fair and equitable distribution of wealth and values?[3]

Furthermore, many problems facing China today, such as technocracy, which has taken roots in China's economic and political system since the 1980s, is an important step towards acquiring what Max Weber has termed a rational-legal basis of political legitimacy, the lack of popular sovereignty and an innate tendency toward an oligarchic meritocracy will eventually weaken the legitimacy of the bureaucratic technocrats. Can China move beyond technocracy? Will China improve political and social equity without sacrificing economic efficiency? Can an optimal balance between efficiency and equity be achieved through proper implementation of equity-maximizing policy?

The answers to these questions are largely dependent on two developments. First, the excessive pursuit of equality and a social welfare system may slow China's economic growth and hinder its performance. It is projected that China needs to maintain an 8 percent annual GDP growth rate in order to provide enough jobs for the new labor forces and migrant rural labor forces. In many areas, the improvement of efficiency remains a major challenge. If China suffers a major economic downtown, the welfare system that is being put in place will become a financial drain on the government's budget.

The second development is the transformation of the corporatist state to a democratic one. As we have seen in the case of community governance, the demand for political equity and participation will challenge the authoritarian rule of the technocrats. What lies ahead is what former Premier Zhu Rongji called a *dilei zheng* (minefield) and is filled with dangers. The current political leaders in Beijing have no doubt that there is an urgent need to promote democratic reform to tackle the equity issue and some have vowed to *shachu yitiao xuelu* (open a blood-filled passageway).[4] But the last thing they want is to give up party control; and every reform proposed is designed to strengthen the ruling capacity of the party the state. So in the foreseeable future, the democratization process will continue to be piecemeal and incremental. One may hope that this kind of incremental change may eventually accumulate into another major breakthrough.

The current consensus within the CCP is that the development of inner party democracy must take precedence over implementing democratic reforms at the national level, and deliberative democracy should take precedence over electoral democracy. As we discussed in Chapters 4 and 5, there are deliberative efforts to rationalize the existing NPC and CPPCC systems and to make them functional institutions of democratic deliberation. Meanwhile, democratic participation in legislative and administrative decision-making has been also opened up slowly. The rising civic activism will continue to test the level of tolerance and boundary lines of the system of managed political participation. There is a learning curve for all parties involved.

According to Nobel Prize winner James M. Buchanan, in a society in which each member is to seek interest-maximization, the only way to achieve Pareto Improvement is through consensus building by all parties whose interests are at stake. If unanimity can be achieved, the social cost will be avoided, and the Pareto optimal is achieved, even though the economic cost of the process may be high.[5] Since actors perceive the game to be zero-sum, even with majority rule in a democratic decision-making process, there will still be some who consider themselves losers. The only hope for Pareto improvement, according to Buchanan, is to build a super majority to minimize the losses.

Now, under the authoritarian technocracy, there appear to be mechanisms available for consensus building. First of all, the People's Consultation Conference provides a place for making "side payment" and interest aggregation. Secondly, the technocrats can serve as policy entrepreneurs to initial policies aimed at "compensating" the losing side. However, public trust in the technocrats has declined due to rampant official corruption. Moreover, the alliance between the technocrats and big businesses may result in monopoly privileges or rent-seeking behaviors.[6] Many technocrats, especially at local levels, are using their powers to maximize their self-interests, either legally or illegally. According to Transparency International, China is now ranked as one of the most corrupted countries in the world, measured by its Corruption Perception Index (CPI).[7] It is incongruous that the system of technocracy which intends to enhance efficiency has become a source of Pareto inefficiency.

Still, the use of entrepreneurial policies and the anti-corruption campaigns may temporarily relieve inequality in various shapes and forms and may even strengthen the regime's legitimacy and the one-party rule for a while.[8] Nonetheless, it will not resolve the issue of equity deficiency in the long run. The reason is simple, the unequal distribution of growth and wealth is not merely an economic one; rather it is an accumulated result of the unequal distribution of political power in the country. The lack of a well-developed civil society and opportunities to participate in the decision-making process are the primary sources of inequity. For instance, some people get rich not because of their business talents, but simply because of their political power and political connections with government officials.

Lack of institutionalized means for people to defend or promote their self-interests is a major barrier to the achievement of social and economic equity. Zheng Chuguang, a member of the Chinese People's Political Consultative Conference (CPPCC), suggests that more delegates should be elected from the disadvantaged or underrepresented groups, such as farmers to fill the seats in the NPC and CPPCC, and peasants should be allowed to establish peasant associations to defend their interests.[9] In modern labor relations, the inability of official trade unions to serve as true representatives of workers has produced imbalance in labor relations, with management wielding excessive amounts of power. Unless labor's right to organize, engage in meaningful collective bargaining, and even to strike are allowed, workers will not get a fair share of the profits of the economic growth.

What This Book Has Accomplished

This book breaks new grounds in several aspects. First of all, it sheds new light on the issue of political legitimacy by a systematic examination of the utilitarian dimension of the subject. While the theoretical underpinning is rooted in Western public choice theory developed by James M. Buchanan, Anthony Dawn, and Amartya Sen,[10] this study examines the relationship between efficiency and equity and the meaning of political legitimacy in the context of Chinese political traditions and political culture. The end result is a new analytical framework and a number of key hypotheses that can be further tested and verified. The main purpose of this book is to seek a better understanding of the inner dynamics of Chinese political development. However, the analytical framework developed will contribute to a more comprehensive theory of political legitimacy.

Secondly, the book has illustrated a contour of the new Chinese state for the early part of the twenty-first century. The return to the traditional Chinese hu-

manism and populism, the reform of the administrative state, the creation of a
welfare state, the modernization of corporatist social control, and the emphasis
on social harmony indicate a new course of Chinese political development. Yet,
it may be a surprise to many Western observers that none of the new development is designed to foster a liberal form of democratic order in China. Instead,
the soft authoritarian state will be the predominant characteristics of Chinese
politics for years to come.

Finally, the study reveals a cyclical pattern of Chinese political development, namely, the rotation of the politics of efficiency and the politics of equity.
This discovery will be an important contribution to the study of Chinese politics.
Unlike the conventional one-dimensional approach towards the study of legitimacy, this study considers the utilitarian-based legitimacy to be two dimensional:
namely, the pursuit of efficiency and the pursuit of equity. The two goals will
compete with each other and form an upward spiral pattern of political development. The rotation constitutes a dynamic political process aimed at achieving
the optimal level of balance between the two seemingly incompatible goals.

Unlike many scholars who perceive contemporary Chinese history as a constant search for democracy, this book takes a very different approach. Based on
a careful analysis of traditional Chinese political theory and history and current
political development, it asserts that the enduring question in political development in China today is no different from what was asked before. The core question remains to be who governs and where do the rulers derive their right to govern. In another words, contemporary Chinese political development is a continuation of the search for political legitimacy. The search for democracy has never
been an end in itself; rather, it is always treated as essentially a tool tailored to
suit the needs of political regimes. It is true the search for democracy is an important part of normative inquiry and empirical endeavor. Nevertheless, for the
most part, China had non-democratic states throughout its modern history. Legitimacy of the different regimes was acquired though ways other than electoral
democracy that was highly valued by liberal political theory. For many years,
the CCP actually enjoyed high level of political acceptance among Chinese
people, and few challenged its legitimacy even though it was not operated on
modern electoral democracy. As Max Weber pointed out, rational-legalism is
only one way political leaders can be legitimized, but certainly not the only one.
A legitimate government is not necessarily a democratic one, and a democratic
government is also constantly facing legitimacy crises. In terms of acquiring and
maintaining political legitimacy, democracy is not a cure all. If someone believes that one day when China embraces electoral democracy, then it will solve
all of its legitimacy puzzles, he or she will be terribly wrong.

In Chapter 1, we discussed a two-dimensional view of legitimacy in Chinese traditional political theory. The original justification is based on tacit consent of the people and the guiding principles are benevolence, rule by virtue, and
fairness. The utilitarian justification is based on the fulfillment of utility of the
people, measured by happiness, well-being, prosperity, and individual security.
The guiding values are benefiting people and enriching people.

To build a parsimonious theory, we borrowed two economic concepts to highlight the two types of value orientations in acquiring political legitimacy, namely, efficiency and equity. Efficiency can be achieved through a functional market economy, technocratic rule and a strong developmental state. Technocracy and scientism in modern time is known for promoting modernization and industrialization. Equity can be achieved through interest articulation, civil activism and political participation and democratic governance where individuals and groups can defend or advance what they considered a fair share of the scarce resources. It is in the politics of equity that one finds democracy and rational-legal choice works the best to ensure fairness and equality.

However, good things do not always go hand-in-hand. There is an inevitable trade-off between the politics of efficiency and politics of equity. Western liberal democracy has developed a sophisticated system of election, interest group representation, and conflict resolution. However, the excessive emphasis on political equity and political pluralism tends to compromise government performance and produce frequent political stalemates and deadlocks. Since China has begun a long journey toward the politics of equity, we will not be surprised to learn twenty years from now that people will complain about the excessive civil activism and a stalled political process, and that the overemphasis on popular appeals led to the explosion of public expenditures on social welfare and deterioration of China's economic efficiency and productivity. By then, the demand for efficiency will most likely return to the center stage of Chinese politics.

Consequently, not only the industrialized democracies suffer from chronic legitimacy crises of inefficiency, but the copycats of the equity-enhancing liberal democracy in the Third World countries also produced many failed states where neither efficiency nor equity were attained though the pursuit of Western-style electoral democracy. Countries like Haiti, Iraq, and Afghanistan were pressured by the West to implement liberal democracy, but their governance situations have been close to nightmares.

In order to have a better assessment of good governance and the changing dynamics of political legitimacy, we must turn our attention away from Western liberal political theories; we should turn our focus on the central question of the all politics, that is, the search of political legitimacy. Chinese traditional political theory provides some useful insights on this issue, and modern Chinese political leaders rely heavily on the traditional cognitive model of political legitimacy. Since legitimacy is rooted deeply in a country's political culture, leaders can frame the communication of political rightfulness more easily with norms and values existed in the past. Consequently, we must give more attention to the traditional cognitive pattern of legitimacy in China and assess objectively its impact on the development of China's political system in our time.

The theoretical framework set out in Chapter 1 can serve as a starting point in our inquiry. Many of the hypotheses developed in this chapter were tested in various chapters of this book and certainly, they can be further tested in other case studies as well. However, before we look into the implications of this new analytical framework, let us summarize the major findings of this study of Chinese political development first.

China's Legitimacy Deficiency

The notion of political legitimacy comprising both original justification and utilitarian justification is not new to Chinese traditional political rulers. Political stability and ruler's staying power ultimately rested on the consent of the people, tacit or in-tacit. To win the hearts and minds of the people, a ruler must tend to people's utilitarian needs, such as security, food, shelter, and clothing. Equally important is the moral base of governance and justice. A number of preliminary conclusions can be generated based on our analyses so far.

1. *Legitimacy is a subjective judgment of deservedness or rightfulness of using political power or governance, and the judgment is made on the original, procedural and utilitarian justifications.*

A comprehensive theory of political legitimacy must be three dimensional to include people's multi-level judgments. The Chinese traditional theory of political legitimacy placed emphases on original (divine rights) and utilitarian (needs-based) justifications while paying little attention to maintain a just process or procedure. This weakness can be explained by the lack of democratic traditions in Chinese political practices and the strong presence of Confucian paternalistic norms. The utilitarian-based judgment can be satisfied by expanded personal space for growth, opportunity to become prosperous, and fulfillment of basic human needs such as food, shelter, affection, etc. The policies designed to encourage economic growth, improvement of productivity, and efficient allocation of resources serve the purpose of consolidating and strengthening a state's utilitarian support of political legitimacy.

Chinese traditional political theory also emphasizes the importance of equality and equity. While agrarianism focused on horizontal equity and asked for equal shares of wealth, Confucianism emphasized vertical equity, namely, those who are unequal should be treated unequally, and rich should be taxed more to help the poor. Political leaders have used various policies, such as land reform or tax reform to promote shared economic equality. This kind of policy tends to promote social harmony and political stability. However, too much equality will sacrifice productivity and efficiency.

With the elimination of monarchical rule and the endorsement of a market economy, the issue of equity is no longer an economic question; instead, it has become a political one. Unlike communist ideology, which emphasizes public goods and collective interests, in a market economy, "men, in a great measure, governed by interest"[11] and self-interests are best served in a political marketplace where competition and bargaining are in action. The answer to that question determines who governs in a society. Political equity demands players in a public domain have a stake in the decision-making process in order to ensure just distributions. Therefore, modern day political crises were often crises of political participation. If the state has no willingness to open up the governing process and provide no institutions to accommodate the needs for both elite and mass participation, then the legitimacy of the state will be in question. As Greek political thinker Aristotle pointed out, "If the people involved are not equal, they will not [justly] receive equal shares . . . that are the source of quarrels and accusations." [12] Equity-enhancing politics, therefore, is a question of democratization, and Chinese political development will have to go beyond their traditional governing philosophies to tackle the issue of political equity.

2. *The dynamics of modern political development lie in the periodical shifts in focus in different ingredients of legitimacy due to the trade-off between different goals.*

The pursuit of equity and equality will lead to a negative impact on efficiency, while the pursuit of equity will lead to compromises on efficiency. A shift in focus, whether it is done through reform, uprising or a revolution, is always a major correction to the negative impact of previous policies. This breakthrough-rationalization rotation constitutes a main dynamic force of change in any politics. The Chinese traditional legitimacy theory considers *ge ming* (revolution) to be the only way for a change of political legitimacy. The efforts to change focus of legitimacy through *bian fa* (reform) most often ended in failure.

The CCP has demonstrated a high level of adaptability in making periodic changes in order to strengthen its basis of political legitimacy. The CCP's rise to power and its transition from a revolutionary party to a ruling party can serve as an illustration of the dynamic nature in the search for political legitimacy. In the ninety years of history of the CCP, its base of political legitimacy has changed at least three times. Prior to 1949, the CCP was engaged in a prolonged struggle for power. The Marxist ideology and revolution itself provided the original and utilitarian justification for its ascendance to power. The founding of the PRC marked the beginning of a new era. The task of modernizing China led to the reliance on performance-based legitimacy. Economic development and the improvement of people's standard of living were the main appeal of the CCP in its effort to stay in power. However, for a while, the revolutionary old guards continued to engage in revolutionary politics and campaign-style mass mobilization which led to the weakening of both the CCP's original and utilitarian justification. China's economic development made some great inroads initially, but soon suffered from stagnation, inefficiency, and wasteful programs such as the Great Leap Forward.

The end of the Cultural Revolution brought China into the second period: the economic reform and opening up. The establishment of a market economy and the coming age of technocracy improved China's economic performance tremendously. In thirty years, the world has witnessed the rapid ascendance of China as a new economic powerhouse. Under the guidance of Deng Xiaoping's pragmatism, the technocrats made most decisions in an authoritarian manner. No time was wasted on debates and discussions (*bu zhenglun*). This single-handed pursuit of growth and development has resulted in a period of unprecedented growth. The size of China's economy quickly surpassed most of the Western nations, and individual per capita income quadrupled in two decades. These remarkable achievements helped boost popular support for the Chinese ruling elite despite the negative impact of the June 4 Incident in 1989. According to the latest PEW survey, the Chinese public's satisfaction to the country reached as high as 83 percent, far exceeding the 48 percent in 2002. The satisfactory level towards its government also reached 89 percent, near all-time high. During the same period, China maintained an average 9 percent of GDP growth rate and the per capita GDP increased 58 percent.[13]

However, the continued existence of authoritarian rule and slow progress in political reforms also posts some serious challenges to the original justification of the technocratic rule. The politics of efficiency of the 1980s and 1990s only helped the enhancement of the utilitarian dimension of the party-state's political legitimacy. Yet, the aggressive pursuit of market-dictated efficiency led to widespread of inequality, immorality, insecurity, alienation, rootlessness, and ruthlessness. Leaders whose trainings were limited to science and engineering had intentionally or unintentionally neglected human distresses and acted more or less in the traditional authoritarian and paternalistic manner in their decision-making.[14] Technocracy has an inborn weakness in legitimacy, namely the inability to achieve equity. Although everyone in China today is better off than what they were two decades ago, due to the efficiency-driving market reforms, a small number of people had most of the economic wealth and political power. This suggests that the lack of equity will be a new social cleavage that will weaken the popular support of the people. The new alliance between the political elite and the new business elite has led to widespread mistrust of government, especially at the local level.

3. *Legitimacy deficiency in one area can be supplemented by the strong performance of another.*

The imbalance in a regime's original and utilitarian justification is a constant feature. But asymmetry with an excess skew line may not necessary lead to political instability. A development state can keep its population at bay for its effective economic management and efficient allocation of resources, or even the use of coercion. A democracy that may appear to be inefficient from time to time can still maintain stable politics if the process of decision-making is fair and open. Therefore, legitimacy deficiency may not necessarily produce a political crisis.

After more than two decades of rapid changes, China's economic system has been transformed beyond recognition. In contrast, the essential elements of China's political system have remained largely unaffected. This lopsided development has created the so-called "China paradoxes." Although the basic framework for a market economy has been put into place, China is still an authoritarian party-state. While economic freedom has become an engine of economic growth, the government retains tight control over the media and political organizations. And even though China has maintained a high-speed economic growth, its ruling elite have kept watchful eyes over the increasing signs of social unrests and political instability.[15]

The "China paradoxes" have puzzled many political observers in the West. After the 1989 Tiananmen Crisis, some Western observers anticipated a rather quick downfall of the Chinese communist regime. Yet this did not happen. Now, two decades later, we hear again the similar predictions of a "coming collapse of China."[16] These predictions, in my view, may be proven wrong for the same reason: it underestimates the ability of the regime to stay in power, and the aptitude of the CCP for adapting to the changing political environment.[17] In addition, the oversimplification over the meaning of political legitimacy also contributes to the repeated failure of forecasting China's political future. Many Western scholars, who were indoctrinated by liberal legitimacy theories, have trouble comprehending the communist's system of legitimation, especially in the context of Chinese political culture and history. As Feng Chen points out, "The theory of imminent collapse was flawed because it treated China as if it were a Western democracy where legitimacy directly determines the continuation of political rule."[18] Furthermore, many studies pay little attention to the multifaceted nature of regime legitimacy. Some have mistakenly believed that only a democratic government can be legitimate. [19]

4.   *A stable government is the one that maintains a proper balance between the original and utilitarian justifications.*

This can be called a "golden mean" between the benefits of efficiency and benefits of equity. Politics in the long haul is always an art of balancing the two desirable goals. After thirty years of successful economic development, stability is still the main objective of the ruling elite. The desire for stability and social harmony has prompted the latest effort to seek proper balance between efficiency, equity and equality.

Many Western observers have been wrong about China for not engaging in meaningful political reform and the failure to liberalize China's politics since the 1980s. It can be argued that during these three decades, China is not ready for an equity-enhancing political model since the main task of the day was to depoliticize Chinese society, eliminate the impact of factional politics that persisted in the aftermath of the Cultural Revolution, restructure the egalitarian-based state socialism, improve China's economic performance, and eradicate poverty. The political correction on the mindset for egalitarianism and the depoliticalization of the Chinese society was the key to China's transition to a market economy. Without these two important changes, China may end up like what Russia is today.

Despite these political changes, there is still an imbalance between economic and political developments. The success of China's economic development has eventually come to the point where the achievement-based utilitarian legitimacy is no longer sufficient to keep the general public being complacent; instead, the aggressive pursuit of efficiency has resulted in the lost of equity, purpose and morality of the development. The authoritarian decision-making has become increasingly incompatible with the growing demand for public participation. As a direct result of these growing discrepancies, civil activism is on the rise and demand for equity is once again a major force for change. The number of mass incidents and the degree of public discontent has risen significantly. Although there is no sign of an immediate crisis of legitimacy, it is something that the current leaders in Beijing are constantly worried about. The open discussion about political legitimacy in the political and scholarly circles and the repeated calls for strengthening of the CCP's social support and governing capability are unambiguous signs of this awareness.

Despite the continued resistance from the core of the CCP leadership, the pursuit of equity in China will be more and more in line with the search for a suitable form of democracy that will enhance citizens' political equity, while at the same time it will keep the compromise to efficiency to minimum. This is the number one challenge in Chinese politics in the next three decades.

Toward a New Chinese Polity

Legitimacy, governability, and stability, as the three most important political goals in effective governance, have shaped the Chinese political development in the later part of the twentieth century and into the foreseeable future. Will China ever become democratic? The rise of civic activism and the coming age of politics of equity are clear signs that democratization is on the horizon. With the goal of achieving modernization by the middle of this century, the political modernization will be a most important goal in the next three or four decades. So we should not doubt that democratization will take place in China, and the time is not indefinite. This confidence is built on our analysis of China's prolonged struggle for political legitimacy. With more and more focuses on building a harmonious society, the maturity of a system of rule of law, and a gradual democratization of the ruling party, the social democracy in China will come naturally.

Nevertheless, many western scholars share a view of uncertainty of China's democratic future. Some believe that the establishment of the technocratic state helps China transform itself from a totalitarian state to authoritarian corporatist one. But this new state shares many similarities of other corporatist governments. First, the ruling party claims to represent the interests of all people. Second, there is a monopolistic interest group for each sector of the society, and all bargaining and consultation will have to be conducted between the ruling party and the monopolistic groups. Finally, the state remains authoritarian in nature since it does not tolerate opposition outside the corporatist social institutions. Civil society is carefully monitored and managed to ensure political control.[20] The presence of a strong state and the imbalance of power among various social groups make the equity-enhancement all the more important.

Will the latest drive toward equity-enhancement and the creation of a harmonious society consolidate or put China beyond the corporatist-style governance? The odds for it are probably very unlikely, at least in the near future. As long as the ruling party knows how to cultivate its political legitimacy, there is no imminent threat to the corporatist political structure. In other words, don't expect CCP leaders to rock the boat and surrender political control voluntarily. What will happen is the continued rationalization of the existing corporatist social and political structure, combined with a certain degree of electoral democracy as well as deliberative democracy.

To what extent will democracy expand in Chinese society in the next few decades under the auspices of one-party rule and a system of corporatist state? The answer to this question is that it depends on the continued growth of Chinese civil society and the maturity of its middle class. An optimistic prediction, based on conventional wisdom, is that economic development will eventually lead to political democratization, or that maybe within the next three decades there will be some kind of transition from an authoritarian corporatism to a societal one. If we look at China's neighbors, such as Japan and South Korea, one may find this kind of optimism does exist. Like China, both Japan and South Korea practiced authoritarian corporatism during their modernization process. In the 1990s, we saw an essential change in state-society relations in the two countries. The number of civil society organizations mushroomed. They started to play a more active role in policy-making and to participate vigorously in the political process. Both countries have moved away from state corporatist control of civil society since then, and are embracing a liberal style of democratic governance, although not entirely meeting the description of a liberal democracy.[21]

Can this be repeated in China? Will China embrace the same kind of liberal democracy? There are two groups of scholars or commentators alike who cast their doubt on this prospect from two different angles. One the one hand, Minxin Pei deplores the causal links between the structural logic of China's "illiberal adaptation" and the democratic future. He argues that because the CCP continues to be autocratic and is interested in retaining control over economic as well as many other aspects of the society to ensure its political survival, gradualism will ultimately lead to a state of "trapped transition" and political stagnation.[22] Martin Jacques, on the other hand, believes that Beijing is destined to displace Washington as the capital of the world's leading superpower, and it can do so without having to abandon Confucian values or Leninist structures to do so.[23] Daniel A. Bell also insists in his book that East Asian political traditions contain morally legitimate alternatives to Western-style liberal democracy.[24] Who is right?

No doubt, China will remain a communist state in the predictable future. This factor alone will make a complete liberal transition more difficult, if it not entirely impossible. However, the Chinese state is facing the same kind of challenges like their counterparts in Japan and South Korea faced in the 1980s and 1990s. The need for legitimacy will serve as the most powerful force for political adaptation. China may resist the idea of liberal democracy, but it does not and cannot resist the idea of democracy.

One way to change the negative view about the corporatist style of governance is by inventing a new analytic framework which may go beyond the corporatist way of thinking. One prediction is that China may attempt to develop its own model of democracy that will best suit its own needs for efficiency and equity, a model that will also unite its past with the present, and a model that will accommodate the needs for a strong state and the needs for a vibrant civil society. In Confucian terms, China needs to develop a "zhongyong" style of governance model that combines a strong state with decentralized democratic politics. John Naisbitt's claim that a new "vertical democracy," which combines the bottom-up democracy with the top-down central command, is emerging in China and is an insightful analysis.[25] Vertical democracy, as an alternative to the horizontal democracy of the west, may also be called by some as "collective democracy" in which traditional collectivism will be combined with individual rights.[26]

The notion of a "vertical democracy" is not entirely new. Aristotle's ideal type of government is a polity–a form of government that infuses oligarchy with democracy.[27] He understood that different understandings of equity lead to two different kinds of government, and a good government is based on the "golden means" and multitude powers.

> Now equality is of two kinds, numerical and proportional; by the first I mean sameness or equality in number or size; by the second, equality of ratios. . . . As I was saying before, men agree that justice in the abstract is proportional, but they differ in that some think that if they are equal in any respect they are equal absolutely; others, that if they are unequal in any respect, they should be unequal in all. Hence there are two principal forms of government, democracy and oligarchy; for good birth and virtue are rare, but wealth and numbers are more common. In what city shall we find a hundred persons of good birth and of virtue whereas the rich everywhere abound. That a state should be ordered, simply and wholly, according to either kind of equality, is not a good thing; the proof is the fact that such forms of government never last. They are originally based on a mistake, and, as they begin badly, cannot fail to end badly. The inference is that both kinds of equality should be employed; numerical in some cases, and proportional in others.

According to Kang Xiaoguang, a well-known scholar in China, Confucianism disagrees with liberalism in that it does not recognize the notion that all men are born to be equal; instead, it is the inequality that leads to meritocracy that has persisted in Chinese history. The legitimacy of meritocracy is rule of benevolence. Unlike liberalism, which considers the state to be a necessary evil, Confucianism believes that state is always needed for public welfare. Men ben idea is the essential value of the paternalistic state.[28] In other words, Kang tries to give a new meaning to the legitimacy of an elitist oligarchic rule. We may not agree with Kang's logic entirely, but his analysis of Chinese political traditions can give us some insight on the cultural influence on a new Chinese polity.

The establishment of the new Chinese policy may be influenced by the so-called democratic-centralism. The CCP has endorsed Leninist democratic-centralism for many years. Democratic centralism calls for "freedom of discussion, unity in action."[29] While the central command has been fully realized, the democratic component of this doctrine is seriously underdevelopment. The key here is that if the ruling party, which serves the core of the new democracy, does not practicing democratic governance internally, how can it be legitimized first to exercise veto powers over popular wishes? Therefore, the CCP is in the process of carrying out experiments in broadening inner party democracy. Since China is historically deficient in its political theory on procedural justification, the endorsement of democratic legalism and institutionalism will help make up that deficiency and solve the problem of chronic political instability and lack of a peaceful transition of power.

No one has a clear picture of the new Chinese polity. The only thing we know is that it is not going to be a full-fledged liberal democracy, even though it may borrow some of its useful elements such as checks and balances. We also know that it is not going to be a majority tyranny or a proletarian dictatorship, like what China used to have under Mao. Some called this type of democracy "the third way."[30] The new policy will be a one-party democracy which infuses certain levels of deliberative democracy with oligarchic elite rule based on the principle of collective leadership at the top and its governing philosophies are still development in nature. The oligarchic component actually represents non-individual based party interests and public interests. It serves as a check on the individual-based private interests. If one takes a structural-functional approach, the one-party democracy is not unthinkable. As David Apter wrote,

A structural approach is useful for comparison partly because it avoids the problem of dealing with the unique. For example, we are accustomed to regarding democracy as uniquely related to a multiparty form of competitive politics. If, however, we consider democracy as a system of rule, a function of which includes public checks on arbitrary power, then it is possible to conceive of situations in which a single party, through its internal factions, serves much the same purpose.[31]

Obviously, the one-party democracy only works if three conditions are met: First, political competition must be legalized within the ruling party. Second, the party must be broadly represented to be an all-people's party. Third, there must be true inner-party democracy.

Polities infusing democratic and undemocratic elements are common in the history of Western political development. If we study the history of the Constitutional Convention of 1787 in the United States, we find abundant evidence of this type of infusion. The framers of the Constitution carefully laid out a republican form of government in which the democratically elected institution, the House of Representatives, was checked by an indirectly elected Senate, a president who was selected by an Electoral College, and an unelected branch, the judiciary. The main concerns of many framers of the U.S. Constitution were to ensure energy (efficiency) and stability for the new government. Alexander Hamilton argued forcefully that there was a need to maintain a powerful and energetic government. According to him,

A government ought to contain in itself every power requisite to the full accomplishment of the objects committed to its care, and to the complete execution of the trusts for which it is responsible, free from every other control but a regard to the public good and to the sense of the people."[32]

The British system also kept an elected nobility house–the House of Lords–as a way to check on the popularly elected House of Commons. Democracy may sound promising, but it can lead to majority tyranny; therefore, Aristotle's concern is justified. A true republic requires a rule of law that protects the interests of both majority and minority. Democracy can only last if the majority can be checked.

In this sense, a monopolistic ruling party, the noncompetitive and undemocratic components, can perform such a balancing act. In recent years, the CCP has firmly established collective leadership which allows a group of power "oligarchies" to govern as a group instead of one paramount leader. The party no longer has to rely on a charismatic leader to maintain its legitimacy. The effort to open up inner party democracy will also help to bring internal party accountability and legitimacy of the "oligarchies." If inner-party factional politics can be recognized and tolerated, then the need for multiparty competition will be further reduced.[33] Hence, the model of the new policy connecting oligarchic rule with democracy may not be the best form of government but is clearly a practical solution to the quest for political legitimacy and the pursuit for stability, eco efficiency, and equity.

In sum, the politics of equity is the politics of legitimization. In the contemporary Chinese political setting, it does involve a significant amount of democratization. However, the extent to which the Chinese political system will be democratized is largely dependent on the formation of a new Chinese polity, a polity that can maintain a balance between democratic participation and deliberation and "oligarchic" elite rule embodied by the persistence of one-party rule, and a workable political solution that will demonstrate some continuity of China's political tradition and culture.

Notes

1. Lawrence D. Brown, *New Policies, New Politics: Government's Response to Government's Growth* (Washington, D.C.: The Brookings Institution, 1983).

2. Adam Smith, *An Inquiry into the Nature and Causes of the Wealth of Nations* (Chicago, University of Chicago Press, 1976), Book I, Ch. 8, 88.

3. John Guinther, *Moralists and Managers: Public Interest Movements in America* (Garden City, NY: Anchor Books, 1976).

4. Wang Yang, Guangdong Provincial Party Secretary, made the remarks in the provincial party committee meeting on December 25, 2009, http://leaders.people.com.cn (accessed January 25, 2010).

5. James M. Buchanan and Gordon Tullock, *Calculus of Consent: Logic Foundations of Constitutional Democracy* (Indianapolis, IN: Liberty Fund, 2004).

6. Anne Kruger, "The Political Economy of the Rent-Seeking Society," *American Economic Review* 64 (1974): 291-303.

7. Transparency International, *Global Corruption Report 2006* (London: Pluto Press, 2006).

8. Thomas Heberer and Gunter Schubert, "Political Reform and Regime Legitimacy in Contemporary China," *ASIEN* 99 (April, 2005): 9-28.

9. Zheng Chuguang, "Social Equity Comes from Equal Representation of Different Interests," *People's Daily*, August 25, 2006.

10. James M. Buchanan and Gordon Tullack, *op cit.*

11. David Hume, quoted by John Ralston Paul, *The Unconscious Civilization* (Penguin Books, 1997), http://www.dhushara.com/book/multinet/saul.htm (accessed January 3, 2010).

12. Aristotle, *Nicomachean Ethics* (New York: Oxford University Press, 1998), Book 5, 1131a23-24.

13. http://www.wforum.com/wmf/posts/1115652142.html (accessed February 2, 2010).

14. The name of the movie is called "Where is the Big Dipper," cited in Guangwei Ouyang, "Scientism, Technocracy and Morality in China," *Journal of Chinese Philosophy* 30, no. 2 (June 2003):177-193.

15. Francois Mengin and Jean-Louis Rocca, *Politics in China: Moving Frontiers* (New York: Palgrave MacMillian, 2002).

16. Gordon Chang, *Coming Collapse of China* (New York: Random House, 2001); Ross Terrill, *New Chinese Empire: and What It Means for the United States* (New York: Basic Books, 2003); Joe Studwell, *The China Dream: The Quest for the Last Great Untapped Market on Earth* (New York: Atlantic Monthly Press, 2002).

17. For example, political scientist Bruce J. Dickson believed that the CCP couldn't transform itself into a democratic party for its lack of adaptability; see *Democratization in China and Taiwan: the Adaptability of Leninist Parties* (Oxford: Clarendon Press, 1997).

18. Feng Chen, "The Dilemma of Eudemonic Legitimacy in Post Mao China," *Polity* 29, no. 3 (Spring 1997), 422.

19. Allan Buchanan, "Political Legitimacy and Democracy," *Ethics* 112, no. 4 (July 2002): 689- 770.

20. Howard J, *Corporatism and Comparative Politics: The Other Great "ism"* (Armonk, NY: M.E. Sharpe, 1982); Philippe Schmitter, "Still the Century of Corporatism?" *Review of Politics* 36 (1974):35-131.

21. Lichao He, "Moving towards 'Societal Corporatism'?–Structural Factors in Civil Society Development in South Korea and Japan," paper presented to the Midwest Political Science Association Conference (Chicago, April 23-26, 2006).

22. Minxin Pei, *China's Trapped Transition: the Limits of Developmental Autocracy* (Cambridge: Harvard University Press, 2006).

23. Martin Jacques, *When China Rules the World: The End of the Western World and the Birth of a New Global Order* (New York: Penguin Press HC, 2009).

24. Daniel A. Bell, *Beyond Liberal Democracy: Political Thinking for an East Asia Context* (Princeton, NJ: Princeton University Press, 2006).

25. John Naisbitt and Doris Naisbitt: *China's Megatrend: the 8 Pillars of a New Society [Zhonghuo Da Sushi]* (Beijing: Zhonghua Gongshanglian Chubanshe, 2009).

26. Chih-Yu Shih, *Collective Democracy: Political and Legal Reform in China* (Hong Kong, Chinese University Press, 1999).

27. Aristotle, *Politics*, translated by Benjamin Jowett, Book IV.

28. Kang Xiaoguang, *Renzheng: Zhongguo Zhengzhi Fazhang de Disantiao Daolu [Rule of Benevolence: the Third Way of Chinese Political Development]*(Hong Kong: Bafang Wenhua, 2005), 119-144.

29. V.I. Lenin, *Report on the Unity Congress of the R.S.D.L.P.: A Letter to the St. Petersburg Workers*, http://www.marxists.org/archive/lenin/works/1906/rucong/viii.htm (accessed December 12, 2009).

30. Wang Lixiong, *Dijin Minzhu [Incremental Democracy]* (Taipei: Locus Publishing, 2006).

31. David Apter, *The Politics of Modernization* (Chicago: University of Chicago Press, 1965), 17.

32. Alexander Hamilton, John Jay, and James Madison, *The Federalist*, no. 31 (New York: Modern Library, 1964), 190.

33. Zhang Weiying, "Bamai Weilai Zhongguo [a Prognosis of China's Future], *Global Think Tank Briefing*, 8 (January 2010).

Selected Bibliography

Aaken, Anne van, Christian List, and Christoph Luetge. *Deliberation and Decision: Economics, Constitutional Theory, and Deliberative Democracy*. Burlington, VT, USA: Ashgate, 2004.

Aday, Lu Ann. *Evaluating the Healthcare System: Effectiveness, Efficiency, and Equity*. 3rd ed. Chicago, Ill. Washington, D.C.: Health Administration Press, 2004.

Alagappa, Muthiah. *Political Legitimacy in Southeast Asia: The Quest for Moral Authority*. Stanford, CA: Stanford University Press, 1995.

An, Pyong-jun. *Chinese Politics and the Cultural Revolution: Dynamics of Policy Processes*. Publications on Asia of the Institute for Comparative and Foreign Area Studies No. 30. Seattle, WA: University of Washington Press, 1976.

Anckar, Dag, Hannu Nurmi, and Matti Wiberg. *Rationality and Legitimacy: Essays on Political Theory*. Books from the Finnish Political Science Association. Helsinki, Finland: Finnish Political Science Association, 1988.

Anderson, B. "Social Stratification in the Soviet Union." *Studies in Comparative Communism* 8, (1975): 397-412.

Anderson, Christopher. *Losers' Consent: Elections and Democratic Legitimacy*. Oxford; New York, NY: Oxford University Press, 2005.

Association of Chinese Political Studies. Meeting (19th: 2006: University of Louisville), Shiping Hua, and Sujian Guo. *China in the Twenty-First Century: Challenges and Opportunities*. New York, NY: Palgrave Macmillan, 2007.

Baber, Walter F., and Robert V. Bartlett. *Global Democracy and Sustainable Jurisprudence: Deliberative Environmental Law*. Cambridge, Mass.: MIT Press, 2009.

Bachman, David. "Retrogression in Chinese Politics." *Current History* 89, no. 548 (1990): 249-74.

Bader, Jeffrey A. "China after Deng Xiaoping: Prospects for Continuity or Change." *Asian Affairs: An American Review* 24, no. 2 (1997): 69-77.

Bailes, E. *Technology and Society under Lenin and Stalin*. Princeton: Princeton University Press, 1978.

Barker, Rodney S. *Political Legitimacy and the State*. New York, NY: Oxford University Press, 1990.

Barnard, F. M. *Democratic Legitimacy: Plural Values and Political Power*. Montreal; Ithaca: McGill-Queen's University Press, 2001.

——. *Pluralism, Socialism, and Political Legitimacy: Reflections on Opening up Communism*. Cambridge England; New York, NY: Cambridge University Press, 1991.

Baum, Richard. *Burying Mao: Chinese Politics in the Age of Deng Xiaoping*. Princeton, NJ: Princeton University Press, 1994.

Baum, Richard, and Alexei Chevchenko. "The State of State" in Merle Goldman and Roderick MacFarquhar, ed, *The Paradox of China's Post-Mao Reforms*. Cambridge, MA: Harvard University Press, 1999.

Bell, Daniel. *Beyond Liberal Democracy: Political Thinking for an East Asian Context*. Princeton, NJ: Princeton University Press, 2006.

Bentham, Jeremy. *An Introduction to the Principles of Morals and Legislation*. New York, NY: Hafner Publishing Co., 1948[1789].

Besson, Samantha, and José Luis Martí. *Deliberative Democracy and Its Discontents*, Burlington, VT: Ashgate, 2006.

Bishop, Donald. *Chinese Thoughts: An Introduction*. Columbia, MO: South Asia Books, 2001.

Bo, Zhiyue. "Balance of Factional Power in China: The Seventeenth Central Committee of the Chinese Communist Party." *East Asia: An International Quarterly* 25, no. 4 (2008): 333-64.

———. *China's Elite Politics: Governance and Democratization*, Series on Contemporary China. Singapore: World Scientific, 2009.

———. *China's Elite Politics: Political Transition and Power Balancing*, Series on Contemporary China V. 8. Hackensack, NJ: World Scientific, 2007.

———. "The 16th Central Committee of the Chinese Communist Party: Formal Institutions and Factional Groups." *Journal of Contemporary China* 13, no. 39 (2004): 223-56.

———. "Hu Jintao and the CCP's Ideology: A Historical Perspective." *Journal of Chinese Political Science* 9, no. 2 (2004): 27-45.

———. *Chinese Provincial Leaders: Economic Performance and Political Mobility since 1949*. Armonk, NY: M.E. Sharpe, 2002.

Bobocel, Ramona, and Aaron C. Kay. *The Psychology of Justice and Legitimacy*, Ontario Symposium on Personality and Social Psychology. New York, NY: Psychology Press, 2009.

Bohman, James, and William Rehg. *Deliberative Democracy: Essays on Reason and Politics*. Cambridge, MA: MIT Press, 1997.

Bonesrønning, Hans. *Efficiency and Equity in Education Production: Empirical Evidence from Norway*. Trondheim: Norwegian University of Science and Technology, 1998.

Bonnin, Michel. "The Lost 'Generation': Its Definition and Its Role in Today's Chinese Elite Politics." *Social Research* 73, no. 1 (Spring 2006): 245-273.

Booth, John A., and Mitchell A. Seligson. *The Legitimacy Puzzle in Latin America: Political Support and Democracy in Eight Nations*. Cambridge; New York, NY: Cambridge University Press, 2009.

Bozóki, András. *Democratic Legitimacy in Post-Communist Societies*. 1st ed. Budapest: T-Twins Publishers in cooperation with the International Center at the Tübingen University, 1994.

Breslin, Shaun. "Do Leaders Matters? Chinese Politics, Leadership Transitions and the 17th Party Congress." *Contemporary Politics* 14, no. 2 (June 2008): 215-231.

———. *China in the 1980s: Centre-Province Relations in a Reforming Socialist State*. New York: St. Martin's Press, 1996.

Brødsgaard, Kjeld Erik, and Yongnian Zheng. *Bringing the Party Back In: How China Is Governed*, Politics & International Relations. Singapore: East Asian Institute, Eastern Universities Press, 2004.

Brown, David. *The Legitimacy of Governments in Plural Societies*, Occasional Paper. Singapore: Published by Singapore University Press for the Dept. of Political Science, National University of Singapore, 1984.

Brown, Michael E. *The Rise of China*, International Security Readers. Cambridge, MA: MIT Press, 2000.

Brunner, George. "Legitimacy Doctrine and Legitimation Procedures in Eastern European Systems." in T. H. Rigby and Ferenc Feher, eds., *Political Legitimacy in Communist States*. New York, NY: St. Martin's Press, 1982.

Canache, Damarys, and Michael R. Kulisheck. *Reinventing Legitimacy: Democracy and Political Change in Venezuela*, Contributions in Latin American Studies. Westport, CT: Greenwood Press, 1998.

Carlson, Allen, and East-West Center Washington. *Beijing's Tibet Policy: Securing Sovereignty and Legitimacy*, Policy Studies. Washington, DC: East-West Center Washington, 2004.

Carraro, Carlo. *Efficiency and Equity of Climate Change Policy*. Boston, MA: Kluwer Academic Publishers, 2000.

Centeno, Miguel Angel. "The New Leviathan: the Dynamics and Limits of Technocracy." *Theories and Society* 22, no. 3 (June 1993): 307-335.

Chan, Anita. *China's Workers under Assault: the Exploitation of Labor in a Globalizing Economy*, Asia and the Pacific. Armonk, NY: M.E. Sharpe, 2001.

Chan, Anita, and Jonathan Unger. "It's a Whole New Class Struggle." *Nation* 250, no. 3 (1990): 79.

Chan, Steve. "Chinese Political Attitudes and Values in Comparative Context: Cautionary Remarks on Cultural Attributions." *Journal of Chinese Political Science* 13, no. 3 (2008): 225-48.

Chen, Feng. *Economic Transition and Political Legitimacy in Post-Mao China: Ideology and Reform*. Albany, NY: State University of New York Press, 1995.

Chen, Jie. *Popular Political Support in Urban China*. Washington DC: Woodrow Wilson Center; Stanford, CA: Stanford University Press, 2004.

Christman, John Philip. *The Politics of Persons: Individual Autonomy and Socio-Historical Selves*. Cambridge; New York: Cambridge University Press, 2009.

Chua, Beng Huat. *Political Legitimacy and Housing: Stakeholding in Singapore*. London; New York, NY: Routledge, 1997.

Cohen, Ronald, and Judith D. Toland. *State Formation and Political Legitimacy: Political Anthropology*. New Brunswick, NJ: Transaction Books, 1988.

Collins, D. C., and J. R. J. Richardson. *Efficiency and Equity Considerations in the Determination of Age Pension Eligibility*, Research Paper. North Ryde, N.S.W.: Macquarie University, School of Economic and Financial Studies, 1984.

Connolly, William E. *Legitimacy and the State*, Readings in Social and Political Theory. New York: New York University Press, 1984.

Cornia, Giovanni Andrea and Julius Court. *Inequality, Growth and Poverty in the Era of Liberalization and Globalization*, policy brief, no. 4, World Institute for Development Economic Institute, the United Nations University, 2001.

Crocker, David A. *Ethics of Global Development: Agency, Capability, and Deliberative Democracy*. Cambridge; New York, NJ: Cambridge University Press, 2008.

Dench, Geoff. *The Rise and Rise of Meritocracy*. Oxford, UK; Malden, MA: Blackwell Pub. in association with *The Political Quarterly*, 2006.

Dewey, John. *How We Think*. Lexington, MA: D.C. Heath, 1910. Reprinted. Buffalo, NY: Prometheus Books, 1991.

Ding, Sheng. *The Dragon's Hidden Wings: How China Rises with Its Soft Power*, Challenges Facing Chinese Political Development. Lanham, MD: Lexington Books, 2008.

Ding, X. L. *The Decline of Communism in China: Legitimacy Crisis, 1977-1989*. Cambridge; New York: Cambridge University Press, 1994.

Ding, Yijiang. *Chinese Democracy after Tiananmen*. New York, NJ: Columbia University Press, 2002.

Dingxin, Zhao. "The Mandate of Heaven and Performance Legitimation in Historical and Contemporary China." *American Behavioral Scientist* 53, no. 3 (2009): 416-33.

Dittmer, Lowell, and Yu-shan Wu. "Leadership Coalitions and Economic Transformation in Reform China: Revisiting the Political Business Cycle" in *Domestic Politics in Transition: China's Deep Reform*, ed. by Lowell Dittmer and Guoli Liu. Lanham, MD: Roman & Littlefield, 2006.

————. "The Modernization of Factionalism in Chinese Politics." *World Politics* 47, no. 4 (1995): 467.

Dogan, Mattei. *Comparing Pluralist Democracies: Strains on Legitimacy*, New Directions in Comparative and International Politics. Boulder: Westview Press, 1988.

Dryzek, John S. *Deliberative Democracy and Beyond: Liberals, Critics, Contestations*, Oxford Political Theory. Oxford: Oxford University Press, 2002.

Eastaugh, Steven R. *Financing Health Care: Economic Efficiency and Equity*. Dover, MA: Auburn House, 1987.

Eastern, David. *A Framework for Political Analysis*. Englewood Cliffs, NJ: Prentice-Hall, Inc., 1965.

Easton, David, and Jack Dennis. *Children in the Political System: Origins of Political Legitimacy*, McGraw-Hill Series in Political Science. New York, NY: McGraw-Hill, 1969.

Elliott, D. "Uncertainties of Chinese Politics." *Newsweek* 110, no. 3 (1987): 37.

Elster, Jon. *Deliberative Democracy*, Cambridge Studies in the Theory of Democracy. Cambridge, U.K.; New York, NY: Cambridge University Press, 1998.

Epstein, Edwin M., Dow Votaw, and California University School of Business Administration. *Rationality, Legitimacy, Responsibility: Search for New Directions in Business and Society*. Santa Monica, CA: Goodyear Pub. Co., 1978.

Eriksen, Erik Oddvar, and Jarle Weigård. *Understanding Habermas: Communicative Action and Deliberative Democracy*. London; New York, NY: Continuum, 2003.

Falkenheim, Victor C. *Chinese Politics from Mao to Deng*, World Social Systems Series. China in a New Era. New York, NY: Professors World Peace Academy: Distributed by Paragon House, 1989.

Farrelly, Colin Patrick. *Justice, Democracy and Reasonable Agreement*. New York, NY: Palgrave Macmillan, 2009.

Feng, Guang. "Yi Ren Wei Ben Yu Yi Min Wei Ben Qubue de Tantao (A Study of the Differences between the Idea of Putting People First and Putting the Governed First)." *Lilun Qianyan [Theoretical Frontline]* 18 (2005): 36-37.

Fewsmith, Joseph. *China since Tiananmen: From Deng Xiaoping to Hu Jintao*. New York, NY: Cambridge University Press, 2008.

————. "Chinese Politics under Hu Jintao." *Problems of Post-Communism* 50, no. 5 (2003): 14-21.

————. *Elite Politics in Contemporary China*. Armonk, NY: M.E. Sharpe, 2001.

Fincher, John H. *Chinese Democracy: Statist Reform, the Self-Government Movement and Republican Revolution*. Rev., expanded ed. Monumenta Serindica No. 20. Tokyo, Japan: Institute for the Study of Languages and Cultures of Asia and Africa, 1989.

Fishkin, James S., and Peter Laslett. *Debating Deliberative Democracy*, Philosophy, Politics and Society 7. Malden, MA: Blackwell, 2003.

Feldman, Jeffrey. *Framing the Debate: Famous Presidential Speeches and How Progressives Can Use Them to Control the Conversation (and Win Elections)*. Brooklyn, NY: Ig Publishing, 2007.

Franck, Thomas M. *The Power of Legitimacy among Nations*. New York, NY: Oxford University Press, 1990.

Fu, Zhengyuan. *Autocratic Tradition and Chinese Politics*. Cambridge, England; New York, NY: Cambridge University Press, 1993.

Fung, Edmund S. K. *In Search of Chinese Democracy: Civil Opposition in Nationist China, 1929-1949*, Cambridge Modern China Series. Cambridge; New York, NY: Cambridge University Press, 2000.

Gamer, Robert E. *Understanding Contemporary China*. 3rd ed., Understanding. Boulder,

Colo.: Lynne Rienner Publishers, 2008.

Gardner, John. *Chinese Politics and the Succession to Mao*. New York, NY: Holmes & Meier, 1982.

Gastil, John, and Peter Levine. *The Deliberative Democracy Handbook: Strategies for Effective Civic Engagement in the Twenty-First Century*. 1st ed. San Francisco, CA: Jossey-Bass, 2005.

Gilboy, George J., and Eric Heginbotham. "Latin Americanization of China?" *Current History* (September 2004):256-261.

Gilley, Bruce. "The Limits of Authoritarian Resilience." *Journal of Democracy* 14, no. 1 (2003): 18-26.

———. *The Right to Rule: How States Win and Lose Legitimacy*. New York, NY: Columbia University Press, 2009.

Goffman, Erving. *Frame Analysis: An Essay on the Organization of Experience*. Cambridge: Harvard University Press, 1974.

Goodman, David S. G. *Groups and Politics in the People's Republic of China*. Cardiff, United Kingdom: University College Cardiff Press, 1984.

Grafstein, Robert. "Toward a Theory of Legitimacy." Ph D. thesis, University of Chicago, 1977.

Gundersen, Adolf G. *The Socratic Citizen: A Theory of Deliberative Democracy*. Lanham, MD: Lexington Books, 2000.

Guo, Baogang, and Dennis Hickey. *Toward Better Governance in China: An Unconventional Pathway of Political Reform*, Challenges Facing Chinese Political Development. Lanham, MD: Lexington Books, 2009.

Guo, Sujian. *China's "Peaceful Rise" In the 21st Century: Domestic and International Conditions*. Burlington, VT: Ashgate, 2006.

———. *The Political Economy of Asian Transition from Communism*. Aldershot, Hampshire, England; Burlington, VT: Ashgate, 2006.

———. *Post-Mao China: From Totalitarianism to Authoritarianism?* Westport, CT: Praeger, 2000.

Guo, Sujian, and Baogang Guo. *Challenges Facing Chinese Political Development*. Lanham, MD: Lexington Books, 2007.

———. *China in Search of a Harmonious Society*. Lanham, MD: Lexington Books, 2008.

———. *Greater China in an Era of Globalization*. Lanham, MD: Rowman & Littlefield Publishers, 2009.

Gurr, Ted Robert. *Why Men Rebel*. Princeton, NJ: Princeton University Press, 1971.

Gutmann, Amy. *Why Deliberative Democracy?* Princeton, NJ: Princeton University Press, 2004.

Habermas, Jügen. *Legitimation Crisis*, trans. by T. McCarthy.Boston, MA: Beacon Press, 1975.

Hamilton, Alexander, James Madison, and John Jay. *Federalist Papers*. New York, NY: Penguin Classics, 1987.

Hann, Alison. *Health Policy and Politics*. Aldershot, England; Burlington, VT: Ashgate, 2007.

Harris, Paul G. *Global Warming and East Asia: The Domestic and International Politics of Climate Change*. London; New York, NY: Routledge, 2003.

Hayek, Friedrick von. "The Nature and History of the Problem," in *Collectivist Economic Planning*. ed., Friedrick von. Hayek. London: George Routledge & Son, 1987.

He, Baogang. *The Democratic Implications of Civil Society in China*. New York, NY: St. Martin's Press, 1997.

———. *The Democratization of China*, Routledge Studies—China in Transition [1].

London; New York, NY: Routledge, 1996.
————. *Rural Democracy in China.* New York, NY: Palgrave Macmillan, 2007.
He, Zengke, Thomas Heberer, and Gunter Schubert. *Cheng Xiang Gong Min Can Yu He Zheng Zhi He Fa Xing.* Zhongguo Min Zhu Zhi Li Yan Jiu Cong Shu. Beijing: Zhong yang bian yi chu ban she, 2007.
Heberer, Thomas, and Gunter Schubert. *Regime Legitimacy in Contemporary China: Institutional Change and Stability,* Routledge Contemporary China Series. Milton Park, Abingdon, Oxon; New York, NY: Routledge, 2006.
Hicks, John. "The Foundations of Welfare Economics." *Economic Journal* 49, no. 196 (1939): 696–712.
Hu, Shaohua. "Confucianism and Contemporary Chinese Politics." *Politics & Policy* 35, no. 1 (2007): 136-53.
Hua, Long. *Hu-Wen Zhiguo Jiemi* [the Secret of Hu-Wen Governance]. Hong Hong: Xinhua Caiyin Chubanshe, 2005.
Humphrey, Mathew. *Ecological Politics and Democratic Theory: The Challenge to the Deliberative Ideal,* Routledge Studies in Extremism and Democracy. London; New York: Routledge, 2007.
Huntington, Samuel P. *Political Order in Changing Societies.* New Haven, CT: Yale University Press, 2006.
————. *The Third Wave: Democratization in the Late Twentieth Century.* Norman, OK: University of Oklahoma Press, 1993.
James, Estelle, and World Bank. Policy Research Dept. Poverty and Human Resources Division. *Pension Reform: Is There a Tradeoff between Efficiency and Equity?* Policy Research Working Paper. Washington, DC: World Bank, Policy Research Dept., Poverty and Human Resources Division, 1997.
James, Michael Rabinder. *Deliberative Democracy and the Plural Polity.* Lawrence, KS: University Press of Kansas, 2004.
Johnson, C. *Changes in Communist Systems.* Stanford: Stanford University Press, 1970.
Jost, John T., and Brenda Major. *The Psychology of Legitimacy: Emerging Perspectives on Ideology, Justice, and Intergroup Relations.* New York, NY: Cambridge University Press, 2001.
Kadlec, Alison. *Dewey's Critical Pragmatism.* Lanham, MD: Lexington Books, 2007.
Kahane, Reuven. *The Problem of Political Legitimacy in an Antagonistic Society: The Indonesian Case,* Studies in Comparative Modernization Series. Beverly Hills, CA: Sage Publications, 1973.
Kaldor, Nicholas. "Welfare Propositions in Economics and Interpersonal Comparisons of Utility." *Economic Journal* 49, no. 195 (1939): 549–552.
Kautsky, John H. "Revolutionary and Managerial Elites in Modernizing Regimes." *Comparative Politics* 1, no. 4 (July 1969): 441-453.
Khan, L. Ali. *A Theory of Universal Democracy: Beyond the End of History,* Developments in International Law V. 44. The Hague; New York, NY: Kluwer Law International, 2003.
Kluckhohn, F. R. and F. L. Strodtbeck. *Variations in Value Orientations.* Evanston, Ill.: Row, Peterson, 1961.
Lakoff, George. *Moral Politics: What Conservatives Know that Liberals Don't.* Chicago, IL: University of Chicago Press, 1996.
Laliberté, André, and Marc Lanteigne. *The Chinese Party-State in the 21st Century: Adaptation and the Reinvention of Legitimacy,* Routledge Contemporary China Series. Milton Park, Abingdon, Oxon; New York, NY: Routledge, 2008.
Lam, Willy Wo-Lap. *Chinese Politics in the Hu Jintao Era: New Leaders, New Challenges.* Armonk, NY: M.E. Sharpe, 2006.

Le Grand, Julian. *Equity and Choice: an essay in Economics and Applied Philosophy.* London and New York: HarperCollins, 1991.

Lee, Ching Kwan. *Against the Law: Labor Protests in China's Rustbelt and Sunbelt.* Berkeley, CA: University of California Press, 2007.

Lee, Don Y. *Traditional Chinese Thoughts: The Four Schools.* Bloomington, IN: Eastern Press, 1990.

Leib, Ethan J., and Baogang He. *The Search for Deliberative Democracy in China.* New York, NY: Palgrave Macmillan, 2006.

Leng, Tse-Kang, and Yunhan Zhu. *Dynamics of Local Governance in China during the Reform Era*, Challenges Facing Chinese Political Development. Lanham, MD: Lexington Books, 2010.

Li, Cheng. *China's Changing Political Landscape: Prospects for Democracy.* Washington, D.C.: Brookings Institution Press, 2008.

Li, Helin, and Xianmin Zuo. *Zhongguo Te Se Xie Shang Min Zhu Yan Jiu* [*the Studies of Deliberative Democracy with Chinese Characteristics*]. Beijing: Zhong yang dang xiao chu ban she, 2008.

Lijphart, Arend. *Democracy in Plural Societies: A Comparative Exploration.* New Haven, CT: Yale University Press, 1977.

Lipset, Seymour Martin. *Political Man.* Baltimore, MD: John Hopkins University Press, 1981.

———. "Some Social Requisites of Democracy: Economic Development and Political Legitimacy." *American Political Science Review* 53 (1959): 69-105.

Liu, Guoli, and Weixing Chen. *New Directions in Chinese Politics for the New Millennium*, Chinese Studies V. 24. Lewiston, NY: Edwin Mellen Press, 2002.

Longe, Oskar. "On the Economic Theory of Socialism" in *On the Economic Theory of Socialism*, ed., B. Lippincott. Minneapolis: University of Minnesota Press, 1956.

Lowi,Theorode J. "Four Systems of Policy, Politics and Choice." *Public Administration Review* 32, no. 4 (July/August 1972):298-310.

Mannheim, Karl. "The Problem of Generations" in *Essays on the Sociology of Knowledge by Karl Mannheim.* edited by P. Kecskemeti. New York, NY: Routledge & Kegan Paul, 1952.

Maslow, Abraham H. "A Theory of Human Motivation." *Psychological Review* 50, no. 4 (1943): 370-96.

Mattei, Ugo. *Comparative Law and Economics.* Ann Arbor, MI: University of Michigan Press, 1997.

McDevitt, Gilbert Joseph. *Legitimacy and Legitimation; an Historical Synopsis and Commentary.* Washington, D.C.: The Catholic university of America press, 1941.

McGuire, Martin C., and Henry J. Aaron. *Efficiency and Equity in the Optimal Supply of a Public Good.* Washington, DC: Brookings Institution, 1969.

McLaverty, Peter. *Public Participation and Innovations in Community Governance.* Burlington, VT: Ashgate, 2002.

Moody, Peter R. *Tradition and Modernization in China and Japan.* Belmont, CA: Wadsworth, 1995.

———. *Chinese Politics after Mao: Development and Liberalization, 1976 to 1983.* New York, NY: Praeger, 1983.

Muncy, Mitchell S. *The End of Democracy? II: A Crisis of Legitimacy.* Dallas, TX: Spence Pub. Co., 1999.

Murphy, Melissa, and Center for Strategic and International Studies (Washington D. C.). *Decoding Chinese Politics; Intellectual Debates and Why They Matter; a Report of the CSIS Freeman Chair in China Studies.* Washington, DC: CSIS Press, 2008.

Murray, Alan. "Will China's Politics Imperil Its Economy?" *Wall Street Journal - East-*

ern Edition 246, no. 94 (2005): A2.

Murvar, Vatro. *Theory of Liberty, Legitimacy, and Power: New Directions in the Intellectual and Scientific Legacy of Max Weber*, International Library of Sociology. London; Boston: Routledge & Kegan Paul, 1985.

Naisbitt, John, and Doris Naisbitt. *China's Megatrend: the 8 Pillars of a New Society [Zhonghuo Da Qushi]*. Beijing: Zhonghua Gongshanglian Chubanshe, 2009.

Nathan, Andrew J. *Chinese Democracy*. 1st ed. New York, NY: Knopf: Distributed by Random House, 1985.

Nelson, Daniel N., and Stephen White. *Communist Legislatures in Comparative Perspective*. Albany, NY: State University of New York Press, 1982.

Nguyen, Quoc Tri. *Third-World Development: Aspects of Political Legitimacy and Viability*. Rutherford,London: Fairleigh Dickinson University Press;Associated University Presses, 1989.

Nino, Carlos Santiago. *The Constitution of Deliberative Democracy*. New Haven, CT: Yale University Press, 1996.

O'Brien, Kevin J. *Reform without Liberalization: China's National People's Congress and the Politics of Institutional Change*. New York, NY: Cambridge University Press, 1990.

O'Flynn, Ian. *Deliberative Democracy and Divided Societies*. Edinburgh: Edinburgh University Press, 2006.

Okun, Arthur M. *Equity and Efficiency: the Big Tradeoff*. Washington, D.C.: The Brookings Institution, 1975.

Park, Han S. *North Korea: The Politics of Unconventional Wisdom*. Boulder, CO.: Lynne Rienner Pub., 2002.

Parkinson, John. *Deliberating in the Real World: Problems of Legitimacy in Deliberative Democracy*. Oxford; New York, NY: Oxford University Press, 2006.

Parsons, Talcott. "Authority, Legitimation, and Political Action" in C. J. Fredrich, ed. *Authority*. Cambridge, MA: Harvard University Press, 1958.

Payrow Shabani, Omid A. *Democracy, Power and Legitimacy: The Critical Theory of Jürgen Habermas*. Toronto; Buffalo: University of Toronto Press, 2003.

Perry, Elizabeth J. "Studying Chinese Politics: Farewell to Revolution?" *China Journal*, no. 57 (2007): 1-22.

Peter, Fabienne. *Democratic Legitimacy*, Routledge Studies in Social and Political Thought. New York, NY: Routledge, 2009.

Pye, Lucian W. "Chinese Politics in the Late Deng Era." *China Quarterly* 142 (1995): 573-583.

————. *The Mandarin and the Cadre*. Ann Arbor, MI: University of Michigan Press, 1988.

————. *The Dynamics of Chinese Politics*. Cambridge, MA: Oelgeschlager, Gunn & Hain, 1981.

————. *The Dynamics of Factions and Consensus in Chinese Politics: A Model and Some Propositions*, [Report] - the Rand Corporation. Santa Monica, CA: Rand, 1980.

————. *The Spirit of Chinese Politics; a Psychocultural Study of the Authority Crisis in Political Development*. Cambridge, MA: M.I.T. Press, 1968.

Pye, Lucian W., and University of Chicago. Center for Policy Study. *The Authority Crisis in Chinese Politics*. Chicago, IL: University of Chicago, 1967.

Quigley, Harold Scott. *China's Politics in Perspective*. Westport, CT: Greenwood Press, 1973.

Ramo, Joshua Cooper. *The Beijing Consensus: Notes on the New Physics of Chinese Power*. London: Foreign Policy Center, 2004.

Rawls, John. *A Theory of Justice*. Cambridge, MA: Harvard University Press, 1999, revised edition.

Rigby, T. H., and Ferenc Fehér. *Political Legitimation in Communist States*. New York, NY: St. Martin's Press, 1982.

Riley, Patrick. *Will and Political Legitimacy: A Critical Exposition of Social Contract Theory in Hobbes, Locke, Rousseau, Kant, and Hegel*. Cambridge, MA: Harvard University Press, 1982.

Roberts, Nancy Charlotte. *The Age of Direct Citizen Participation*, Aspa Classics. Armonk, NY: M.E. Sharpe, 2008.

Roemer, John E. *A Future for Socialism*. Cambridge, MA: Harvard University Press, 1994.

Rogowski, Ronald. *Rational Legitimacy: a Theory of Political Support*. Princeton, NJ: Princeton University Press, 1974.

Rosenberg, Shawn W. *Deliberation, Participation and Democracy: Can the People Govern?* Basingstoke, England; New York, NY: Palgrave Macmillan, 2007.

Rostbøll, Christian F. *Deliberative Freedom: Deliberative Democracy as Critical Theory*. Albany, NY: State University of New York Press, 2008.

Schecter, Darrow. *Beyond Hegemony: Towards a New Philosophy of Political Legitimacy*. Manchester; New York: Manchester University Press Distributed exclusively in the USA by Palgrave, 2005.

Schmitt, Carl. *Legality and Legitimacy*. trans & ed. by Jeffrey Seitzer. Durham, NC: Duke University Press, 2004.

Schoem, David Louis, and Sylvia Hurtado. *Intergroup Dialogue: Deliberative Democracy in School, College, Community, and Workplace*. Ann Arbor, MI: University of Michigan Press, 2001.

Sen, Amartya. "Markets and freedom: Achievements and Limitations of the Market Mechanism in Promoting Individual Freedoms." *Oxford Economic Papers* 45, no. 4 (1973): 519-541.

Shapiro, Ian. *The Moral Foundation of Power*. New Haven: Yale University press, 2003.

Shi, Zhiyu. *Collective Democracy: Political and Legal Reform in China*, Academic Monograph on Chinese Politics. Hong Kong: The Chinese University Press, 1999.

Shook, John R., and Joseph Margolis. *A Companion to Pragmatism*, Blackwell Companions to Philosophy 32. Malden, MA; Oxford: Blackwell Pub., 2006.

Simmons, John. "Justification and Legitimacy." *Ethics* 109 (July 1999): 739-771.

Smith, Graham. *Deliberative Democracy and the Environment*, Environmental Politics. London; New York, NY: Routledge, 2003.

Sniderman, Paul M. *The Clash of Rights: Liberty, Equality, and Legitimacy in Pluralist Democracy*. New Haven, CT: Yale University Press, 1996.

Snow, D. A., Rochford, E. B., Worden, S. K., and Benford, R. D.. "Frame Alignment Processes, Micromobilization, and Movement Participation." *American Sociological Review* 51(1986): 464–481.

Solomon, Richard H. *Mao's Revolution and the Chinese Political Culture*, Michigan Studies on China. Berkeley, CA: University of California Press, 1971.

Somboon, Suksamran. *Buddhism and Political Legitimacy*, Chulalongkorn University Research Report Series No. 2. Bangkok, Thailand: Research Dissemination Project, Research Affairs, Chulalongkorn University, 1993.

Sugarman, David. *Legality, Ideology, and the State*, Law, State, and Society 11. London; New York, NY: Academic Press, 1983.

Sun, Zhe. *Quan Guo Ren Da Zhi Du Yan Jiu, 1979-2000: a Study of the National People's Congress of China*. Beijing: Fa lü chu ban she, 2004.

Swanson, Matthew. *The Social Contract Tradition and the Question of Political Legiti-*

macy, Studies in Social and Political Theory V. 25. Lewiston, NY: Edwin Mellen Press, 2001.

Talisse, Robert B. *Democracy after Liberalism: Pragmatism and Deliberative Politics.* New York: Routledge, 2005.

Teiwes, Frederick C., and Warren Sun. *The End of the Maoist Era: Chinese Politics During the Twilight of the Cultural Revolution, 1972-1976.* Armonk, NY: M.E. Sharpe, 2007.

Thaxton, Ralph. *China Turned Rightside Up: Revolutionary Legitimacy in the Peasant World.* Yale, NJ: Yale University Press, 1983.

Thornton, Patricia M. "Crisis and Governance: SARs and the Resilience of the Chinese Body Politic." *China Journal*, no. 61 (2009): 23-48.

Tones, Keith, and Sylvia Tilford. *Health Promotion: Effectiveness, Efficiency, and Equity.* 3rd ed. Cheltenham, UK: Nelson Thornes, 2001.

Tsur, Yacov, and Ariel Dinar. *Efficiency and Equity Considerations in Pricing and Allocating Irrigation Water*, Policy Research Working Paper. Washington, DC: World Bank, Agriculture and Natural Resources Dept., Agricultural Policies Division, 1995.

Tubilewicz, Czeslaw. *Critical Issues in Contemporary China.* New York: Routledge, 2006.

Turner, Timothy J. *Local Government E-Disclosure & Comparisons: Equipping Deliberative Democracy for the 21st Century.* Lanham, MD: University Press of America, 2005.

Unger, Jonathan. *The Nature of Chinese Politics: From Mao to Jiang*, Contemporary China Books. Armonk, NY: M.E. Sharpe, 2002.

Valadez, Jorge M. *Deliberative Democracy: Political Legitimacy and Self-Determination in Multicultural Societies.* Boulder, CO: Westview Press, 2001.

Vidich, Arthur J., and Ronald M. Glassman. *Conflict and Control: Challenge to Legitimacy of Modern Governments*, Sage Focus Editions 7. Beverly Hills, CA: Sage Publications, 1979.

Voitchovsky, Sarah. "Does the Profile of Income Inequality Matter for Economic Growth? Distinguishing Between the Effects of Inequality in Different Parts of the Income Distribution." *Journal of Economic Growth* 10, no. 3 (2005): 273-296.

Walder, A. "Career Mobility and the Communist Political Order." *American Sociological Review* 60, no. 3 (June 1995): 309-328.

Wang, Chuanmin, and Xin xing chu ban she (Beijing China). *The National People's Congress: Highest Organ of State Power.* China in Brief. Beijing: New Star Publishers, 1998.

Wang, Gungwu, and Yongnian Zheng. *Reform, Legitimacy and Dilemmas: China's Politics and Society.* Singapore, Singapore; New Jersey: Singapore University Press;World Scientific, 2000.

Warren, Mark. *Deliberative Democracy*, Documentos De Trabajo / Doctorado En Ciencia Política. México, D.F.: FLACSO, Sede Académica de México, 1999.

Weber, Max. *Economy and Society*, ed. by G. Roth and C. Wittich. Berkeley, CA: University of California Press, 1968.

Wei, Pan. "Toward a Consultative Rule of Law Regime in China." *Journal of Contemporary China* 12, no. 34 (2003): 3-43.

Wei, Shan, Zhang Qi, and Liu Mingxing. "Bargaining for Less Democracy: The Role of the State in Grassroots Elections in China." 2004/04/14/2004 Annual Meeting, Chicago, IL.

White, Lynn T. *Legitimacy: Ambiguities of Political Success or Failure in East and Southeast Asia*, Series on Contemporary China. Singapore; New Jersey: World

Scientific, 2005.

Wilson, Richard W., Sidney L. Greenblatt, and Amy Auerbacher Wilson. *Moral Behavior in Chinese Society*. New York, NY: Praeger, 1981.

Womack, Brantly. *Contemporary Chinese Politics in Historical Perspective*. Cambridge, England; New York, NY: Cambridge University Press, 1991.

Wu, Fengshi. "Environmental Politics in China: An Issue Area in Review." *Journal of Chinese Political Science* 14, no. 4 (2009): 383-406.

Xie, Qingkui, et al. *Zhongguo Zhengfu Tizhi Fenxi [A Study of the Chinese System of Government]*. Beijing, China Radio and Television Publishing House, 2002.

Xing, Guoxin. "Hu Jintao's Political Thinking and Legitimacy Building: A Post-Marxist Perspective." *Asian Affairs: An American Review* 36, no. 4 (2009): 213-26.

Yan, Jinfen. *Utilitarianism in Chinese Though*. Quebec: World Heritage Press, 1998.

Yang, Guobin. "The Internet and Civil Society in China: A Preliminary Assessment." *Journal of Contemporary China* 12, no. 36 (2003): 453-475.

Yongnian, Zheng. *The Chinese Communist Party as Organizational Emperor: Culture, Reproduction and Transformation*, China Policy Series. New York, NY: Routledge, 2010.

You, Ji, and Australian National University. Research School of Pacific Studies. *Jiang Zemin's Leadership and Chinese Elite Politics after 4 June 1990*, Working Paper. Canberra: Strategic and Defense Studies Centre, Research School of Pacific Studies, Australian National University, 1990.

Young, Stephen M. "Post-Tiananmen Chinese Politics and the Prospects for Democratization." *Asian Survey* 35, no. 7 (1995): 652-667.

Yu, Keping. *Globalization and Changes in China's Governance*, Issues in Contemporary Chinese Thought and Culture. Leiden; Boston: Brill, 2008.

Yue, Tianmin. *Zhengzhi Hefaxing Wenti Yanjiu [A Study of Political Legitimacy*. Beijing, Zhongguo Shehui Kecue Chubanshe, 2006.

Zelditch, Jr., Morris. "Theories of Legitimacy" in John T. Jost, Brenda Major, ed. *The Psychology of Legitimacy*. New York, NY: Cambridge University Press, 2001.

Zhang, Le-Yin. "Market Socialism Revisited: the Case of Chinese State-Owned Enterprises." *Issues and Studies* 42, no. 3 (September 2006): 1-46.

Zhang, Xiaowei. "Elite Transformation and Recruitment in Post-Mao China" *Journal of Political and Military Sociology* 36 (Summer 1998):39-57.

Zhong, Yang. "The Logic of Comparative Politics and the Development of Political Science in China." *Journal of Chinese Political Science* 14, no. 4 (2009): 335-42.

———. "Legitimacy Crisis and Legitimation in China," *Journal of Contemporary Asia* 1, no. 1 (1996):201-220.

Zhu, Yunhan. *How East Asians View Democracy*. New York, NY: Columbia University Press, 2008.

Index

About the Author

Baogang Guo received his Ph.D. in political science from Brandeis University. He is associate professor of political science at Dalton State College, and president of the Association of Chinese Political Studies (ACPS, 2008-2010). He is also a research associate at the China Research Center in Atlanta, Georgia. His research interests include comparative public policy, political culture and political legitimacy, and Chinese and Asia politics. He coedited a number of books, including *Toward Better Governance in China: Unconventional Pathway of Political Reform* (2010), *Dancing with the Dragon: China's Emergence in the Developing World* (2010), *Thirty Years of China-US Relations* (2010), *Greater China in an Era of Globalization* (2010), *China in Search of a Harmonious Society* (2008), and *Challenges Facing Chinese Political Development* (2007). His research articles appeared on *Asian Survey, Journal of Chinese Political Science, Modern China Studies, Journal of Comparative Asian Development, Twenty-First Century,* and *American Journal of China Studies*.

Breinigsville, PA USA
13 September 2010

245234BV00002B/5/P

9 780739 122587